Spiritually Reached...
Why Me?

One Woman's Search For
The Meaning Of Her Life

by
Beryl Ann Fangue

Visit www.booksurge.com to order additional copies.

APPRECIATION...

is extended to my wonderful daughter,
who has always been there for me,

and

to my professional artist son,
whose talent still amazes me,

and

to Chris for his computer expertise

and

to my Spirit Guides and Angels,
for helping me through my difficult life,

and

to my special doggie friend and
constant companion "Ronnie Bonnie",
for always being at my side,

and

to all those magnanimous Spirits, from
the "Other Side", whom God must have sent
to help rejuvenate my memory,
so I could write this book.

INTRODUCTION

Don't know about you, but I have for the most part been unfulfilled in this lifetime. However from childhood, it was my feeling that I was put on this planet, during this particular span of time to do something special. But no matter how hard I tried, how many pursuits I followed, how many of my talents I applied during my lifetime, the answers did not come.

"Why am I here?" "Am I on God's path?" "Is this all there is?" These are the questions that remained unanswered for me--that is until I was spiritually "reached" in 1994. Since then, I have become aware of a future, that has been revealed--a personal future for me and mine, that is truly an awakening.

But along with this "spiritual out reach" from the "other side", also came more of my questions. Why me, I asked? What made my life so noteworthy, that I became a candidate for something so special? After all, like me, multitudes of people have also been unfulfilled in this materialistic world, with it's stringent rules of society, the impact of unyielding religious dogma, the pursuit of the almighty dollar, and mankind's general inhumanity to it's fellow man & woman. So, similar-- or even worse--devastating experiences are felt by many other people too. Therefore, again I ask this question. "Why me"?

Therefore, in an effort to understand if my personal lifetime of ups and downs might possibly have led to my qualifications to be "spiritually reached", I have chosen to write about certain of my decades long memories, that might hold this answer. Of course, such recollections are often on a bitter sweet path, filled with pitfalls and traumas, that often lay dormant in our mentality for many years. I call that place "File 13". Indeed, so deep are these bad events filed--buried in our psyche--that it could take another traumatic event to kick start these recollections.

In addition, the reader will discover (sometimes little known) vignettes of family, regional and world history, that have contributed life ingredients, during the seven plus decades of this lady's life. Indeed, the text of this book contains recollected experiences, observations and recorded personal points of view--all relative to this author's make-up as a person of age 75.

This book was written to perhaps help others, who may be going through similar situations in their lives. It is meant to allow the readers glimpses into the circumstances that molded this particular lady's character, so that they can decide for themselves whether or not this author is worthy of having such a spiritual connection.

So, for better or worse, welcome to this trip down my memory lane.

CONTENTS

CHAPTER - 1
I Didn't Ask For This.....Or Did I ?

"You must move from this place.....it will not be safe here in the future!" These are the telepathically expressed words, that resounded in my mind one fine morning in March 1994, while I was making my bed.

"What is this?" I thought to myself. For no one was there with me anywhere in my house at that moment in time. So, I dismissed it as perhaps a figment of my imagination and continued on with my chore--that is until I heard it again.

"Pay attention to us....we are sent from God, and we have a message for you!"

At that moment, I became alarmed, and sat myself down on the edge of the bed, to consider what was happening to me. I hurriedly peered out of my bedroom window and saw the sun reflecting off of the palm tree fronds and the sun beams highlighting the deep green leaves of my orange trees growing outside. It was as if I wanted to assure myself that no one was at my window, trying to play tricks on me. But no one was there.

Returning my gaze back into the bedroom, I assured myself that no one was there either, and then I ventured to reply to what I had telepathically heard.

"Who....or what are you?"

Needless to say, I felt somewhat foolish. For it was as if I was talking to myself. And I couldn't help thinking how I must be losing it, because I was obviously hearing voices from sources that were not visible. Such a thing had never happened to me before. After all, I was a reputable 62 year old woman--mother & grandmother, a decades long newspaper columnist, author of well-researched historical novels and now editor/publisher of my own monthly newspaper. Thus, I was definitely not known to have such flights of fancy. So, what was happening to me?

Once again, the voice came. "We are your Guides, and must advise you that your path in life is some place else. So, you much sell this house and move elsewhere. We will direct you!"

Upon hearing these words, I realized that this was actually happening. I was indeed hearing--no, not hearing, but absorbing these words within my head. It was not through my ears, but a telepathic communication. However, when I realized what their communication had imparted to me, I became adamant about this bill of goods, that "they" were trying to impress upon me, about moving.

Moving? No way, I thought, from this great four bedroom house on a large property with a pond out back, and located only 25 miles from the Gulf of Mexico beaches of southwest Florida! This was to be my final house, my retirement home where I would live until my time was up on this planet. No way was I ever going to move!

"You must be kidding me," I exclaimed. "I love it here, and will never move from this place! You have the wrong gal....go tell somebody else to move! Because you are barking up the wrong tree here."

Imagine that, I thought. I was actually talking back like that to some unseen force, who for all I knew might just be capable of sending a bolt of lightning to do me in. But I couldn't help it. It took me all my life to finally get to this great place in SW Florida, and now I am expected to believe that God is not happy with my living here?

"No!" They answered, obviously a bit irritated with my tone. "You are the one, whom we are supposed to reach--to tell you to move away from here. In the future, this region will not be a safe place to live, and you are expected to go on into older age. There are other human souls, who are also being reached. But they are not our charge... you are!"

"Go away," I shouted to what I considered to be invisible entities. "Leave me alone. I do not want to move.....I refuse to move!" To this, they replied.

"We have been with you from the very beginning when you came into this world, and we will be with you until the end of your human life, so we will never go away from you as long as you are in your soul's container body here on earth. So, you can never make us go away!"

After that first day's exchange with these entities, who claimed to be my "Guides", I tried to go about my daily business and block them out as much as I could. Most days, I could do this. But sometimes, they would bombard me with their entreaties, to take heed of them and listen to what they were trying to tell me.

Finally, one day when I was alone in my home, I decided to hear them out. It was either that, or I would continue to be plagued with that uninvited telepathic voice. So, I spoke as if into the empty air of my living room, thusly.

"Tell me, why it is so necessary for me to hear you out? But let's be perfectly clear about this, again! I'm letting you know up front, that no matter what you say I have no intention of moving any place else."

There was silence at first, and I initially thought that they had indeed gone away. But not so, because they soon replied. "There are plans you have to accomplish for God, and there are things you are supposed to do before you cross over. But this place is not where you are supposed to accomplish what your destiny dictates."

"If this is true, " I continued. "Why me? Why must I be the one, needed for that particular future?"

"You are a communicator, and your abilities are needed elsewhere. Also, you have to accomplish certain things, so that your seed can go on, after you are gone from this life. Besides, God knows your heart."

Needless to say, I was astounded by that answer, but I persevered. "What do you mean about 'my seed'? And what am I expected to do, to make these things happen?"

"Certain of your seed, we mean certain of your family members, who came through you, are supposed to go on with their lives after you have left this earth. But in order for those selected ones to continue with their lives, you must assure their survival by your efforts. It will not be an easy task, but we will direct you. So, you must do what we say."

After that exchange, I decided to play along and ask a more direct question. "O,K., so you say I have to move. Well, just so I can understand all of this, where do you want me to move?"

"Get out a map of Georgia," they directed, "and we will show you."

Wow, Georgia, I thought! I would never have guessed that state. But I did as they asked and scrounged around until I found a proper Georgia map, and spread it out on the dining room table. "It is a big state," I said to them, pointing out the obvious.

"Indeed it is," they replied. "Look above Atlanta at the smaller towns up there. When you come to the right one, we will tell you."

So, I directed my eyes across the northern region of that state as I was told, taking note of the names of each town. But for some strange reason--or maybe not as it turned out--my eyes kept coming back to one particular town about 50 miles north of Atlanta, off of Interstate 75.

"That is it....that is the area where you must move!" Their resounding words filled me with so many questions, that I didn't know where to begin.

"Let's get this straight," I began. "You want us to sell this lovely house here, end our businesses, pack up everything we own and move to a new state--to an area where we have never been before, where we know no one and have no logical reason to move there?'

"Exactly," was the reply. "Your destiny lies there. But this will not be your final destination. There is still another home, not far from there, yet to come."

As I mulled this over in my mind, I pointed out the obvious to these unseen voices. "You know, I have a husband. Granted, if I would go along with this plan, how in the world do you expect me to convince a man, who mostly deals with logic, to accept this strange scenario? What should I say to my hubby--we have to move to another state, because some invisible entities tell me that we have to do this? So, you will have to stop your business, as will I, and go along with this strange plan, even though it makes no sense to you?"

"That is right. You must approach him with this information....and believe it. He will finally come around." They continued, as I began to get more exasperated.

"No...no...no, we will not move! What you ask is too much! We have all our money tied up in this house and our two businesses. How can you or God or anyone ask us to do this? Besides, it costs money to make such a move, not to mention the obstacle of getting another place to live at the end of this illogical road. Besides, I ask you again, why me? Go find someone, who is more devout than I am--someone like a Mother Theresa type, someone who literally spends most of their time in church praying. You must know, that I am a fallen Catholic, who hardly ever goes to church anymore."

"We have already told you, that you have the communicative ability that is needed elsewhere. God knows that you constantly have Him in your heart, and have always believed. You have never lost your faith in Him. But some of those, who are in constant church attendance are not always the best candidates to do God's bidding. Only God knows, who is strong enough and right for a particular job." This was the answer I received to my heart-felt entreaties.

For days after this exchange, I once again tried to shut them out. But it was no use. They would not give up. In fact, they made my life miserable, trying to get into my mind with their constant directives--so much so that it was interfering with my work and my behavior around the house. So, finally I shared this with my husband, who upon hearing this illogical tale, looked at me like I had really gone off the deep end. So, my work was cut out for me--trying to convince him that this was real. Besides, why would I make up such a thing? But he refused to even consider that this was indeed real.

For weeks, this state of affairs went on, until finally I had had it and knew instinctively that I had no choice in this matter.   Then I approached my husband with these words.

"I know this directive is aimed at me and you just happen to be my husband. But apparently they are not reaching you--only me. So, since this is wearing me out emotionally, I simply cannot fight this any longer. But I do understand your feelings in this matter, and do not blame you. However, I have no choice, but to do as I am being directed. So, we will have to separate, and I will make this move. I will settle with you on my share of this house, so you can keep it."

The expression on his face, upon hearing my words, was one of astonishment. However, it finally sank in for him--that I was indeed serious about this.

For days afterwards, my husband mulled this situation over in his mind, and apparently decided that I was important enough to him, that he would believe what I had said. Also, he fully realized that I had made up my mind to do this--with or without him!

So, it was decided and I told my spiritual sources this. Of course, they already knew what had been said between us. After all, they know--and have known-- everything about me from the time of my birth. They had previously informed me of this. So, I asked how we should go about this life altering change; what is next?

"Put your house up for sale and as soon as you can, take a journey up to that region, so you can see the area where you will be moving. Get an idea of what housing is available up there, and remember when you decide on a home, it must have a fire place and basement."

I considered these words for a moment, and asked about the fireplace and basement. After all, we lived in south Florida where hardly anyone had fire places--

much less basements. But their reply did make sense to me.

"In times to come, there may be power failures, so you will need a source of warmth. The basement is to allow more room for possible others, and for protection from devastating storms."

Again, that made sense, for I had heard that tornadoes often skip scotch over that region. So, basements are often the only source of safety for many, who have to deal with such weather. But I hastened to tell them the following:

"Any place we get will have to have a fenced in backyard, for our four dogs. I am not leaving here without my dogs!"

We had three males and a female, that had been our doggie friends for years. So, the possibility of leaving them behind would be non negotiable. "Baby", a Terrier mix female was almost age 14, "Chipper", our male smaller Terrier mix was already 14. "Frisky", our Cairn Terrier was about 12, and "Dandy" a Boston Terrier was the youngest at 5 years.

"No, you will leave with only one of your dogs-- Frisky . The others will not be going with you to your new home," was their reply.

Upon hearing those words, I just about lost it! "No....no....no! How can you do this to me? How do you expect me to give up so much, and now even my beloved dogs? You ask too much of me. That's it....I am not going without my dogs. I don't care what you say....I am not leaving them."

"Everything will fall into place," was the reply. "Even though you cannot see it now, it will happen. Now, after you put your house up for sale, go buy an RV."

Talk about being astonished upon hearing this! Words cannot express my thoughts at that moment. Why, I asked myself, at such a time after being given all of these other incredible dictates, would anyone ask us to do such an obviously foolish thing? This is especially because it will stretch us to the limit monetarily, just to make this move. So, why should we buy as big a ticket item as an RV at this time?

As if in anticipation of what I was going to literally scream at them, they beat me to it. "You will need the RV to live in for a while, after you make this move. You cannot see the logic in all of this now, but God does not deal in logic. God is all powerful and can make anything happen when needed. You are to accept what we are telling you, and go along with it. In times to come, you will understand why all of this was necessary."

Well, we went ahead and put our house on the market, and proceeded to cease our businesses in preparation for this gigantic (seemingly totally illogical) move that we were told was a part of my destiny. However, I couldn't help but wonder how many people would even consider doing such a thing--to disrupt a way of life they had come to love. Why, even most of those ultra religious folks, who almost live in church, would probably draw the line at such as this, I thought. Yet, we were doing this literally on blind faith. But I remained adamant about my dogs, and kept in mind that I would look for a house with a fenced yard, so they could be with us.

As it turned out, it took two years to sell our wonderful house. I can't imagine why it took so long, because it was a notable property. However, since so much spirituality has entered my life, I have come to believe that a house will only sell when certain people, who are pre-ordained to live there, come along. No matter how many potential buyers walk through, only those spiritually selected ones will eventually be allowed to buy.

But during this time of waiting for our house to sell, I saw for myself several of my guide's predictions come true. My beloved dogs were a part of that scenario.

One day, as I was washing dishes at my kitchen sink, I gazed out of the window there and saw three of my dogs, laying in a line outside along my flower bed edging, in obvious somber moods. They were all looking toward under my window, just about four feet from where they lay. There was "Baby", "Friskie" and "Dandy", but I did not see "Chipper" anywhere with them. So, I immediately dried my hands and went out the back door to look for him.

Then I saw what these three dogs were looking at. It was "Chipper", laying there against the house under that window. I went to him, to see what was wrong. But he did not respond. Then I realized, that he had died right there.

My heart sank with sorrow, for I loved that dog. But what was so astounding to me was that he had not even displayed any symptoms of being sick. Yet apparently, he had just lied down and quietly passed away. And it was as though the quiet respectful behavior that had been displayed by my other three dogs--their behavior which had drawn me outside--could have been likened to mourners at a wake for someone they loved.

Then, months later I had to take "Dandy" to the vet, because he had an enlarged growth on his rear side. The prognosis was grave. He had a tumor, that even if removed the Veterinarian could not guarantee that he could get all of it. So, reluctantly I had to do something that has laid heavy on me all these years. I had to have him put down, so he wouldn't suffer.

Also as directed, we did in fact purchase a 34 foot RV during this time. How this would fit into the plan still escaped us. But we did get some enjoyment from it, going on short trips, while waiting to move. In addition, we drove it up to north Georgia on our investigative search to get the lay of the land up there. Before we left, I boarded "Baby" at a kennel, and upon our return we picked her up and she appeared to be her old self. So, I gave her a bath and that night as usual she slept in her cushioned doggie bed in the garage. The next morning, when I opened the kitchen door into the garage and went over to her bed to give her a morning doggie treat, I was astounded. She lay there, with legs outstretched and her eyes staring blankly out in space. I knew then, that she had died in her sleep. I cried over her loss so much, as I had done for the other two, that it is hard to describe. To think we had lost three beloved dogs in a handful of months--one after the other.

Some people would say that they were all getting old (except for Dandy), and this was to be expected. But I refused to believe that, because this was too much of a coincidence to accept. As it turned out, only "Friskie" was left, even though he was not by any means the youngest. But he was the only one prophesized to move with us.

As for the RV reason, it soon came to light why this directive. Our Florida house finally sold, but we could not find the right house for us up there. So, we contracted to have an appropriate house built--complete with fireplace and basement. But it would take four months to build. So, we contracted for a big commercial moving van to come and take all our worldly possessions away, to be stored in a storage unit near where our new home would be. Then, hubby drove the RV to north Georgia,, pulling our packed Plymouth van, and with me following in my packed Pontiac Grand Am, pulling a small full trailer. Thereafter, we had to live in the RV for those four months, while waiting for the house to be completed.

So, these prophesized happenings--the things that previously seemed incongruous to me--were becoming real. This was even including some years later, when I started writing a newspaper column for the local paper up here in north Georgia. At that time, it appeared that my printed words had helped jump start a local county political party.

I was one of those people, who was so against the invasion of Iraq. And I wondered why I seldom heard about others, who felt as I did. So, I wrote a column entitled-- "County Democrats....Where Are You?" And then many people, who believed as I did, seemed to come out and be counted. Afterwards, I heard from many in the local Democrat Party, which had become somewhat dormant thereabouts. It was as if many of them were just waiting for something to bring them all together, after that devastating election in 2000. It was that election, when Democrat Al Gore won the popular vote, but Republican George W. Bush was literally awarded the presidency by court decision. This left a lingering bitterness for Democrats, a feeling of being robbed, that has lasted to this day.

Afterwards, I became involved in the rejuvenation of this county's Democrat Party, all the while continuing to write columns against the Iraq War. In fact, I was honored for my efforts by being awarded that county's "Democrat of the Year 2004" trophy. Words escaped me (and these seldom do) at receiving this heart warming honor.

So, here again was another example of those spiritual predictions coming to pass. Because I was driven to put my communicative efforts toward a worthy cause, I did indeed make a difference, as I was supposed to do.

As an addendum to this unusual story of prophesies becoming reality, there is even more to consider. During the great years we spent living in SW Florida, my daughter and family had moved to our neighborhood down there too. So, it was an ideal family situation, with two dear grandchildren residing only a few blocks away. However, when I was directed to move to Georgia, and I shared this with my daughter, who had a bit of precognition herself, she believed me. So, when faced with the information about where we were living not being safe in the future, she convinced her husband to ask for a transfer. And after much consideration on his part, which must have been hard for him, as he loved living in SW Florida too, he did so. As it turned out, his transfer came through rather quickly--to a nearby town above Atlanta , also near I-75. So, this meant that he would have to start work up there, before their Florida house sold. So, my daughter and her young children stayed behind, to sell the house. But it was not for long.

Another key player in all of this was my good friend Doris, whom I had come to love after I moved to SW Florida. She was an astrologer by profession, and had a psychic gift as well. I used to share what was being told to me with her, and she concurred that these directives were valid and I should pay attention. She had also previously reported to me, that where we were living would not be safe in the future. The only question being, how far in the future? However, she and her husband did put their house up for sale, about the same time that we did.

When I asked my "Guide" about the sales of our three houses, they had this to say. "Your daughter's house will sell first. Your house will sell next. And Doris will leave later."

True to my guide's predictions, my daughter and hubby had a buyer for their house within a couple of months. But our house took two frustrating years to sell. So, hubby and I did not move to north Georgia until early August 1996.

As for my friend Doris and her hubby, their house was still on the market when we left. And it was so hard to leave my good friend behind. However, I felt that it would be just a matter of time until we would all be living in nearby towns in north Georgia. But I was wrong!

In October 1998, I phoned my friend Doris, who was still living in SW Florida. It was then that I got one of the shocks of my life. Her sister answered the phone and told me this.

"Doris had started coughing up blood one day, and was rushed to the hospital. There, they discovered she had lung cancer, which had spread extensively to other parts of her body. So, there was nothing they could do. She was then sent to hospice, where seventeen days later, our dear Doris passed over."

My grief, upon hearing this news, was horrific. I knew Doris was a life long cigarette smoker, and I had begged her time and time again to quit. But I was still not prepared to accept her sudden passing. After all, she and I had been born in the same year and the same month, and I had expected to share our friendship for many more years to come. But then, I recalled the words of my "guide", and it made sense.

"Your daughter's house will sell first. Your house will sell next. And Doris will leave later."

☆ ☆ ☆

Since first being "reached", I have been told several other things that are supposed to be on my personal path in the lifetime. There are some things I can relate, and other things that I cannot talk about. But one question still nags at me-- "Why me?"

I can concur with wiser heads than mine, who have asked (not in exactly the same words)--how can we hope to understand the present or aspire to the future, unless we have learned from the past?

So, this is what I am endeavoring to do-- learn from my past.

☆ ☆ ☆

CHAPTER - 2
To Begin With..... I Was Born

Let's face it, 1932 was not the best of years wherein to be born. After all, it was in the depths of America's Great Depression. But nevertheless, I came into this world at 1:15 AM on a December day (weighing 8 pounds), and in a seen-better-days "shot gun" house on Fourth Street in Berwick, Louisiana. But I was fortunate early on to have good parents, for Mae and Howard were indeed just that—loving parents for me and my brother Sonny.

However, like millions of Americans in those Great Depression years, we were very poor by most standards. But so were most other folks too. However, I was rich in the love of my parents and extended family, so much so that as kids my brother and I really did not think of ourselves as ever being poor.

I offer this early background check on me, to let you know that not all of my life was dotted with unfortunate choices. Fortunately, the lessons learned in my earlier years must have gone far in helping me through the bad times yet to come in adulthood. Because there were many bits and pieces of joyous memories sprinkled here and there in my childhood.

But now, after struggling on my life's path, which took me precariously to this aged point in time, I have learned so much along the way. Now, I truly believe that we choose our life's path before we come into this world, with the goal of experiencing for God, so that our soul can be elevated further. And usually it takes multiple lifetimes of living, in order to reach our soul's more elevated status. Some of us choose easier life paths, whereas more ambitious souls often chart difficult lifetimes, that are oftentimes traumatic.

I have considered this concept seriously, and decided that I was probably under some kind of deluded influence, when I chose my life here on earth this time around. For even though my childhood had it's gratifying moments, my adult life was filled with more pitfalls than most.

It is with this realization, that I write this book, hoping to show others, who fall down along their life's path, that they too can pick themselves up, brush themselves off and start all over again. After all, I did it!

✳✳✳

But then, I am descended from hardy French-Acadian people (today referred to as Cajuns), who began to carve out productive land in south Louisiana, back in the late 1700s, after the English had expelled them in 1755, from their ancestral land in Acadia (now Nova Scotia, Canada). However, these earlier ancestors refused to be defeated, even after finding their way to the south Louisiana region and being faced with conquering that swampy land, infested with alligators, snakes, and subject to many serious hurricanes. So, perhaps I could say that some of those "will do" genes have trickled down to my generation. Thus causing me to never give up. Whatever the reason, I am honored to be descended from such courageous people, whom I wrote about in my CAJUN ODYSSEY books.

Of course, that "get up and go" spirit of entrepreneurship apparently existed in previous generations on both sides of my Acadian descendant family lines. But the struggle continued on for subsequent generations of these earlier people. In this regard, my parents did tell me bits and pieces of their earlier life, and the lives of their parents. Such stories will attest to this legacy, making evident the revelations which helped to shape this lady's character, and also afforded a better understanding of those, who came before, and the impact they have had on this author.

One such story took place in the late 1920s, when my mother was still in high school. She resided just west of Patterson, Louisiana, on land that her father farmed. The family struggled on this farm, but mother did tell me, that for the most part she and her siblings were happy. Of course, being one of ten children, her prospects in life for anything more ambitious than marriage and motherhood were just about non-existent. This is except for one opportunity, that came her way.

Mother used to tell me about a grand plantation mansion, that stood on several acres along the shores of Bayou Teche, just a couple of miles down the dusty road from their farm. Everyone did indeed marvel at the grandeur of that elegant big house, where rich people lived. Those wealthy folks were Harry & Margueritte Clark Williams. He was a millionaire lumber tycoon and aviation pioneer, with his own small airfield, that had been carved out among the vast fields of sugar cane. Their mansion was located just across the gravel road from his air field.

Harry's wife was a beautiful silent movie actress, who made some 40 movies during her career. She met Lieutenant Harry P. Williams, just after the First

World War and they subsequently married. Besides the grand home on the bayou near Patterson, they also had an elegant home in New Orleans, where they became part of that city's society. During those years, they also socialized with the likes of Buddy Rogers and Mary Pickford of silent movie fame.

Williams and his partner Jimmy Wedell—a famous aircraft designer and air racer—participated in several air races and competitions, breaking many records in that era. Unfortunately, they both met untimely deaths in airplane crashes—Jimmy in 1932 and Harry in 1936. So, after his death, Margueritte sold the Williams' family stable of existing airplanes to the fledging Eastern Air Lines, for use in their mail service between New Orleans and Houston, Texas. At that time, Eastern Air Lines' owner was Eddie Rickenbacker.

But I do digress. So, allow me to retrace back to those late 1920's years, which was the time when that teenage girl (Mae)—my Mother—apparently became acquainted with the lady of that grand mansion—Margueritte. I do not know how these two met, since they were from two vastly different worlds. Even though Mother never elaborated on their initial meeting, she did express to me how proud she was, that this elegant lady "took a liking to her", and would chat with her on frequent occasions.

That is how Mrs. Williams found out that my Mother had aspirations of becoming a registered nurse. Of course, Mae knew this to be an impossible dream for her, as her parents could certainly not afford to make that happen. However, it turned out that Margueritte offered to pay for her nursing school training, as soon as Mother graduated from high school. My, what a wonderful opportunity had been offered to Mae!

Unfortunately, it was not to be, because Mother met my daddy Howard, just before her Senior year. And he wanted to marry her, but was not prepared to wait for her to finish her last year of school—much less for Mother to accept her wealthy patron's offer of higher education. So much for Mother's grand career opportunity!

But I do believe, that all of her life she never forgot about that special opportunity she lost. And it would have been an apropos calling for her, as she was always a caring woman, who relished in taking care of others. However, it was apparently not to be.

Yes, in the late 1920s Mother and Daddy met. But he lived in Berwick, about eight miles from her home. So, this meant Howard had to have access to some wheels, in order to court Mae. But first she said that he had to learn to dance. If he didn't, she told him he could "hit the road". After all, she came from a family of dancers, and it was often said that those Landrys' could certainly dance! So, the handwriting was on the wall for him, and apparently no sacrifice was too much for him to make for her. As a result, their courtship was a toss up between this couple either attending silent movies, with her little sister or brother going along with them as chaperons, or going to those Saturday night "Shindigs" at the dance hall on Main Street in Berwick. This is where folks from all around used to move to the musical renditions of those swing bands, that would come all the way from New Orleans for such gigs.

Now remember, this was in the time of prohibition, so no spirited drinks were allowed to be sold at these dances, or anywhere else for that matter. But there was a lot of "pop rouge" drunk at those dances, and it was said that all those thirsty dancers downed a lot of it. So much, it was said, that they could literally feel all of that pop swishing around inside of their tummies every time they did a "Charleston" or two.

However, not withstanding the prohibition law of the land back then, everybody knew that there were other sources for alcoholic beverages—or reasonable facsimiles thereof. Yep, heard tell that most of the young guys took advantage of what was for sale behind the "green door" or red door, or brown door, particularly after hours at certain local drug stores in the area. Legend has it, that they went to such places to buy a mixture of grain alcohol and food coloring, that was all the rage. Then there was that sweet little old lady in town, who brewed and sold her special alcoholic gin concoction out of her bath tub. And some people wondered why prohibition did not work!

Naturally, the proper young ladies in those days were never expected to indulge in spirits. No way, for it was reserved for guys, who adhered to the lyrics of a popular song. That song proclaimed—"Lips that touch liquor will never touch mine." So much for women's rights then.

The wedding day for my parents finally arrived on March 1, 1930. What a terrible time to wed, at the beginning of the Depression. From reports, my Mother was radiant in her beautiful pink lace flapper dress, that Daddy had bought for her. But then he was still flush with money he had earned from the previous trapping season, after which he had bought a brand spanking new 1929 Chevy Sedan for $850. Of course, by then everything had gone up, as his previous car had only cost $640.

She was 18 and he was 22, as they embarked on their sea of matrimony. Later, they set out by boat to Mosquito Point, to spend winter months at their trapping camp, where Daddy had been so successful the previous year. He had indeed brought in many muskrat and mink pelts. Back then, it was common practice for folks to spend November, December, January and February at their camps. Such a camp was little more than a one room wooden shanty on stilts (with no electricity and only cistern water from the rain for their use). These camp structures were built above the marshland, that rim the Louisiana coastline. And it was even common practice for children to be taken out of school, so they could be with their parents for those winter months, in order to help with the family trapping pursuits. On most years, the trapper's take was good, and the pelts were of fine quality. Unfortunately, on other years, those people did not fair so well.

As it turned out, the winter after my parents were wed proved to be one of those bad years, and many families came back in to face bills, which they could not pay. It had been commonplace back then for businesses to extend credit for groceries and supplies, to trappers at the beginning of the season. This was done, with the expectation that when the pelts were brought in and sold, the bills would be settled. But even in addition to it being a financially disappointing trapping season, it must have also been a strange adventure for newly married Mae. Of course, Howard had already experienced a couple of trapping seasons out there in that wide open marshland. But she had not yet seen what trapping camp life entailed.

So, her first winter season out in that vast marshland, in a one room stilted shack, with only a kerosene heater, and a kerosene stove for cooking, must have been difficult. But she did tell me, that there was a good side to it all. After all, they were newly weds—even though on what could be construed as a not-so-glamorous honeymoon.

However, there was a multitude of wildlife everywhere in those hundreds of miles of seemingly endless marshland. She said, that brown pelicans would light on the wharf in great numbers, and when one would come right up to her, she would put a whole fish in it's mouth. Also, setting traps for blue crabs, which were so abundant at the end of their little wharf, was another of her favorite pastimes. This was while Daddy was trudging the marsh paths in his hip boots, checking his traps. He used to tell us how hard that was, sometimes sinking above his knees in the mud. And then having a hard time, pulling his legs out of the mud to set on harder ground, in order to go on to the next trap. In those days, muskrats and mink were the desired species. Unfortunately, decades later another species was introduced into this swampland. It was the Nutria, which became so prolific, that it edged out the other more valuable species—thus pretty much ending trapping down there.

Whenever any boat would pass on the waterway in front of their camp, they would wave and shout a welcome. These could be the boats of other trappers coming and going from town, or fishermen on their way to Four League Bay, Atchafalaya Bay, or any of the countless waterways that dotted that coastline. People were so trusting back then, and anyone passing by in a boat would often time be invited to stop in and have a cup or coffee, or even a meal—in spite of the fact that most of those people were strangers. Because visitors were so few for such long spans of time, the company of any new people was an unexpected delight, and a break from the monotony of marshland trapping life.

The only other exciting event was when a grocery/ supply boat would come by and stop at the camps to sell their wares.

But reality crept in, when they returned from that season. The pelts they had worked so hard to get did not equal enough money to settle the debts, that they had incurred. In addition, all returning trappers from that season, came back into a continuing era of the depression, where jobs were almost non-existent. Thus, my parents' first year of marriage left much to be desired. Because they were in such debt, they had to sell that 1929 Chevy for $300, to help settle some of the creditors. But they persevered, and life went on.

✫✫✫

Remembering back when I was a child in the decade of the 1930s, I can still recall that little three room house where I was born. It had a front porch and a lean-to small room off the kitchen in the rear, where the ice box was kept. From time to time, the ice truck would come by and sell my mother a block of ice (5 or 10 cents worth) to be put in that ice box.

There was a beat up old Ford truck, that came by occasionally, loaded with fresh vegetables just picked from the garden of that farmer, who owned the truck. When it stopped on our street, all the ladies from the houses thereabouts came out to buy some of his produce. Remember, this was long before these times of frozen foods and super markets. Such things were unknown in those days. In fact, most folks in this small town kept a few chickens in their backyards for eggs and an occasional meal of baked chicken (only on Sunday).

Mother and Daddy kept a large hog in a pen in the backyard. They were fattening him up for eventual slaughter, from which to get salt meat, sausage, ham, pork chops & roasts, boudin, hogs head cheese and such. But my Mother had treated that pig as a pet (which was a no-no in those days). She used to feed him by hand every day and scratch his back, so after he was slaughtered, she would not eat any of that meat.

Mondays were considered "wash days" by most women in our area. That meant it was "white beans and rice day". Because washing on a wash board, wringing out the wet clothes and hanging these on outside lines to dry, was very labor intensive, so most women of those years would put a pot of white beans, with onions and salt pork, to slow cook on the stove on Monday mornings, for the family meal later. But back in my grandma Azalie Landry's day, the family wash was done outside in a large black iron vessel, placed on an open fire. Happily, by the 1940s, most ladies had up graded to electric washing machines with wringers.

I remember Dr. Aycock, the parish doctor from Franklin down the highway a few miles. He was the one, who came to the homes when someone was sick or to deliver babies, as he did for my brother and me. He would arrive in his time-worn car, that had seen countless miles, during his St. Mary Parish home visits. He would arrive with his well worn leather doctor's bag, inside of which was a stethoscope, forceps and other medical tools, as well as any medications he could fit into that bag. So, if there were complications with the birth of a baby or if a very ill patient needed emergency hospital resources, that were deemed necessary for certain life-threatening ailments, there was little recourse for help. This is because the nearest hospital was far too many miles away.

Therefore, some times in birth cases, when complications arose, the patient or the baby—or both—died. Back then, such deaths were accepted as part of life, and chalked up to "God's will". Afterwards, life simply went on. Because most folks in the Great Depression lived very hard lives. And there was always the pursuit of putting enough food on their tables and clothes on the backs of other family members, the responsibility for whom was ever present.

When my brother Sonny was born (like me at home), it was on the day after Christmas 1935. Decades later, Mother told me that she had exhausted herself on that Christmas day, when she had cooked a big dinner, with a baked bird and the trimmings. She added that her belly was so big, that she had trouble moving around the kitchen. As a result, it was her opinion that this over exertion had brought on her labor. Turns out, my brother weighed over 9 pounds at birth. So, it was a very long and difficult delivery for my Mother.

Throughout her painful labor, Daddy sat on the front porch, and couldn't help but hear it all through the thin walls of that house. It was then, that he came to a decision. So, after it was all over he told my Mother that this was the last time she would be put through this pain again, as he did not want her to have anymore children. What a great guy he was, having so much empathy for his wife. Truth be told, my Mother always wanted a third child, but Daddy would not hear of putting her through child birth again.

In those depression days, most couples were obviously trying not to have big families, because they couldn't afford to support many children. As it was, my Daddy's older brother said to him when they announced my Mother was expecting their second child.

"What's the matter with you.....what are you thinking?"

This Uncle and his wife was one of the couples, who had only one child then. So, I have often wondered about these small families, because I knew several such couples—even in my extended family, who had only one child during those years. And I wondered how they accomplished that. After all, this was way before the pill or other modern contraception devices. Later in life, I asked an Aunt of mine how she managed to have only one child., to which she replied.

"We were careful....very careful!"

After Sonny's birth, when mother and child were deemed healthy enough, and while the doctor was there, my parents asked him to circumcise the baby. So, the doctor merely laid baby Sonny on the kitchen table and proceeded to do the circumcision, while the baby screamed and cried from the pain. That's the way things were done back then, with little to no fanfare.

My family's little shotgun house was right next to the brand new Atchafalaya River bridge, that had been under construction for a while. Before that time, traveling across that wide river involved taking a ferry that ran at different intervals. The year of this bridge's much anticipated completion was 1932, and to mark that year, it was engraved in large size onto the concrete at the foot of this bridge, on both sides of the river. It was so prominently shown on the bridge, right next to our house, that Dr. Aycock apparently took this as a sign and suggested to my mother that I be named "Bridget" But apparently, she had other ideas.

The most important Louisiana leader of that time was Huey P. Long. Ever since his reign, even to this modern day, his critics have been very vocal in painting him as an unethical man. True, history tells us that he did, indeed, use unorthodox methods in pursuit of getting things done. But to many of the people of Louisiana back then, he was a god. After all, he built bridges where there had been none, had hundreds of miles of highways constructed where before there were deplorably rough byways. He pushed through laws that afforded school children free books and free lunches. So, no matter what people may think of him as a controversial historical character, we have to admit that he made Louisiana a better place in which to live.

My Daddy was a hard working young man in those days. He was of small frame and probably weighed no more than 135 pounds in the 1930s. But he was a "go-getter". After I was born, he worked at the Shell Crusher company, located about nine blocks from our house on the other side of town. Each day, he would walk there, get in line with many other men to lift and carry 100 pound sacks of shell dust, to be loaded on trucks and rail cars. At noon, he would then walk the nine blocks home to eat his lunch. Afterwards, he would hurry back to the plant site to work the rest of the day. He did this six days a week, and he did not dare miss a day of work, because there were desperate out-of-work men standing around, just waiting to take his job if he did not show up. And he endured all of this for ten dollars a week. This was at a time, when one week's pay was needed just to pay the rent, with only 30 dollars left to pay for the family's needs.

During my childhood in the 1930s, I can honestly say that there were simple happy memories for us kids, as our parents shielded us from the ugliness that prevailed in that era of desperation for the multitudes. We only knew that no one in our town went hungry.

They planted gardens, fished and held on to any menial job available. But there is one particular day that is etched in my memory, when I was a child.

That day, a strange man (I later learned that he was a "hobo"), came to our back screen door and knocked. We had seen such men, meandering and hitch hiking along the highway and railroad tracks. But now here was one, with whom we were face to face. Back then, no one kept their doors locked during the day, so it was a shock to see such a stranger suddenly appear at our back door. I remember him well, standing there with his hat in hand. His clothes were soiled and scruffy and in much need of mending. And his face looked as if he had not shaved in many days. Those eyes of his were so sad and without any trace of glimmer, with only sheer desperation reflected there. He carried a bundle over his shoulders, probably containing all of his worldly goods. But his manner was polite, as he stood there and talked in a respectful manner to Mother through the screen door. My recollection of his words were something like this.

"Mam, could you possibly spare a piece of bread for me, as I haven't eaten in a couple of days......and if there is some chore I can do for you in payment, I will do it."

My Mother, a young adult and quite a pretty woman in those days, expressed no alarm at the sudden appearance of this man at her door. Instead she told him that if he would wait there, she would make him a sandwich to take with him, and while waiting he could turn on the faucet on the side of the house for some water if he was thirsty.

In a few minutes, she handed him a paper bag in which were a couple of sandwiches, and told him there was no need for any chores in payment. She wished him well, and he thanked her profusely. Then, he went on his way.

Many years later as an adult, I learned that hobos in the 1930s, who stopped at houses to get a handout were usually really in need. This was because so many of these men had become financially destitute due to the stock market crash back east in late 1929. Thereafter, throughout our country, many previously well-to-do folks lost everything, and as a trickled down effect, companies closed, businesses were ruined and banks failed. So, many men left the big cities, which no longer held any opportunity for them, and they traveled mostly by hopping freight trains to the south and mid west. Most of them were good people, who were in search of a place that held some hope for them to begin again.

So, it was common practice for these wandering men, to ask for food and water wherever they could, since they had no money. One of the habits they became known for in this regard was to tie a little piece of cloth to the fence post at the houses, where they had been fed. This was to make it easier for other men, who were bound to come the same way, to be alerted as to which houses were their best bets for a handout. I remember that we did not have a fence post, so I suppose that man couldn't leave any such evidence of my Mother's kindness, to alert those who came afterwards.

✢✢✢

I also learned many things about my parents' lifetime before I was born. A most important event was about the influx of the "Spanish Flu", which hit the world back at the end of World War One in 1918. It killed over 20 million people. The soldiers came back from that European war, and returned to their homes all over the USA, never suspecting that they were also carrying something terrible back too—the Spanish Flu.

So, later on in my adulthood, I asked my Mother about that event. I had seen documentaries about that terrible pandemic, where people in cities were wearing white masks on their faces whenever they went out in public. This was an effort to keep from getting that flu. Because as it turned out, there were probably few families that did not have it hit in their midst or among folks in their friend's families—so "catching" was it. In cities, all places where the public gathered (theaters and even churches) were closed in an effort to curtail the spreading of that terrible disease. As it turned out, Mother said that it hit her family too.

She was a young girl at the time, so her younger siblings were not as yet born. But according to her, she and her five older brothers and sisters—as well as their Mother—came down with that flu all at the same time. I wanted to know, who in the world took care of them, especially since their Mother was sick too? It turned out the Department of Health sent a colored lady practical nurse, to help them. And there was a happy ending for at least this one family, as all of them survived that horrible disease. Upon hearing this story, I told her that for this woman, who helped them in their time of need, to have risked her own health in the process, was remarkable. I further remarked to her, that they should have worshiped the ground that lady walked on.

Yes indeed, it is amazing that folks back then even lived into adulthood. Because it was such a different era, when for the most part people depended so much on time trusted medicinal home remedies, that had been passed down for generations. Foremost of these were the doses of Castor Oil we kids had to endure at different times of the year. A dose of this was supposed to clean us out from within, and make us healthier. Well, I am here to tell you, it certainly did clean us out!

Since researching Castor Oil in recent years, I have discovered that it does indeed have healing properties. But it is especially so, when used in compresses on the exterior of the body—not within, because it is too harsh internally. However, back in those days just about all kids were subjected to those internal doses, every few months. For me, I shall always remember those horrific big tablespoons full of that oily fluid. But to make it better, Mother would hurriedly give me something to drink as a chaser. In my case, it was either orange juice or coffee. As a result, it took me many years before I could tolerate drinking orange juice. And as for coffee, to this day, I cannot stand the taste or the smell of that beverage.

But many things were so different, all those decades ago. I faintly remember, as a child, noticing the time one of my aunts came to visit us. To my childish eyes, this usually slim lady had suddenly put on a lot of weight. I asked Mother about why my aunt looked so much bigger than usual. The answer I received was that she had just put on a few pounds, but would be losing these very soon. And so it was. Because weeks later, the next time my aunt came to visit, she appeared back to her slim self. And she was holding a new baby in her arms—a baby who seemed to have materialized from out of nowhere! This seemed so strange to me. But I realized later, that this was the way a woman "with child" was referred to, should youngsters ask questions. Never, in that era did anyone say that excluded word—"pregnant"—as it was apparently taboo. And absolutely nothing remotely having to do with "sex" was ever discussed in polite conservations.

There are other apropos topics, that are worth mentioning here. Personally, I have found that this expression, "everything old is new again", certainly has merit. This is because after my parents became more affluent, we moved into a house, that had beautiful varnished & waxed hardwood floors throughout. To her, it was so important that her floors shined. Thus she became a slave to this waxing & buffing chore, for it was never ending. Ever since then, I decided that I would never allow such a household chore to dictate my life.

But it was in the 1960s, when wall to wall carpeting became the status symbol in homes. And it was so in my Mother's house too, as my parents had all those beautiful varnished floors covered with plush carpet. It seemed to be a sign to everyone that they had "arrived" and were "with it", in regard to the latest trends. And they were not alone, as almost every family I knew succumbed to the wall to wall carpeting trend.

Nowadays, it has become trendy to have hardwood bare floors as a status symbol. But somehow, I simply cannot buy into that, as those memories still remain for me. Besides, carpeted floors are a lot warmer in the winter.

Ah yes, my treasure trove of memories seems to stream out of my psyche in a never ending flow, as I endeavor to remember. For there are even many historic events, that should never be forgotten, and indeed be told to the new generations. Case in point— those particular interesting historical happenings, that affected so many families, not only in the south, but in the rural northeast, east and mid west. Those were the "Orphan Trains", that made such an impact on family life before my generation, and also impacted my own extended family.

Beginning in 1853, a remarkable minister named Charles Loring Brace observed so many children in New York City, who were literally living on the streets. They had been deserted to fend for themselves. And they lived in horrible conditions, sleeping in doorways or wherever they could find a bit of shelter. Most of them begged for coins in the street so they could eat. Some sang and danced on the street for those passing by, in hopes of a coin or two. They generally lived miserable lives, with no hope for any better conditions. Some had been put in overcrowded orphanages, which were almost as bad as being on the streets. So, Minister Brace took on the task of saving as many of these children as he could. His Children's Aid Society organized trains, and with the help of financial donors, thousands of unwanted children were transported to the countryside—to small towns and generally rural regions of this country, where they could hopefully be taken in by good families and given a better chance at life.

As a result, countless trains transported these needy children westward, to new homes. Later, other charities took part in this too—Sister's of Charity in Boston was one of those. This program continued for 75 years, ending in 1929, after having transported some 150,000 homeless children. So, these re-located children played a big part in the dynamics of our country's history.

As I said, this historic event also touched my own family. Because my Aunt Dorothy, who married my

Daddy's older brother, was one of those children. Yes, she was a child from an Orphan Train, that stopped in Morgan City and Berwick. After the children on board were brought out at the train station for folks there to consider for adoption, she was chosen by a local family. For the children, who were not chosen there, they went back onto the train, which continued to the next town, and then the next, until all the kids were selected.

However, because of those children's background information—or lack thereof—few of them knew anything about their biological families. And this came back to cause problems for Aunt Dorothy. For years later, after her husband passed over and she had been a widow of some years, she wanted to do some traveling. So, she and another Aunt of mine signed up for a European trip. But for this, Dorothy needed a passport. However, she had no legal proof of birth, so was denied a passport. She tried to get some documentation back east, from where she had been originally transported when a child. But there were no documents, attesting to the fact that she was even born in this country. I never did learn how she persevered in this regard. But I do know that she did eventually go on her European vacation. Perhaps, the federal government made a special dispensation for those children from the Orphan Trains. We can only surmise, that some bureaucracy with a heart must have intervened on behalf of all those thousands of orphaned children, who grew up to be good citizens of our nation.

But looking back, I cannot help but wonder how most children of that era ever grew up into adulthood— orphaned or not. Because in those days, there were so many childhood illnesses, for which there were no inoculations. Such ailments as several types of measles, as well as mumps, chicken pocks (to name but a few) were considered something that all children had to endure—and for recovery, their parents just had to hope and pray for the best. For there were no childhood preventative shots for any of those maladies then. But there was one childhood disease, that was at the top of the list of potential horrors for children in those times. It was Polio, which was better known as Infantile Paralysis.

In that era, back in elementary school when I was to be in a play, the teacher had cast me as a poor little crippled girl on crutches. Well, when my Mother found out what part I was to play in that drama, she hit the roof. Because so paranoid was she about giving her approval to any role where her child would be portrayed as a cripple, was never going to happen. So, even though I wanted to do the part, she told the teacher in charge in no uncertain words to cast some other child in that role. Her attitude was understandable, because so in fear of Polio inflicting her children was she, that even a hint of seeing her child on crutches was an abomination for her.

Yes, parents were really paranoid about Polio in those days. There was already one girl and a boy (whom we personally knew)—just a couple of years older than me—who had been stricken with Polio in our town. They were both bed ridden for a time, and when they were well enough to walk, they could not—not without the help of heavy metal braces on their legs, along with crutches to get around. Later, they were forced to use those horrific heavy leg braces to walk all the time. Thus, they had been permanently crippled for life by the terrible disease.

The pity of it all was that no one knew how poliomyelitis was spread to some children, while leaving others unaffected. In the southern region of our country, it was reported, that polio would strike mostly in the late spring or early summer, while reports from that era showed the northern states being hit with this mostly in late summer and fall. But no matter when Polio struck in a community, people became terrified that it could happen to their children. So, it is understandable why my Mother lived in such fear of that terrible disease striking her children—and she was not alone in this anxiety. Because there was probably no home, where this fear did not exist in those days. Yes indeed, we should all thank God for Jonas Salk and his Polio vaccine!

✵✵✵

CHAPTER - 3
Early School Daze and World War-II

My memories of attending school in the late 1930s faded somewhat in adulthood. But these days at this more aged point in my life, bits and pieces are coming back to me. As so many Seniors discover, with age comes more recollections of long ago times. And I have to admit that I can concur with this, as these days I now find myself remembering more about previous times of the past.

All the girls back then wore dresses or skirts and blouses. I was particularly well dressed, because my mother used to sew pretty little cotton dresses for me. And later in high school, my Grandma sewed for me, too. I would draw a formal design on paper, go get the cloth needed to make this design real, and bring it to my talented Grandma Oceania Fangue, who put it all together from my drawing. Thus, I always wore an original self-designed creation for every prom and homecoming dance I attended.

But during early elementary school, still in the Great Depression era, I recall having only a few home made dresses, a pair of lace up shoes for school and a pair of (usually black patent leather) dress shoes for church. However, I was far better off than some kids I knew. There was one girl in my class, who had only two school dresses for an entire year. She would wear one dress on a particular day, and the other dress on the next day. In between the days, her mother would launder and iron the other dress, so her daughter always had a clean dress to wear.

Then there were some very poor kids, who lived down the river road and had to walk at least two miles to school. For there were no school buses then. Usually, they came to school in their bare feet the entire school year, because they owned no shoes. Sometimes when it was cold, their teachers and some of the other kids would have sympathy for those boys, and bring a pair of their male sibling's hand-me-down, out grown shoes, for them to wear. Those boys wore patched up denim overalls, which back then only really poor kids wore to school. It would have been difficult for those children to ever imagine, that in the distant future kids and even adults would seek out and buy such worn looking, frayed denim pants to wear—and pay outrageously high prices for such. Because in those days, denim pants were only meant for men and boys to work in—not to wear as their attire for school, church or any social occasion. Indeed, wearing worn denim pants at such times would have been like wearing a badge that announced to the world their poverty, and that they could not afford anything better.

During those years, when so many people were poor, most took baths very seldom. This was because few houses had bathrooms with running water—much less hot water heaters.—something we all take for granted these days. So, taking a bath meant bringing out the big metal wash tub into the kitchen, hauling water from the faucets in buckets, boiling some of it on the stove to mix with the cold water in the tub, so as to make the water temperature tolerable.

Then there was a hierarchy of sorts, when it came to which kids would be allowed to go first for a bath in that tub. I faintly recall a time when a few of my cousins, my brother and I were staying the night at the home of Grandma Landry (my Mom's mother). This was so our parents could attend a dance a few miles away. It was a Saturday night—"bath night". So, Grandma prepared the bath water in her old wash tub in the kitchen, and made us line up for our bath. We were just young kids then, but it was generally accepted in those days, that the oldest always went first.

So, that meant my Cousin Betty had this privilege, as she was the oldest kid there. Afterwards, it was then my turn, as the next oldest. After me, it was my brother Sonny's turn, then cousin Jade, and finally it was little Beverly's turn to bathe. Looking back, I can't help but wonder how dingy that bath water must have been by the time young Beverly had his turn.

However, that was the way it was, because the work involved in replacing dirty bath water with fresh water for each kid would have been too labor intensive to accomplish, without wearing out the grown-ups in the process.

Back then, the older ladies usually wore their hair in a bun at the nape of their neck, and wore "comfortable" lace up shoes and dowdy dresses, that made (age forty plus) matrons look so much older. But the younger women and girls in those days tried to emulate the Hollywood movie stars they saw at the movie theater about once a week, if they had the few coins it took for admittance. The movies were about the only escape most people had from the hum drum lives they lived— that is except for the Saturday night events at the dance halls.

But for many gals, not only was bathing once a week the norm, washing their hair more than once a week was not always possible. Mostly, they used the cistern rain water to wash their hair weekly. However, they managed to find still another way to keep their hair as clean and presentable as possible in between. Every few days when their hair began to look oily, and they were unable to wash their hair, they would sprinkle corn meal all over their head and then brush it all out. Amazingly, the corn meal took that oily look away, and rejuvenated their hair for a few more days.

I relate all of these tidbits, about the everyday living of some folks in those days, for the purpose of enlightening the reader about the oftentimes little known things about people's lives in that era. It is important to consider that such humble beginnings have been known to influence people for the rest of their lives—even into their future, when times for them would become more prosperous. So, for many people, who lived through the "Great Depression" years, as well as World War-II, these experiences molded their character for all time. And for many who lived productive lives in their futures, they were assured a notable place in the "Greatest Generation".

As for many of us born into the decade of the 1930s or before, it is understandable that our very character came to absorb many of the lessons learned when we were young. But then, lessons learned about being frugal, valuing the worth of what little money we had, as well as becoming self-sufficient and respectful of our elders, these aren't exactly bad traits to carry throughout life.

However, my care free childhood as I had come to know it, came to a screeching halt on that memorable Sunday of December 7, 1941. That day has been etched into my memory for all time. My cousins, brother and

I were out running and playing hide and seek under the Spanish moss hung giant live oak trees on my grandparent's property in Patterson, when we became out of breath. It was an unusually warm December day, so we decided to go into the kitchen for drinks of water. As we bounded through the kitchen screen door, I saw Mother, Grandma and a couple of my Aunts gathered around the radio, apparently listening intently to what was being said. When she saw us come in, Mother quickly motioned toward us to be quiet. So, we tip toed in and sat on the floor to listen. As the words from the radio began to sink in, I heard Grandma cry out in alarm. She was followed by emotional exclamations from Mother and her sisters, as they voiced their dismay. After their initial alarm my Mother turned to us, and explained what had happened.

The Japanese had attacked our country and we were at war, she informed us. I could see that these grown-ups were more concerned than I had ever seen them. It was not only the realization that our country was now at war, but there was more to be concerned about. Grandma's sons (my Mother's brothers—not even yet in their 20s), who were currently serving in the Civilian Conservation Corps (CCC), would probably be among the first ones to be inducted into the army. As it turned out, their concerns proved to be true. Because these two young men were indeed immediately inducted into the army at the start of that war. Thereafter, two more of my Uncles, my Mom's nephew and several older cousins were also called up to serve. And serve they certainly did—seeing duty in England, France and the South Pacific.

The draft was instigated in that war, and I dare say that there was probably not one family, that did not have at least one member in the service. So, seeing those little red and blue on white background flags hanging in the windows of almost all houses, became common place. There was one star imprinted in the middle of some flags. This meant that a family had one young man in the service. But some families had flags with two, three and even four stars depicted thereon, to show how many of their own were serving.

Yes, World War-II was a conflict that affected everybody in this country and in nations all over the world. It was indeed a war like never before in our country's history. So, it took all of us pulling together in order win—not only overseas, but on the home front as well.

As a result, even we young kids were expected to play our part, too. So, the home front during those war years in the early 1940s became a whole different scene from what we all had been used to. Civilians planted Victory Gardens on even the smallest of plots in their backyards, so they could grow some of their own food to feed their families, because so many things were rationed. Yes, gasoline, sugar, butter, rubber tires and meat (to name a few things) were rationed. And there was no chocolate candy to be bought anywhere. For my family to have even a chance of getting a few small bottles of Coca Cola, we had to write our family name on a reserved list down at Pete's corner grocery store. In this way, when the weekly delivery came, we would be allowed to buy six small cokes—only six to a family, no more.

As for all those commodities, like butter, sugar, meat, etc., it didn't matter how much money you offered, stores were not allowed to sell any of this to you, unless you had enough ration coupons, along with the money, to buy this stuff. So, everyone was at the mercy of the little ration stamps in those booklets, which were issued to each family on a regular basis. Also, war bonds were a big thing then, because that money went to finance the war. As a result, just about every head of household man regularly authorized that his employer automatically take out $18.75 from his pay check, for that $25 war bond. I say $25, because that is what it would eventually be worth if you kept it for ten years. I always remember after the war, when my Daddy showed me those stacks of war bonds, that he had accumulated during all those years. He had bought several of these with my brother's and my name on these. Many years later, especially after I got married, he gave me the ones with my name thereon.

Looking back, I recall all those aging cars that kept on going on the home front during the war. There were no cars available to be bought at all between 1942 and 1945. The major car manufacturers had retooled at the beginning of the war, and made tanks, army trucks, jeeps and any vehicle needed for the war effort. So, every family car was expected to keep on going, causing many folks to literally hold their collective breathes, hoping that nothing on their car would break down. Nothing, that is, they couldn't fix themselves. Hopefully they also wished there would be no need for a new part to be replaced, as few standard automotive parts were available then, either. And you never saw as many patches on inner tubes, as there were then.

But there was one outing my family took in 1943, that I shall always remember. Daddy and Mother saved enough gas ration stamps, that would be needed for our little vacation weekend to Grand Isle—some 112 miles south. It was the first time my brother Sonny and I had ever been to a real beach, to the sandy beaches of the

Gulf of Mexico. We were so excited, even though each rental cabin on the beach had black-out curtains in all the windows, that we had to make sure were covered after dark. But all we kids could think about was running over that sandy beach and into the salty waves of the Gulf.

However, when we saw the beach at the water line, it wasn't as nice as we had envisioned. There was all manner of debris, that had been washed up from tankers that the German subs had sunk, just a few miles offshore. And there were large pools and splotches of icky black crude oil everywhere along that beach. Mother didn't want us to go into that water, but nothing would stop us. We ran into the waves of the Gulf like little wild Indians, shouting with delight all the way. But it wasn't until after an hour or so of splashing in those waves, that we came out and looked at ourselves. Our bodies were almost completely covered with splotches of sticky black crude oil. Daddy had to go and purchase some kerosene, so Mother could literally give us a kerosene washing. That seemed to be the only thing that would take that terrible crude oil off of our bodies.

But through it all, we kids really had a good time on our first outing into the big salty water. These days, no one would ever think of going into such water, nor would they even want to walk on that beach, which was so strewn with all manner of debris from sunken vessels. I am amazed when I recall those times, and realize how close those German submarines regularly frequented the waters along our coasts.

Indeed, German submarines literally laid in wait regularly for those oil tanker ships, coming out of Texas ports, that were destined for Great Britain. Many of those ships regularly plied the Gulf waters, very close to our shores for a couple of years into the war. And there is no telling how many of our ships the German subs sank.

I have memories of large sacks of flour, chicken feed and such being sold in those war years—not within burlap sacks, but in sacks of varied cotton, flowery printed, calico cloth. This served two purposes. One was for the sack to obviously hold whatever it contained. The other purpose was that it allowed the calico cloth of the sacks to be further used—to be sewed into dresses and shirts for children and adults alike. Thus, little to nothing during that war was ever wasted. We, civilians, were expected to make things last and to do the best with what we had. It was our patriotic duty to support our military people, who were so courageously fighting the war on several fronts. So many commodities were needed by our armed forces overseas. Things like chocolate candy, soft drinks, meat, butter, etc. were also supplied to them—to make their lives just a little better. As for we civilians, in addition to the above, we were expected to mostly do without such things as new leather shoes, new clothes, candy—things that made our lives better. We simply had to "make do" with what we had, as well as make everything last longer.

But everyone seemed all right with that, because in our own way, "doing without" was our way to help win the war. As for gasoline and new tires for family cars, we were all expected to be satisfied with what ration coupons would allow us to buy. We were expected to stretch those coupons as far as possible. So, there were no "joy rides" for us. There were no unnecessary trips to neighboring towns anymore. The car was only used for Daddy to get back and forth to work, and maybe across the river a couple of times each week to attend a movie.

There (in addition to the radio and newspapers), we could keep abreast of what was happening through the news reels. So, it seemed that our family life revolved around whether or not we had enough ration coupons to do anything, anymore.

I remember one time when my Mother had saved a number of ration coupons for sugar and butter, so that she could once again make a home made cake. Wow, was that the best tasting cake ever! Considering that we kids had to do without candy, cake and pop, any offering such a my Mother's was indeed a treat for our "sweet tooth". Unfortunately, such treats were few and far between.

My little brother Sonny and I would take his red wagon, and like many others kids, pull it all over our small town in search of things that some people threw away. We collected such things as discarded newspapers, old rubber tires, useless inner tubes and scrap metal, which were all valuable items to be turned in at the scrap drive receiving stations, to be sent to factories and subsequently made into new tires, ammunition, vehicles and other items for the war effort. So, civilians of all ages did their part on the home front.

There was an even more personal side to all of this for me. As a young Girl Scout in 1942, I recall a special project our troop had. On such occasions, I and my two best girl friends at the time, Gaylen & Helen, and the rest, made box lunches and brought these to the train station, where the trains usually stopped to wait for the railroad draw bridge over the river to close, before the train could proceed. You see, during those war years there were countless Southern Pacific trains, containing untold numbers of soldiers, who were being transferred to certain coastal locations before going overseas.

So, we little Girl Scouts would bring our box lunches, along with the appreciation letters we had written and included, to the depot. And when the train stopped we would hand these to any of the uniformed soldiers, who were literally hanging out of those train windows to receive our gifts. I can still recall so many of their young faces then—all looking like they were mostly still in their teens and others barely in their 20s. All of the faces of those still innocent young soldiers just lit up with glowing smiles, as they received our box lunches and envelopes. Little did they have any inkling of what awaited them in that horrible war. Their smiles—still to this day—are etched in my memory, as they shouted their thanks to us from those train windows.

Even as long ago as that time when I was about ten years old, still those memories are with me. Our house was almost five blocks from the railroad tracks in our town. But often times in the dead of night—when the wind was blowing in our direction—I could hear the lonely whistles of so many of those Southern Pacific trains, transporting countless young recruits to various ports of embarkation. This went on month after month, and turned into years, when those muted train whistles could be heard all over our town, at all hours of the day and night. Indeed those muted train whistles seemed to take on an eerie resonance, as if permeated with so much sadness.

Even on rainy nights, sometimes I could still hear those sorrowful whistles. And that was no little thing, considering our house had a corrugated tin roof, where the sound of rain drops was noisily enhanced. But then there is really nothing that has ever given me more of a feeling of protective coziness, than sleeping in my second floor room under that tin roof. However, no matter how comforted my slumber might have been then, my feeling of well being was oftentimes subdued, because I could not shake the feeling that I was so privileged, when countless others had to fight, suffer and die in that terrible war.

Yes indeed, there are so many memories still alive and well in my memory bank about that era, recollections that resonate about the home front in those war years. Yet another of these memories had to do with a particular project my Mother insisted I accomplish. Whenever she would get a V-Mail letter (that is what they called those then—"V- For Victory") from her brothers and cousins, she would of course reply immediately. But she would also sit me down at the dinning room table and insist that I also write letters from me to all of them. At first, I resented that chore. But after a while it came easier for me, and when I would get a V-Mail letter from some of them in reply—especially to me—it made the effort all worthwhile. Looking back, I do believe that this was the very beginning of my writing career, and it is all thanks to my memorable Mother.

Amazingly, many years later my Uncle John told me how much he appreciated my letters, because as a soldier all letters from family members represented their lifeline from back home. He also said later in life, that his experience in the army in England and France was the most memorable time for him in his entire lifetime. Because he was an army cook he did not go over in the first waves of invasion day on the shores of France. Military support groups always were deployed after the beachheads were for the most part secured.

However, all military people after serving on or near the front for a certain time were rotated and allowed an R&R (Rest and Rehabilitation) leave. And amazingly, his group was sent to the French Riviera (Cannes and Nice)—previously the playground of the rich and famous! Imagine, if you will, all of those young American soldiers suddenly being brought into that wealthy people's fabulous domain. Before the war, this area in the south of France was known for formal gaming casinos, first rate lavish hotels along glittering promenades and pristine beaches.

Then, enter all of those young American soldiers, to whom the Army had issued each a "Welcome To The Riviera" booklet, before they occupied their lavish rooms in those posh hotels. It was to serve as a guide to this foreign realm into which these soldiers had suddenly been plunged. But in this booklet, they were admonished thusly.

"We are set up to make your stay here as pleasant as possible, to subject you during this period to a minimum of regulations and in general to give you the chance to relax and rest. On your part we ask of you one thing— that you so conduct yourself as to reflect credit on the service to which you belong. The facilities placed at your disposal have been put into first class condition for your use and occupancy. There are others to follow you. Therefore, your care and consideration will make it better for them if you do your share to help keep these facilities in good condition and restrain from any action of a destructive nature."

As a result of that R&R experience, when he (as only one of those young soldiers) was treated to this special time, most soldiers like him also probably looked at that experience as one of the best times of their lives. So did my Uncle John. Of course, it is not difficult to see, considering most of these men before the war had never even traveled out of their county or parish in the USA.

And now, they were experiencing facilities geared for privileged ultra rich people—with Uncle Sam picking up the tab. How great was that for them? But Uncle John was special to me, as he had replied more to my letters than the rest. And he later joked about his time on the French Riviera, when he had left the troubles of war for just a little while, and related how well he got along with the French girls there.

Being a great jitterbug dancer in those days, along with having a happy personality, must have certainly helped him attract girls. But he had the advantage of being from that region of South Louisiana, where thousands of people still spoke French—albeit a Cajun French dialect. In fact, he was reared in a household where Cajun French was spoken everyday. Why, even his parents could not speak English. So, it certainly must have been easy for him to converse with the people on the Riviera.

Imagine those guys, promenading along the thoroughfares of Monaco, sitting in the sunshine of Monti Carlo's Mediterranean sun, sipping cognac and vermouth at sidewalk cafes? What a great experience they had, and so deserving for them—before having to return to that war.

Speaking of dancing, this seemed to run in my family, as it was a special part of our lives. Personally, as a teenager I lived for those teenage Friday night dances, and wanted to attract guys, who actually knew how to dance. For this gal was one, who could have "Danced All Night", as the song goes.

How I remember the first dance party I was invited to, at age 13 in 1945. My best girl friend was having a birthday party and we were expected to wear formal long dresses. I had a navy blue taffeta dress, trimmed with little red velvet bows, that Grandma had made for me. And I was so excited, literally counting the days until it was time for the party. Finally that Saturday came, and I awoke not feeling too well. But I blamed it on my just being tired. When afternoon came, I wasn't feeling any better. However, I was determined to hide it from my Mother, who would certainly make me stay home from the party if she suspected I was not well. I felt a bit feverish, so, I laid down on the couch to rest—just for a little while—in preparation for the big night.

Of course, back then whenever we kids ran a fever it could have meant a number of things. Because in those days, there were no series of childhood inoculations for us, to prevent early diseases. On the contrary, as I said before, getting the mumps, chicken pox and a couple of strains of measles were viewed as something every kid had to endure. It was looked upon as a kind of rite of passage for youngsters to get through.

So, I lay there on the couch feeling weak from a fever, which I realized was now invading my body on this special day. And my mind was full of "what if". What if my Mother kept me from going to the party because of this? I was so looking forward to celebrating my friend Geraldine's birthday at this first dance party for all of us. I so wanted to be with her, along with Gwen, Jo Ann, Molly, Juanita, Earl, Donald, A.J. and the rest of the kids.

As I mulled all of this over in my mind, it was then that I saw her coming! Mother entered the living room and hurriedly came over to me, asking—"Why are you lying down in the middle of the day?"

I knew she asked this incredulously, because I was usually such an energetic youngster, I never did that. Then she laid her palm on my brow—that dreaded hand of her's, which always seemed to diagnose us kids as if by magic. All of a sudden, she pulled her hand back in a jerky motion and her eyes opened wide as she exclaimed. "You are burning up with fever!"

At that point, I knew I was sunk! Now, the party was just an unattainable dream for me. Because with fever, I knew there would be days of bed rest and being medicated.

She brought her thermometer and put it in my mouth. It turned out, that I had 103 degrees of fever. Yet amazingly, my love of dancing was trying, as it turned out in vain, to convince my body that I could still go to that party.

"Give me some aspirin, Mom, and I will be all right." I implored of her, as she replied.

"Oh no, this will take more than just aspirin. I am taking you to the doctor now!"

"Does this mean I can't go to the party?" I asked, pleadingly.

Well, of course, my hopes had been dashed, and she did indeed take me to the doctor. But when he examined me, he was perplexed as to what was causing this high fever. And he was just as astonished as we were, when he finally ventured an educated guess that it might possibly be Typhus Fever!

"What is that?" My Mother asked, as she saw the dreaded look on the doctor's face.

None of us had ever heard of this disease, but it appeared that the doctor had, and from the tone of his voice we knew it was bad, and he made that clear, as he replied.

"I can't be sure, because some testing has to be done for a valid diagnosis. And since there are no medical facilities in these towns, where this child can be treated for such a rare disease, if in fact she has it, she will have to be taken to a hospital in New Orleans."

So, I was immediately driven to New Orleans—two hours away in those days—where I became a patient in the Baptist Hospital for three weeks. And it was true. I did in fact have Typhus Fever, which in the USA in those times was considered a rarity. Because that disease was known as one of the plagues, that wiped out millions of people in Europe and other countries in the world, back in history, it was certainly to be feared. Other than studying about this malady during Medical School, it is doubtful that any of my doctors ever imagined they would actually be treating this horrific disease.

During the course of my treatment, we heard more about what had happened to me. Typhus Fever—known as one of the plagues throughout history—is contracted usually by the bite of a flea off of an infected rat. Horrors, for my Mother, who was appalled upon learning this, as she was such a scrupulous house keeper, and certainly there were no such vermin ever in her house. But it was a fact, I had contracted this somewhere!

We all learned that Typhus Fever is a virulent disease, which was usually associated with over crowding and filth. After contracting this disease, and if patients could survive the accompanying effects of skin eruptions, delirium, vomiting, severe headache, lesions, rash and a very high fever that could last up to two weeks, they might survive.

Luckily for me, Penicillin, a powerful antibiotic which was obtained from certain green fungi that grew on stale bread and decaying fruit, had been discovered years before. And it had been much used on wounded military people during the war. It was also used to save the lives of countless people, afflicted with Typhus and other terrible maladies, after they were rescued from those atrocious German Nazi concentration camps in Europe. Finally, it came to be used widely in the civilian sector, for seriously ill people. So, let's face it.....Penicillin saved my life too!

While enduring those painful injections every three hours around the clock for three weeks at that New Orleans hospital, I learned that two other people had come down with this same thing in my town. The Health Department investigated and found that none of the three of us had anything in common. We were not related and we did not know each other. Finally, they tracked down the one place that we had all frequented. It was that old beat up theater on Main Street in Berwick—that dilapidated structure, probably built at the beginning of the 1900s, and used as a dance hall for many years, long before they made a movie theater out of it.

In those days, there were few health department restrictions on most public places. I am distressed to admit just how bad that place was, and yet we still frequented the movies there. As kids, we used to attend matinees there. We would curl up with our legs on our seats, in that dark place with the flickering light, so we could keep our feet off of the floor. This is because we could hear the rats scampering up and down the isle and under our seats. We giggled about this among ourselves, and would you believe, we would throw popcorn kernels on the floor for the rats to eat. How stupid we kids were then, when we regarded such harmful things as fun!

So, the place of commonality was discovered— where three people had been infected with this terrible disease. It is amazing that there were only the three of us infected, when you consider how many people went there regularly. Luckily, there was not an epidemic as a result. After that, the owners were instructed to gas the place and then tear that building down to the ground, because it had become such a threat to public health.

☆☆☆

Yes, there were bits and pieces of both good and bad memories during the 1940s. But I have vivid recollections in 1942 and 1943, when as kids we played together in that lot (over-grown with tall weeds), across the street from our house. Back then, we kids were always being indoctrinated with hatred for the Germans and Japanese, through movies, slogans on posters and radio persuasions, etc. And the boys mostly received fake rifles, military helmets and walkie talkies for Christmas and birthdays. As a result, it was logical that most kids back then played games called "war". It was my brother Sonny, Cousin Bobby, little Tom from down the street, and me. Even though I was the oldest of our group and a girl, they begrudgingly allowed me to play with them. But I was not allowed to have a rifle. However, I could be on their "front lines" as a nurse, in my fake army nurse outfit I had received for Christmas. Go figure!

I also remember us kids debating, from the point of view of real soldiers, as to which side we would rather be captured by—the Germans or the Japs (as everyone called them back then). We had heard horrendous stories of atrocities perpetrated on captured soldiers and civilians, that it was a toss up for us, as to which enemy would be worse.

One of my notable memories after the end of the war, was when Mother bought me my very first pair of high heel shoes. Those were navy & white spectator pumps—just like the ones Bette Davis wore in that 1939 movie, "Dark Victory". What a grown-up feeling those high heel shoes elicited in me, whenever I would parade in front of a full length mirror—so pleased with myself.

But on the whole, during the first two years of the war, there was so much bad news for us in my generation, as well as for my parent's and grandparent's generation to endure. However, we were always bolstered by the radio speeches of our strong leader, Franklin Delano Roosevelt. For he usually made us feel so much better, with his words of comfort and hope for a victorious future. That is why on April 12, 1945, when his life ended, we were all so devastated.

People cried tears of sorrow, and walked through their daily duties in a depressed mood—having trouble accepting that he would no longer be leading our country and the world. It was like a beloved person in our family had passed away. And in reality this was true. For he had become a cherished member of American families.

✡✡✡

CHAPTER - 4
Segregation In My Old South

As a child of the 1930s and 1940s, I saw my share of the inequality around the area, wherein I lived. But from what I can remember, the people I observed—among my extended family members and others in my town in south Louisiana—they did not act as outlandishly as what was being reported about many hard core segregationists in other more northern regions of the state. For it appeared that there was more such unrest in those regions, as well as in Mississippi and Alabama.

Back then, segregated folks were referred to as "colored people", and even if they had only a very small percentage of Negro blood in their heritage, they were listed on birth certificates as "Negro" or "Colored". But in many cases, some of them were so light skinned, they could have passed for white, if they chose to—and many did.

Today, we are expected to refer to all African-Americans as "black", but it is difficult for me to do so. This is because, to my eyes, most of these folks are not black, but are of different degrees of skin color—ranging from light tan to dark brown. For most, it is the result of generations of forced sexual intermingling, usually (through no fault of their own) instigated by the "Master of the plantation", when their ancestors were slaves in the old south.

Speaking of that era before the Civil War, when slavery was so wide spread in the southern states, I discovered something about my ancestors. While doing research for two of my previous books (CAJUN ODYSSEY I & II), I ran across much family information about that period of our country's history. Some of it, I must say, was a bit distressing for me.

Indeed, for someone like myself, a southern woman of many generations' heritage, and one who looked with so much disdain on segregation in my generation, this new genealogical discovery was upsetting, to say the least.

It was interesting for me to learn about my Daddy's mother's line of people, who helped to settle south Louisiana and contribute to it's progress. Yes, certain of my ancestors settled along Bayou Dularge, one of those extensive waterways, the courses of which run through many miles of marshland into the Gulf of Mexico. Before settlers came there, it was mostly low lying cypress swamp land, inhabited by many species of wild creatures in that wilderness. But there were some strips of somewhat higher land along that bayou, which could support farming. So, that was where they settled.

Afterwards, these hardy people—through years of hard work—did well on that land. So well, in fact, that their efforts resulted in eventual land ownership on both sides of that bayou. Eventually, this section came to be called Dularge Plantation, where fields of sugar cane thrived. But they did not accomplish this alone. For I leaned that my ancestors owned 22 slaves.

This revelation was disturbing for me. On the one hand, I was pleased that I came from this line of such ambitious hard working people, who eventually amassed some wealth. But on the other hand, I couldn't help but be saddened at the thought of my ancestors being slave owners.

However, I kept in mind that through much of my research into that slave era, there were reports about many slave owners being benevolent people. Usually, most of us have only heard about those really bad plantation owners of that era. However, it is a little known fact, that there were countless others, who treated their slaves reasonably.

Therefore, it is with this realization that I have come to terms with having ancestors, who owned African slaves. So, I can only hope that my people were good to those people—treating them with kindness, during that unkind era.

Unfortunately, even into my generation our country had not come to accept that the descendants of those African slaves were people in their own right. They were emancipated American citizens after the Civil War, and should have been treated as such. But even when I was a child, so many decades after the Civil War, this was still not the case. Inadvertently, when still a youngster, I saw a newspaper photo of a particular incident, where a colored man was hanged from the girders of a bridge over Bayou Lafourche, some miles away from where I lived. This was such an appalling realization for my young mind to accept. For even in childhood, I had so much ingrained empathy for the colored folks in my town. They were always kind to me, and my Mother used to chat almost every day with that nice colored lady, who walked by our house on her way to town.

Her family lived across the street from the Berwick school, and my family lived a block away. When I started school, all the white kids walked there—some from across town, because there were no school buses. But my brother and I were considered lucky, that we only had a block to walk. However, that nice colored lady's kids, who lived just across the street from that school, had to walk eight blocks and cross the railroad tracks to attend the colored school.

The government used to refer to that unfair set up as "separate but equal". But what a lot of baloney that was! For you only had to see that the "colored" school, with it's shabby appearance and it's used books (left over from white schools), to realize that it in no way could ever come up to the standards of that attractive red brick elementary school, where we white kids went.

But still, the colored folks in my town accepted this as their only recourse, and never as a youngster did I ever hear of any disturbances in our community, resulting from their frustration.

There is another of my childhood experiences, that particularly stuck in my memory from the time I was in elementary school. One day, my Daddy took me by the hand and we walked up the street to a restaurant along the highway. Today, we would call such a place a "diner". But back then, it was referred to as a "blue plate special" type of eatery.

This was a treat for me, having lunch with my Daddy—and no one else. That was indeed a rare occasion, because Mother always cooked and we all ate together. And what was even more rare, was to buy lunch in a restaurant in those days. This is something rarely done, because most of the people of that era did not have extra money to eat out. But this was a gathering place, where locals sometimes had to grab a fast, cheap sandwich or plate lunch. It was the type of cafe, that could have been likened to so many such establishments in countless small towns all over our nation. There was no fine dining there, no frills, no cloth table cloths, no gourmet menu.

It was a no nonsense type cafe, where home cooking was the specialty, and the hamburgers were tasty.

But that day was one to remember for me, and I felt special. Daddy and I walked through the cafe door and onto the floor's much scuffed, dingy linoleum. Then we sat down at a table, covered (as all the others were) with similar checkered oil cloth.

It was then that I saw something I had never been privy to before in my young life. Along the outside wall of this cafe, there was a window with a wide shelf where the sill normally would be. The waitress had opened the glass window and was talking to a colored man, who was apparently conversing with her from outside. He gave her some coins, and then she handed the man a paper bag, which appeared to hold sandwiches. She then pulled down the window glass and went to take orders from the people in the cafe. It was then that I noticed, as I struggled to look through the window, that the man had walked to a strip of grass where he sat down, took out his food and began to eat. He was not alone there, for two other colored men sat on the grass too, eating their lunch in a shady spot—away from that hot summer sun.

I looked up at Daddy and asked him this. "Why do those men have to eat their lunch outside? Why can't they come in here with us to eat?"

He said something that I shall always remember. "That's just the way it is."

But then, segregation was a part of life in the south in those days. We were used to seeing separate water fountains, waiting rooms, rest rooms and such. Why even at that old Main Street movie theatre, colored people could only be seated in the balcony.

However, here I was a child of the old south, growing up and living in that region all my life until later adulthood, yet I could never accept this way of life, that was so blatantly unjust. Therefore, I never ever fit the definition of a "Southern Belle", who accepted segregation as her due. On the contrary, it was appalling to me.

There is another instance of many years ago, when I worked in an oil company office. There was a congenial older colored gentleman named Henry, who worked as the janitor there. He and I used to talk everyday, and I so enjoyed his wit and sense of humor. Every morning, I would come into my office and Henry would pop in to see if I needed anything done. Sometimes, he could see that something was bothering me. And why not? Being the bread winner for two young children and myself on the salary they paid single women in those days of the late 1960s, was an everyday struggle. Mostly, I tried to hide my problems, but Henry could sense my distress on occasion.

One day he asked me why I was so down that morning? I guess he caught me at a bad time, and I begin to complain how I needed $500, to complete a management correspondence course I was taking. And I didn't know how I was going to obtain this. That was in the days when there was a double standard—one criteria for males and one for females. A man in my head-of-household position would have easily been granted a small bank loan. But for women, it was not permitted, as we divorced gals were considered unreliable. So, it was up hill all the way, and at the time, it seemed to me that the harder I strived to better support my children, there were always road blocks in the way.

Henry considered what I said and spoke his words of consolation to make me feel better. Then he left to do his duties in another part of the building. But soon, he came back into my office and offered these words to me.

"Ms. Beryl.....I want to help you. So I will loan you the $500."

Taken by surprise, I looked at him with amazement. Then tears came into my eyes. I was not shedding tears of despair, or sadness, but tears of gratitude that a person such as Henry, whom I knew must not make much money either, would extend to me such an offer. Of course, I thanked him profusely and told him how overwhelmed I was at such generosity on his part. But I couldn't accept his kind offering.

After realizing how much Henry thought of me, it gave me the strength to find another way to get that money. For if a man such as Henry held me in such high esteem, as a fellow soul worthy of his trust, then I simply had to convince myself that I could rise above yet another obstacle, and I did. But to this day, I have never forgotten Henry—one of the few really selfless, magnanimous gentlemen I ever met in my entire lifetime—this time around.

But back around 1972, attitudes about black and white separation still were quite evident in some circles. However, I always tried to instill in my two children, to think like their mother thinks in such matters that involved race. Indeed, I wanted them to treat all people fairly and to conduct their lives in this manner. I thought that I had succeeded until one day after a parade had finished, wherein my daughter played in the high school marching band. After it was over, she phoned me to ask a question.

"Mom, the parade is over....is it all right if I bring some of my band friends home for refreshments?" To this, I said of course.

"But two of them are black....is that a problem?" She asked.

I was amazed, that she would have to ask that question, as she well knew my views. So, I quickly replied.

"You know you don't have to ask that. All of your friends are welcome in our home."

Over the many decades I have lived so far, I have often wondered if the empathy I feel for those once segregated folks might stem from previous lives I may have lived on this planet. As a believer in reincarnation, I know that cell memory from a previous life sometimes plays a part in the shaping of a person's attitudes in this present lifetime.

So, who knows? Perhaps I lived the life of a slave previously in times of long ago, in the old South or elsewhere. This could be the reason I feel so strongly about this subject. Whatever the reason, for me, this has been much food for thought over the years.

✡✡✡

CHAPTER - 5
Dress Rehearsal For Life

High School and College days should very well be considered as our "dress rehearsal for life". Yes indeed, the situations we encounter during those formative years prepare us, somewhat, for many of the things, that we are yet to encounter in adult years.

My graduating class of 1950 was a particular milestone, because that year marked the first time twelve years of school were required, in order to finish. The graduating classes before 1950 only had to attend for eleven years. Looking back at this, I have to admit that it was just as well, since most of us really needed that extra year of school. It was especially so for me, because had I finished with eleven years, it would have been at age sixteen (because my birthday fell in December). And sixteen would have been absolutely too young. As it was, I finished twelve grades at age seventeen.

Reminiscing in my old high school year book is always a journey through nostalgia. Our class motto was "Our future is not in the hands of fate, but in ours". Also, a sampling of popular songs of that year was depicted on certain pages. There were songs like "The Old Lamplighter", "Remember Me, I'm The One Who Loves You", "A Little Birdie Told Me That You Love Me", "Buttons And Bows", "Some Enchanted Evening", "Open The Door Richard", etc. And there was a special quote printed underneath the photo of every graduating senior, which was supposed to denote something about the personalities of each. Mine read

"Romance is always young". Take from that what you will.

But along with all of that came some sadness, when I remembered what happened to some of my classmates after they went on into their lives. My lovely cousin, whom I speak of in another chapter—that pretty young girl, who was on the basketball team and always had a ready smile for everyone—eventually just gave up on her life several decades later. The quote under her photo read, "For all that is fair, is by nature good".

Then there was a most memorable, handsome young man, who seemed to have had everything going for him. He was Student Council President, in the Future Business Leaders of America, a cheerleader, and was voted "Most Popular" by his classmates—not to mention, that probably half the girls had a crush on him. The quote under his year book photo read—"The greater the man, the greater his courtesy". And yet unbeknown to any of us, he must have been troubled even back in his high school years, although none of us ever suspected such a thing. After graduation he went on into his new life, much like the rest of us. But then, just a few months before our tenth class reunion, which was set for the summer of 1960, he picked up a gun and shot himself.

I shall never forget how distressed all of us felt, and what a loss this was for everyone who knew and loved him. Indeed, for such a wonderful young man, with his whole life ahead of him, to do such a thing was difficult—if not impossible—for any of us to comprehend. And the loss, due to his untimely passing, cast a pall over our previously much anticipated reunion that summer.

All of these memories came to mind recently, while looking through some of my old high school memorabilia. It was then, that I came across a program for our 1960 reunion. Among all the familiar names of classmates and teachers printed thereon, I noted the back page "Memorial" for this much missed fellow classmate—in memory of whom I had been asked to compose a tribute—which I quote as follows:

"Surely, we will each choose to remember him in a special way—as a fellow student, as a good friend, as a pal and a great sport, as a member of our armed forces, as a husband, son and father. Although we grieve his departure and think of him often, we wonder if perhaps he might have pondered words such as these.

"Life is but a venture into joy and sorrow.
Moments of adventure, then regrets on the morrow.
Often, to me it does seem, that to live is to race.
Is contentment only a dream? No... there must be
a place!"

Those words were my humble contribution to honor him. And it is my hope, that he was there at our reunion in spirit, and that he approved of my literary offering.

You know, just reading these decades old words caused me to realize a flood of recollections in regard to this former classmate of mine. Strangely, I can still visualize his face, his smile and his wonderful personality, that so endeared him to everyone.

His passing was the first loss of a former classmate, that any of us had experienced in our young adult lives, and it hit us all very hard. Nowadays, almost 60 years since our graduation day in 1950, it would probably be difficult to gather enough of the beloved people, who are still alive today, in order to have another reunion.

Because a majority of faculty and student body souls from yesteryear have already left this planet.

However, for those of us, who are still going on with our lives, it is none the less difficult for us to appreciate, that those bitter sweet younger years were all part of our soul's learning experience in this lifetime—in preparation for more tribulations to come in our lives.

Speaking of learning several valuable lessons during high school—both good and bad—there were many. A couple of these instances taught me a lasting lesson. One of those happened one day when I was standing at my locker. A fellow student of mine in our junior class came up to me and proceeded to ask me a question. She was not a girl, whom I associated with much. Indeed, we did not travel in the same circles. She was considered a "jock" type girl, who played on the basketball team, and was generally interested in sports. I, on the other hand, was interested in music, literature and dancing, and could care less if they ever played another basketball, football or baseball game, ever. Yet, here she was, seeking me out all of a sudden.

But I could tell by the urgent look in her eyes, that she was desperate. However, I could not imagine why I had suddenly become so valuable to her. But I soon learned what she wanted.

"I need your help....for my next period class. I have to have a poem to turn in.... and I couldn't come up with one. You are so good at writing....it comes so easy for you, but it is so hard for me. Would you write me a few lines.....so I won't fail?"

Well, I thought to myself how ironic it was for this girl to suddenly want a favor from me, when she usually seldom ever gave me the time of day. But being the soft hearted person I was, it was difficult for me to dismiss the distress reflected in her eyes. And even though I protested that I should not be doing this for anybody, I gave in. I then hurriedly scribbled a few lines of poetry, off the top of my head, and handed it to her. She thanked me, and then hurried on to her class.

It turned out, that shortly thereafter our English-Literature teacher was expected to select the best poem and short story, which had been turned in during the semester. These were to be submitted to be judged among the best high school students' literary efforts in a state contest, that was sponsored by a big New Orleans newspaper.

Well, would you believe, the teacher selected the poem, that I had hurriedly written for that girl, as the one to be sent into that contest. And guess what? That poem won first place—but with the other girl's name on it! The poem I had turned in—the one I had spent so much time composing—never even got an honorable mention. Thankfully, my short story, which the teacher had selected to enter, did win first place in it's category. But it was a hollow victory for me.

As the teacher read the results of that contest in front of the class, I looked over at that girl, who had signed her name to a poem she had not created. However, she could not meet my gaze, so embarrassed was she. I guess at the moment we were both wondering how we were going to handle this situation, when at assembly for the entire high school the next day, we would be expected to walk up there in front of the student body and faculty, to accept our medals.

I knew my teacher well enough to realize, that she was certainly aware that this girl could not have created that bit of poetry on her own. Indeed, our teacher knew both our writing styles, not to mention that this girl was barely sliding through that class. So, it could be that (unbeknown to either of us), the teacher decided to teach both of us a lesson.

And so it came to pass, that when our individual names were called as winners in each our category, we marched up there and accepted the awards. For we were both trapped. If I complained that I had written that winning poem and given it to the girl I would be in trouble, and if that girl admitted it was not her work, she would be in trouble.

On another occasion, to add more fuel to this fire of compassionate giving away of my talents to others, who benefited from my efforts, there was even another instance in this regard. A particular football player boy in my high school class—one whom I had started first grade with—had also asked such a favor from me. And magnanimous me, feeling sorry for him as well, hastily scribbled a short poem, that he could turn into English/ Literature class. And as fate would have it, he also won a plaque for that poem, which I had written for him.

But apparently he was not embarrassed about accepting that award, as the girl has been. On the contrary, he seemed quite pleased with himself, at having accomplished such—with no qualms as to how he had dishonorably achieved that award. In fact, on a recent occasion where our paths crossed after all those decades later, he proudly told me that he still had the original copy of that poem I wrote for him, along with the award he received for it back then.

So, after those sad experiences for this aspiring—but naive—writer, I vowed never again to compose anything for someone else to put their name on it. Looking back, I consider those experiences as more valuable, but distressing, lessons that I had to learn. Subsequently, this lesson became very ingrained in me. So much so, that many decades later when a woman had the nerve to ask me to ghost write a book for her—with her name as author thereon—I exclaimed in no uncertain words, that only I have the right to put my name on anything I write for the rest of my life.

One of my ambitions in high school was to be selected as a Homecoming Maid. I could care less about being Queen, because I did not have the connections needed with the football squad, to ever aspire to that. But there was a chance I could be voted in by the students, when they voted on ten girls for that gig. So, as a Junior I campaigned hard, only to learn after the votes were counted from the student body, I had not made the cut. With that news, I remember spending almost an entire weekend, crying from disappointment.

However, afterwards in my senior year, which was my last opportunity, I decided to take no chances with those students, who professed to be my friends, and then stabbed me in the back by not voting for me. The rules stated, that each girl had to sell a certain number of football season tickets, to make her eligible just to be on the ballot. So, I went out and sold more football season tickets than anyone had ever done in the history of that school. And I didn't even like football! As a result, the principal and teachers were amazed at this, and decided because of my diligence, that I would not have to be voted on. Thus, I was automatically appointed a Maid in the 1949 Morgan City High School Homecoming Court. Mission accomplished!

This was another of my "learning experiences", that proved valuable during my lifetime. Because of this, as well as many other hurtles I had to overcome in life, it became my belief that if you want something bad enough, you will figure out a way to accomplish your goal. Along with this realization, I also learned not to trust others to get me where I wanted to go, because people could not always be depended on to be in my corner. In some cases, I found that I could only work hard and trust my own God-given abilities and perseverance— especially in those cases when I didn't know who my real friends were.

However, throughout this entire lifetime of mine, I always had this ingrained sense of justice, so I tried to fight against what I deemed as injustice whenever I could. In June of 1950, right after my high school graduating class collected diplomas, the Korean War was declared. So, several of the boys in my class were drafted or enlisted for that war. Of course, several went on to college—knowing full well, that if they dropped out they would be drafted.

Three years later, after my brother graduated from high school, the draft was still in effect, even though the Korean War was over. So, he opted to go on to college, knowing full well that the draft was still hovering over his head. Even so, after a year of college, fully realizing that it would only be a matter of time until he was drafted, Sonny did in fact put his higher learning on hold. He decided, that he might as well get it over with, so he joined the Army for two years. Quite simply, he did not want to have that eventuality hanging over him indefinitely.

After his basic training, he was shipped over to South Korea, to do guard duty on the 38th Parallel, which marked the boundary line between South Korea and Communist North Korea. Our Mother, upon hearing her only son was going to such a potentially dangerous place, literally lived each day with dread during that time. Because there was always the threat, that the

North Koreans might resume that war. And what made it worse was that my brother seldom wrote letters to any of us. Of course, he was never much of a letter writer—not like me at all in this regard. So, as a result of his lack of communication with his Mother, both Daddy and I had to endure her emotional upsets daily. Finally, I had enough and decided to do something about what I considered an injustice for my Mother. It was then, that I wrote letters to his commanding officer and to his chaplain. I asked for their help in impressing upon my brother the harm he was doing to his Mother. I felt at the time, that Sonny would really be mad at me for doing this, but I could not take it any longer—seeing Mother in such emotional pain.

Because of my actions, as he related to us later, he was indeed reprimanded by his commanding officer, and counseled by his chaplain, about his lack of letter writing. Thereafter, we saw a marked change in the mail delivery to my parent's home from him. So, to my brother at this later point in time, I would like to say that I am sorry for any discomfort I may have caused you back then. But I cannot, because this needed to be done, for our Mother's sake.

✫✫✫

A young woman I knew once said to me. "Beryl, you are such a dreamer."

At the time, I felt like she was selling me short. It was as if she thought my head was filled with frivolous fancies, that could never be attained. However, I soon came to think of that definition as something worthwhile. This something represented to me, that I was indeed a "dreamer"—someone, who would not settle for the status quo, but who would strive for better. And this is what I have tried to do.

Obviously, this also meant that I would not follow the crowd—even back in my high school days. This was brought home to me at my tenth high school reunion in 1960. One of the girls I had graduated with came over to speak to me. I recognized this pretty classmate of mine right away. And I also remembered that she had been the only Jewish girl in my class, which reminded me of the empathy I had felt for her back then. It had appeared to me in those long ago years, that her sense of sadness seemed to be ever with her. I guess this was due to her not being allowed to take part in many social events in high school. Indeed, because her father would not allow her to go out with any gentiles, she had to refuse a football captain, who had asked her to a big dance. So, I always remember, having a special feeling for her loneliness—that loneliness, which seemed so obvious sometimes. Now, here she was, seeking me out some ten years later. But why?

I soon found out, when she spoke to me. "Beryl..... you were always so nice to me in high school....and I have always remembered your kindness. It meant a lot to me, and I want to thank you."

Needless to say, I was astonished, but gratified, that this classmate of mine had so valued my kindness toward her all those years ago. It just goes to show that by my not going along with the so-called in-crowd cliques back then, most of whom usually ignored her, my consideration toward her contributed something that she continued to value.

Oh yes, many of us look back at our high school days—either with relish or disdain. For certain young men, who excelled at football, basketball, track, wrestling or baseball back then, this was their so-called fifteen minutes of fame. And upon going out into the real world, such a young man soon found that no one cared how many baskets he made, or touch downs he ran, or home runs he scored, or school sports records he attained. For few of a boy's achievements later in life could ever match those moments of sports accomplishments in high school. And no matter how many years some of those boys had left to live, for most of them their moments of glory were long gone. About all such boys had to remind them of those days were the trophies on their shelves and sports write-up clippings in scrap books, that their Mother's kept.

But for high school girls like me, who lived to go to those Friday night teen dances at the gym, we counted conquests differently. I recently pulled out my old five year diary, that my brother Sonny gave me one Christmas, when I was in ninth grade. Would you believe, that I had written something in that diary for every day of those years? Although the handwriting had faded, it was mostly legible, and I noted the kind of score I kept back then. For each dance I attended, and there were many, I noted in my diary how many boys had asked me to dance on a particular night. This is not to say how many times I danced with each one, but how many different ones asked me. Those numbers ranged from 10 to 13, to my all time high number of 17 individual boys, asking me to dance at one event.

Ah yes, there were some good memories of high school, and I shall always hold these close to my heart. Of course, there were also many traumatic tests of character in school, and we did not always pass those with flying colors. Yet, despite the emotionally traumatic stuff, that felt like the end of the world for some of us, most of us overcame those trials with just a few bruises, in order to go on into adulthood.

As for some of we teenage girls in high school, there was a particular problem. Let's face it, this nation seems to have such a predilection with "big boobs", that it makes it difficult for young girls, who are not particularly endowed with notable breasts in their teens. In the 40s and 50s, this was the case too. Many teen girls began to wonder if they would ever develop those womanly attributes. Of course, back in the 1930s, this was not a problem, because most folks then were just happy to get enough food to eat and to afford clothes on their backs. In the 1920s, as my Mother related to me, the style was flat breasts. So, the girls used to tightly bind their breasts with cloth, to make those look flatter. Go figure!

Recently, I heard someone remark wisely to a teenager, who was crying about something that happened to her in school—something that seemed so devastating to her.

"Remember......it's only high school", he said to her. And I thought at the time how apropos were those words. But as we now know, those four years serve as an introduction to adulthood.

However, unfortunately if a teenager is hurt and put down enough by others in those formative years, the stings of such verbal assaults and disappointments can be carried with them for the rest of their lives. Thus recollections of such could detrimentally impact a young person's sense of worth as adults.

However, I like to believe that most of us are strong enough to survive high school, and not carry all the unpleasant baggage with us into later life. Personally,

I have to agree with that great lady Eleanor Roosevelt, wife of President Franklin Delano Roosevelt, when she spoke these wise words.

"Nobody can make you feel inferior without your permission!"

✰✰✰

After graduation from high school, it was time for college. My Daddy and Mother really wanted me to go to college in Lafayette, as it was the closest one to our town—73 miles away. It was accepted that most graduates from our school would attend there, except for those few who went to LSU in Baton Rouge.

I have to say, that after graduating from high school, I really did not have a clue as to what I wanted to do with my life. Besides, career options for girls in my day were few and far between. But it was so important, especially for my Daddy, that I go to college. You see, he had only been afforded a fourth grade education, because he had to quit in order to help his widowed mother support the rest of the kids. So, it was such a source of pride for him to be able to say, that he was sending his daughter to college. Therefore, I went mostly because I didn't want to disappoint him.

But considering that my talents were in the artistic, writing realm, I knew there would be no jobs in this category for me in my towns, if I pursued this. So, looking at this logically I knew my choice had to be Business Administration and Secretarial Science, because becoming a secretary or a nurse (which I had absolutely no drive to be), would be my only options for a job later. Let's face it, society then expected that girls should get some schooling, but in the end they would eventually become wives and mothers, so extended higher learning was deemed not necessary, as their future husbands were supposed to take care of them.

In 1950, would-be students applying to most colleges did not have to take extensive state-mandated tests, as they do today. Back then, if you had at least a "C" average and your parents had the money, you were in.

However, my heart really wasn't into becoming a college student at that point. So, in my session with a college counselor, who was helping me with my schedule for the Freshman year, I questioned a few things. I asked why it was necessary for me to have to take Business Administration-1, Typing-1, Short Hand-1, etc. all over again, when I had already had those courses in high school? She told me it was necessary, to see how much I had learned.

This seemed redundant to me, so I implored of her to allow me to take the second courses in those categories (usually only done in the Sophomore year). She answered, that this was quite simply not allowed.

"Please!" I implored of her. "Let me try, for the first month. If I can't keep up, I will admit it and change to those first courses."

After seeing how adamant I was, she relented and scheduled me for those second year subjects. As a result, my schedule was so jam packed, that I literally had to run from one classroom to another, which were spread out all over that campus. And this schedule was so full, that those first few months literally almost wore me out. In fact, I lost five pounds the first month, and I couldn't afford to do that, as I barely weighed one hundred pounds. But one thing was for sure, I do remember always being just about the first one in line, when the cafeteria opened—so hungry was I from all that running. But I did it! I survived that Freshman year and came out of it with Sophomore accomplishments to my credit.

However, during that year something happened—something that has always made me wonder "what if" for me, if I had made a different choice. One day during typing class, there was a U.S. government recruiter, who came to speak to us. We were told about the new Pentagon building, that was being completed in Washington D.C., and the government was looking for girls from all over the USA, who could pass their typing tests and be accepted to work there. Any girl, who would be accepted, was to be afforded a suitable apartment to be shared with another girl who would also be working at the Pentagon. So, those of us, who thought they could pass the 90 word per minute typing test being offered at the local newspaper office in Lafayette, were advised to sign up and try out.

It only took a minute for me to think about this, before I (along with several other girls) signed up for that test. As it turned out, I passed the test and was given a packet of important looking papers, that I was to bring to my parents for their approval. Afterwards, the ball would begin rolling for all who were accepted to go to D.C.

Would you believe, my parents were thrilled at this wonderful opportunity for me, and I was too—for a little while. But it was then that the impact of this awesome change in my previously protected life brought me back to reality. I knew I would be home sick, for my family and friends—and would I really be able to handle living in such a big city?

So, just days before I was scheduled to leave, I chickened out! Looking back at that missed opportunity, and often wonder how different my life would have turned out, if I had accepted and followed through.

Afterwards, it was back to school where I felt so stifled. At that college, they were so protective of female students—especially Freshmen. Curfew each week night was 8:PM. On Friday nights, we could stay out until 10:PM, and on Saturday nights it was 11:PM. Wow, I look back at that Freshman year as merely doing time with studying, going to class, with little to no social life.

That is why I took the Greyhound bus every Friday afternoon after class, to go home for the weekend, where I had so much more freedom. Back then, every Saturday night I could go dancing at one of the local night clubs. There were so many really good live bands, that would regularly play at those places.

At the beginning of the 1950s, there were even really famous bands that were passing through in those days, from New Orleans to Houston. And they used to stop midway to play in our towns. After all, the Shell Inn, which boasted of having one of the best dance floors around, and the Hub Club were often the sites of very special big band attractions.

This was still in the "Big Band" era, before Rock and Roll became the norm. So, we dance fanatics in our small towns had the privilege in those days of dancing to such famous groups as Tommy Dorsey, Jimmy Dorsey, Gene Kruper, Wayne King the Waltz King, and more.

Ah yes, those were the days!

✩✩✩

CHAPTER - 6
Happily Ever After?

There we were, the three of us sitting in my living room rocking chair, in front of the TV on New Year's Eve 1958. We were seeing in the new year, my five month old baby girl, me and my baby son, who was still growing in my belly and yet to be born.

That pathetically sorry picture has stayed in my mind all these years, for it was probably the most miserably lonely evening of my life. And where was their Daddy—my husband who should have been there with us? Well, for him it was just another night of extensive alcohol drinking at some bar down town, where he usually caroused with his drinking buddies. But then, such behavior had become the norm for him in this marriage. But even on New Year's Eve, I asked myself? Shouldn't he have made the effort to be there with the three of us—at least on this special night? Wasn't anything sacred to him? Did he not have any sympathy or empathy for us?

The tears fell from my eyes, as I watched and listened to the whistles, fire works and shouting from those masses of festive people on TV, as they celebrated that event with such joy. I continued to cry, when I realized that I was apparently to be the only parent in their lives—the only parent my children could depend on, because their father was certainly not there for them. Even though with the passing of each year, I held out hope that this man would become a better husband and father. But my hopes were always dashed.

So, his behavior on that night was par for the course—no different than what it would continue to be like, during what turned out to be twelve years of marriage. He was a drinker when I married him. I knew that! But foolish naive me thought I could change him! But he only got worse. Then I thought that after the children came, he would change. It didn't happen then either.

I learned many years later, that no one can change an alcoholic unless he or she decides to make up their own mind to change. So, I was trapped! I say trapped, because in those years, divorce was frowned on by society and the Catholic church, wherein we had been wed. Besides, if I did that, how would I support my children? Women did not make much money in those days. True, I had loving parents, and I knew they had so much sympathy for what I was enduring—even though I kept most of that reality from them. For it would only make them worry more. Besides, I did not want to admit failure, and become a charity case for them. So, I continued to endure the status quo, unfortunately for years to come.

Marriage was difficult enough in the 1950s, when all of we ladies were expected to be so perfect. In modern times, the decade of the 1950s is usually so nostalgically portrayed as an era of really "Happy Days" for everyone. But don't you believe it! Yes, except for the Korean War of a few years duration at the beginning of that decade, we were at peace. However, it was a strange kind of "peace", when you consider the ever present concerns about the Cold War with Russia, that had reared it's ugly head.

Of course, for the most part, folks were enjoying a new age of advantage and economic well being in their everyday lives. Black and white TV ads portrayed housewives with every conceivable kitchen appliance then available. In those commercials, women were shown doing housework with beautifully styled hair, wearing high heel shoes w/hosiery, along with a string of pearls and in a fluffy dress with can-can slips. To believe these ads, was to believe, that housework and child rearing was so easy, with little obvious exertion involved. And get this, on TV, the kids were always portrayed as perfectly clean and well mannered little darlings. What a crock of nonsense, that was!

Take it from this lady, who was one of those young wives & mothers of that decade. The reality behind those portrayed happy days was, in truth, a myth. Women of that era were expected to play the part of "Mrs. Perfect"— the subservient wife, great mother to her children, good daughter for her parents, wonderful neighbor and citizen, as well as a devout church member. In other words, we were supposed to be all things to all people—to the exclusion of who we really were as individuals.

There were even many articles printed, that outlined what was expected of women in the 1950s. Those outlines in depth reflected the prevailing male macho slanted attitude thinking in those days. Of course, this was meant for women, who did not work outside of the home, which was the majority of gals in those days. Because usually any wives, who had jobs outside of the home, were frowned upon as being neglectful of their family's needs.

Some suggestions advised wives to always have dinner ready whenever her husband came home. Before his arrival, she was expected to freshen up and look good for when she greeted him. And she was to make sure the house was clean, that the children were washed and in fresh clothes and they were warned not to be unruly when their dad came home.

It was also advised, that no matter how hard a day she might have had, she was always expected to put her concerns away and greet her husband with a smile—as if she did not have a care in the world. If he came home late, or even stayed out all night, she should not complain. After all, to the prevailing way of male thinking in that era, this should always be forgiven. Because his wife should count her concerns as small, compared to what difficulties her husband might have had at his job that day.

Further advice suggested, that when he did come home, he should always have the most comfortable chair in the living room, with a drink waiting for him on the coffee table. She should also be there to fluff his couch pillows and massage his tired shoulders, while he unwinds. Also, offering to take off his shoes, would be an expected gesture.

After all, as this advice stated, a wife's goal was to make his home a place of peace and refuge from the working world. Even if she had what she regarded as important things to discuss with him, she should not bother him with such things at that time. Let him talk first, it was suggested, because what he had to say was so much more important than anything the wife may wish to impart. A wife should always remember that he is the master of the house, and his judgment should never be challenged. She should feel comforted in her beliefs that he will always use fairness, when dealing with her, the needs of the household, and in reprimanding the children. A wife was expected to be subservient and have no right to question her husband. After all, the advice back then stated, a good wife should always know her place in the family.

Shades of the "Stepford Wives"! The underlying moral to this ridiculous advice of almost 60 years ago, would probably be construed by females of today, as a perfect doctrine for a male dominated society. And that is what existed all those years ago—a male dominated social hierarchy. It was the "women's liberation" era which really took hold somewhere in the middle 1960s, before so many women woke up and took a real good look at themselves and at the kind of life they had been made to accept, usually with little say in the matter. It was in that decade, particularly, that many women began to realize that they should be heard as to where their lives were headed. So, they started to assert themselves.

Emerson once said. "Is not marriage an open question when it is alleged, from the beginning of the world, that such who are in the institution wish to get out, and such as are not, wish to get in?"

As for what women really, really want in this life, it is a fair shake—respect, consideration and a chance to excel on an even playing field. For too long, they have been taken for granted and imposed upon. History reflects this as reality. Indeed, it does pain many a feminine heart to always hear of the great MEN, who "won the west" or the east, or the south, or wherever. Does anyone ever stop to wonder why no one thinks about where these men would have been, without all of those brave pioneering women at their sides? Why is it always the male pioneer, who is deified—and his wife is forgotten?

Thankfully, it took that 1960s era of feminine awakening, before things started to change as to how many married women viewed themselves. And almost 50 years later, it is still resounding as having been a "wake up call" of huge impact.

✡✡✡

Originally, my first husband and I were high school sweethearts, and both of us loved to dance. In fact, he was considered to be one of the best dancers around. Also, back then I felt that I really loved him. Besides, we had fun together. So, we were married when I was 19 and he was 20, in that quaint old wooden St. Stephens Catholic Church, where I had been baptized.

It was a beautiful June 22 day in south Louisiana, marred only by the usual hot humid temperature, that we all were used to enduring at that time of year. For in 1952, no one had air conditioners in their homes. Only the best movie theaters and the big department stores in New Orleans were air cooled. I remember seeing the signs at those store entrance doors, which read like this. "Refrigerated Air Inside". This was their attempt to get people to come inside and cool off, and hopefully do a bit of shopping while there. And it worked every time, for I cannot begin to describe how it felt for those of us, who were seeking such a cool refuge, to step inside and get relief from that notoriously humid, hot summer air. As for those cool movie theaters, folks used to go there, not only to be entertained, but to get a couple of hours of relief from the heat.

Yes indeed, it was hot in those Louisiana summers, with little to no relief available. But even whenever my mother and I went to New Orleans in summer on the Greyhound bus to do some shopping, we would still always dress up for the trip. After all, we were going to the big city and wanted to look our best. Ladies then always wore their best clothes to travel—suits or nice dresses, hats, gloves, purses, high heels and hosiery (except during WW-II when no nylons were available to buy). But we suffered all day long, walking Canal Street from store to store, enduring the foot pain from those high heels. However, we always knew that we would soon become refreshed so much by going into those refrigerated air department stores.

Somehow, on my wedding day of all times, I couldn't stop thinking about those shopping days and that cool air. This was because of the hectic activity in the house that morning. It was due to the hustle and bustle of activity that was going on in the house, where I had lived almost all of my life. It was really hot in the house that day, with so many people cooking in the kitchen. They were busy preparing food for the reception, which was to be held at the house after the church wedding ceremony. Several of my mother's sisters, my Grandma and others were working so hard to prepare food for that event. As a result, the attic fan which was supposed to give some relief from the heat only succeeded in stirring the hot air around. It was then, that I wished we could have had some of that refrigerated air in our house.

But I also marveled at the fact, that all these women in my extended family were working so hard, just for me—so as to make my day a special one. They had even told me that morning to lie down so I would be rested and fresh for the ceremony, which was to come. This made me feel so useless at the time, seeing them exerting themselves while I was resting. Many days later, I learned that the reception had indeed been a big success. The church ceremony was at 11:AM, followed by the reception at the house, which overflowed into the back and side yards. The men had set up a bar under the carport, and used a Cajun pirogue boat as a container for ice, to keep the beer cold. And it seemed that a good time was had by all, at this lively event, which lasted from 11:30 AM and ended at 11:PM, when the last guest finally left. Wow, that was certainly an almost

12 hour long party to remember. I am only sorry I did not get to enjoy my own reception.

However, for me, I had to play the part of the bride in this elaborate saga. My special wedding dress awaited me—that lovely white dress, which back then was considered a symbol of the bride's virginity. And I was certainly worthy to wear white, because I was indeed a virgin. So, when it was time to get dressed for the big event, I donned my special patio length white lace over taffeta dress, with layers of marquisette slips underneath. I wore white satin high heel pumps, with a crown of pearls on my head, which held the mid length white lace bordered veil in place on my head. My three bridesmaids (Geraldine, Marion & Jade) wore brocaded satin patio length dresses (pastel blue, pink and green), died to match pumps and wide lace matching hats. Everything was in readiness for this big event, as we left for the church.

Daddy, who looked quite handsome in that white coat/black pants tuxedo, which was quite fashionable during those years for summer weddings, stood at the church door with me, as we awaited our walk down the aisle. But I sensed some sadness coming from him, as he was about to literally give his daughter away in marriage—a marriage that I knew he certainly did not approve of.

Just then, the organ begin to play the music, which was our cue to begin. So with my hand on his arm, Daddy and I took our first steps down that church aisle. At that moment, I experienced an overwhelming feeling of dread. I already felt as if I was in a trance, a feeling that all of this was like play acting a part in a dream, and I would soon wake up and it would all be gone. Then a strange thing happened to me in that instant. Just as

I took my first step, a voice in my head said (loud and clear), "What are you doing here?" To this day, I have always remembered those words in my head, and looking back it appeared to be a warning about the mistake I was making. But on that day, I pushed it back into my mentality, because I had to get through the ceremony, reception and then go on my honeymoon. It was certainly too late now to change my mind, I thought.

After the photos, cake cutting, toasting, I excused myself to go change. Mother came into my room, to see if I needed any help, and (I guess) to wish me well. My new suit and blouse fit well; my matching hat was already on my head. And at that moment, I felt pretty good about myself, as I stood there in my snazzy new high heels—looking into the full length mirror and assessing my appearance in all of this new finery. My purse and gloves were laying on the bed, waiting to be picked up on my way out. My suit case was already downstairs. All that was left for me to do was to throw my bouquet from the top of the stairs to those waiting bridesmaids and friends of mine, who were hoping to catch it. After this, it would be on to the car and off on my honeymoon trip to Florida.

Yes, I thought to myself, I am ready to leave. But beyond my obvious outward appearance, there was a nagging inner feeling that I was far from ready for what lay ahead of me. So, as mother busied herself, tidying up my room I got up the courage to ask her something.

"Mom, don't you have something to say to me—something I need to know before I go away? After all, now that I am married shouldn't you have some advice for me?"

"Oh Beryl Ann," she answered, in that tone she used when she was perturbed with me, because it was only at such times that she referred to me with my middle name. "Certainly you should know what you need to by now. After all, you probably listened to other girls talk, and know what to expect. All I can tell you is that you have to do everything you can to keep your husband happy. Listen.....they are calling us. It's time for you to go."

That was the end of that, and the closest we ever got to having any kind of meaningful mother- daughter talk. But in those days, it was rare that girls were ever talked to about sex. In fact, at around age 13, most girls were given a little booklet, that showed them what to do when their first period started. I suppose this was so that mothers of that era would not have to personally discuss such an embarrassing subject.

About the only actual "sexual" information, that my classmates and I probably ever got was when our school deemed it mandatory for junior high students to go to a special showing of a matinee at the movie theater. It was a film, depicting high school kids, who made out and the girl got pregnant. Of course, we already knew that should that ever happen to any of us, we were ruined for life, and would have to leave town for good. But the other short film we saw after that story was a film depicting actual pictures of people in the last stages of venereal diseases. This was especially traumatically horrible for all of us kids to view.

But all of this was meant to scare the wits out of us, so that we would never have sexual encounters. However, this was so traumatic and over the top, that a lot of emotional damage was probably done as a result of that distressing film.

Thinking back, I can't remember the word "sex" ever being voiced in front of us kids at home by our parents, or at school by our teachers. And it was expected that virgin girls were to be trusted to just say NO! I remember when I was 17 and 18, whenever I would go out on a date, as I was going out the front door my Mother would say to me—"Don't do anything bad, because your Daddy will never forgive you."

She really knew how to get to me, because the very thought of my Daddy, never forgiving me for anything I would do, was too distressing for me to contemplate.

But isn't it ridiculous how girls were reared to always say NO, but on their wedding night, they were expected to drop all inhibitions and become ready sexual partners? This one sided state of affairs certainly contributed to the sexual hang ups of so many women and girls, back then.

So, I went into this marriage as a totally unprepared naive young woman, who didn't have a clue as to what she was getting herself into. When I became engaged, my family tried to reason with me. This could have been likened to the words of an old song—"They tried to tell me I'm too young"—and they tried, and they tried, and they tried! But I thought, that I knew better. Besides, all my girl friends were getting engaged and married, and I didn't want to be considered an "old maid". Can you believe it, even at the beginning of the 1950s, if a girl was not married by age 21, she fell into that category. This is another example of how the stringent dictates of society literally caused many young people to marry—when they were absolutely not ready.

When I got engaged, my Daddy pleaded with me not to marry that young man. He said, "Don't marry him.....I'll support you for the rest of my life if you call off this engagement."

Of course, at the time I just figured that my parents did not think he was good enough for their daughter.

But then, do any parents really think ANY man is good enough for their daughters?

So, it was off on my honeymoon I went, in his old Chevy coupe, looking to the future through the eyes of a totally innocent young girl. As for my wedding night, it was a total disappointment! And I couldn't help but wonder—"Is this all there is? Is this what I will have to do from now on? Is this what so many people refer to as such a loving, fulfilling experience? What have I gotten myself into?"

That honeymoon didn't last long, because after two nights into our trip, the car's transmission went out. So, we had to spend one day waiting for repairs, which took all of the rest of our trip money. Then it was back home for us. This journey was over, and for me it seemed like a terrible beginning to our married life, that was supposed to be so special.

However, it was pretty much accepted in those times, that you would do the best you could with what you had to work with. To put it quite simply, newly married girls had to struggle toward making a marriage work as best they could. After all, there was no alternative acceptable for young brides in those days. It was kind of like that old saying—"you made your bed, now you have to lie in it."

I guess all those warnings, which certain loved ones of mine tried to alert me to beforehand about marrying too young, began to hit home, big time—early on into my marriage. Indeed, I recall my new husband's own Mother, at the reception, when she took me aside and looked at me with her sad eyes—all the while trying to tell me to be strong in my marriage. She also expressed her hope to me, that I would not have to go through what she went through. Although, I knew only too well how much she loved her first born son, whom I had just married, she also knew his short comings. This is because he "took after" his father, whom I already knew was a "drinker" too, and was also lacking as a good husband. And it was obvious, my new husband even inherited the good looks of his Dad. So, it was apparently her fear that this oldest son, who favored his father so much, might also display the short comings, that she had to endure.

Thinking back to all the weddings I attended, before my own, I always wondered why so many of the bride's women kin would always cry at the weddings of these young girls. It wasn't long before I realized why. This was probably because many of these older women already knew so much about the struggle, stress, pain and endurance, that might become a part of married life for many of their beloved daughters, granddaughters, sisters, aunts, etc. Thus, they were each saddened at the prospect of such things possibly happening to their young, innocent and beloved girls, whom they had protected from birth.

Personally, I had come from a good home, with loving parents, and a dependable Daddy, who made sure his wife and children had what they needed to live as well as it was possible for him to provide. There was no cussing, shouting or screaming in our home. There was no smoking there either, and my mother made sure that there was little discord in our home atmosphere. For she detested discord among her loved ones. If we had something to complain about, we did so when urged to explain. Indeed, I was so blessed with an exceptional home life. Then, I got married!

And it was just a short time after the nuptials, when I was plunged into a foreign (to me) atmosphere. My new apartment home became a place where my new husband used several objectionable cuss words on a daily basis, whenever he felt like it. He was an almost constant cigarette smoker, and there was always a gray haze of smoke hovering within most of the rooms of all the homes we had together. And he disrespected me in so many ways, much too often, without any regard for how it made me feel. Added to this, of course, was his abusive behavior whenever he got drunk.

But I was determined to be as good a wife as possible, even though what I feared most began to come true, almost from the beginning of this marriage. His habitual alcohol drinking became more frequent. Knowing that someone you are to marry already has a drinking problem is one thing. But actually living with such a person is an entirely different and devastating scenario.

His drinking at local bars with several of his guy friends, who were also big drinkers, became more pronounced. And these late night events, when he would stagger in usually after 2:AM, happened as much as three times a week, which became the norm in this marriage. And it was expected then, that a wife was not supposed to complain, because it was a macho thing that prevailed—in that era when men were expected to rule the roost.

Even after the babies were born, this continued. Consider that he never changed one diaper on either of those babies, and seldom if ever personally fed them a bottle—not that I can recall. So, he was living up to this macho image. And as their Mother, I had it all on my shoulders.

Back then, C-Section births were not at all common. But for me it was necessary. You see, in 1958, doctors and hospitals would x-ray expectant mothers one month before their supposed due date, to make sure the baby could fit through the birth canal. This was long before ultra-sound use. In the case of my daughter, her head appeared on the x-ray to be much too big to get through my pelvic area. It was obvious on the x-ray they showed me. So, a C-Section would have to be performed. Back then, once a woman had the first C-Section, all subsequent births would be that way. So, my son's birth was also to be the same. But his birth turned out to be a far more difficult one, than his sister's was.

This was because neither the doctor, nor I, could decide on the length of my pregnancy for this second baby, and we could only take an educated guess. So, June 1 was the agreed upon date for this C-Section. However, as it turned out, we guessed wrong, because this baby was taken too soon. So, my son came into the world prematurely, very underweight and with breathing problems, due to poorly developed lungs.

Remembering back to that time, as I lay on that operating table, when the doctor cut me open to get him out, the baby did not cry at all when they took him up out of me. This was a very bad sign. This necessitated the baby being hastily taken away, to be worked on by a medical team. Due to his undeveloped lungs, every breath he took was a major undertaking for that tiny little being. So, it was necessary to put him in an incubator, to be watched closely around the clock for a week. After his birth, I was in too bad a shape to see him at all. But I was told later, that during those days and nights, this baby's struggle to live was ongoing. Each breath was a great undertaking for him, in that depleted little body of his. But he struggled to heave his gray shriveled tiny chest to the extent of it's limited capacity, in an effort to consume enough oxygen to sustain his life.

As for me, well I was not fairing so well either, after that surgery. Since I had (what they used to call) a spinal block, I was awake the whole time. After they took the baby away, I could see the doctor and nurses working feverishly on me, trying to stop the bleeding, that was becoming life threatening. As I looked up at them, they all appeared so distressed, and I wondered why, because I was feeling so good at the time. But my mental alertness was fading. I could feel that too. And then there was a sense of floating away, without a care in the world, amid all of this hectic activity. I suppose this could have been considered the start of an "out of body" experience—a near death event. I can certainly say this about that. If that is what it feels like to bleed to death, I was amazed at how serene it felt and how glorious was the light that seemed to be around me.

However, the medical team did get my bleeding stopped, and in the following days I was on my way toward healing, during the next week I spent in that hospital room. Meanwhile, my new son was down the hall in an incubator, and as soon as I felt strong enough to shuffle down that hall, I was allowed to look at him through the glass. It was the very first time I actually saw him, and now I couldn't even hold him. But I was appalled at how bad he looked—not at all how my first child had appeared after birth. My son had a gray pallor, his skin was wrinkly from loss of muscle tone, every breath he took was difficult, and he was so small.

But he was alive! Even though few expected he would have lived that long. But not me! I remember, after they had stabilized me, following that extreme bleeding episode, my family came into my room to see me. In spite of my weakened condition, I was happy that I had given birth to a little boy. Now, I had a girl

106

and a boy—all I ever wanted. But when I looked at the faces of my family members, I could see that they were not happy. They couldn't even look me in the eye. Even the doctor displayed much the same behavior.

"Why is everyone so sad?" I inquired of them from my hospital bed. "Isn't it wonderful, we have a baby boy!"

It was then that the doctor told me, that my baby was not expected to live, and that I should prepare myself for the inevitable.

"No....no," I exclaimed. "He is going to live....I just know it!"

Apparently, I was the only one, who felt that way. So, after they all left my room, I had a talk with God and pleaded with Him to let my son live. I do not know if that carried the necessary weight for this success, but the next day my little baby took a turn for the better and began to breathe stronger.

At the end of a week, we were able to take him home. I shall always remember how traumatic it was, to be handed (for the first time) my own baby. He was so delicate, that it was almost like holding a small breakable doll. And there I was, being given the awesome responsibility for this tiny baby. Other than my Mother, no one wanted to hold him, because he was so fragile. Even my husband refrained from holding his own son, thinking that he might break him. But through thick and thin, that baby made it. And this mother always had faith that he would survive, even when everyone else had no hope.

After we were discharged from the hospital, it had been previously agreed that we would all stay at my parent's house—my husband, my baby girl, my new baby and me. This was so my Mother could help me take care of this new baby, as well as my ten month old daughter, and myself, who would have to spend weeks getting well from that C-Section.

However, things did not go as planned. My ten month old, still in diapers, also had to have a nightly feeding, and the new baby had to be fed every two hours, around the clock. My Mother tried to accomplish this for the first couple of days, but I could see that it was just too much for her. So, I announced that we were all going home, and I would take care of the babies. Not a good idea, of course, since my husband was useless when it came to taking care of his own children. But nevertheless, I was insistent, because I didn't want to be responsible for wearing my Mother down anymore.

So, it was back to our house for the four of us. Needless to say, our bedroom was quite crowded, with a large baby bed for my daughter and a bassinette for the new baby. Of course, I could get little rest, having to get up every two hours to give bottles and change diapers, as well as having to take care of a nightly feeding for my ten month old. And not one time did my husband, who was asleep beside me, offer to get up and do these things, so I could get some much needed rest. I was still hurting from that major surgery, but he didn't seem to care. There was one particular time that I remember vividly, when the new baby started to cry at his appointed time for his feeding, and I had just fallen asleep. I awoke with a start, and struggled to get up out of bed, but my body would not cooperate. So, I lay there for a few minutes, while the baby cried, and then I shook my husband awake, so he could do something.

"The baby is crying again," I said to him. "Would you get up and give him a bottle and change him? I just feel so weak......I don't think I can do it this time."

As he groggily turned toward me, he gruffly replied. "Just let him cry...he will finally stop after a while. Go back to sleep!"

With this, my husband turned over and promptly fell back to sleep. So, in that moment it once again became agonizingly evident, that it would always be left up to me to take care of these children, as I certainly could expect no help from him. It was obvious, that no matter how badly I felt, he would not help me. From that moment on, I mustered all my inner strength to overcome any physical pain and fatigue I might have, in order to continue taking care of my children, night and day.

But what was even more difficult for me, during all those 12 years I spent in that marriage, was having a drunk man come home in the early morning hours, after his nights of heavy drinking, and then push himself on me sexually. Any woman, who has ever endured a drunk man doing this to them, well knows how degrading that is. Even after the babies came, this behavior sometimes occurred as much as three times a week. What a blessing it would have been for me, if he had only just passed out after coming through the door, in his alcohol induced state. But no, that was never the case, for there was still more for me to endure. And of course, there was no recourse for wives like me in those days, because a wife's plight then was to be at the mercy of her husband—no matter what his condition. It appeared that such situations were just regarded as part of a woman's duties then, as an unwritten wife ownership addendum to the marriage license.

As for this wife, it mattered not whether I felt ill or was just too worn out, particularly when I was taking care of two babies (ten months apart, all by myself)—which turned out to be the hardest work I ever did in my entire lifetime. None of that seemed to matter for that drunk husband, who had "needs". For yours truly, it was quite simply a case of having to pay a sexual price, against my will each time—just so he could leave me alone, so I could get some much needed sleep.

Yes, any woman, who lived such a life of forced sexual subservience, could not help but feel degraded whenever this would happen, which for me was after all those drunken episodes of his. It felt akin to being raped over and over again. So, my disdain for him mounted, to the point where I resented him for the rest of his life.

Recently, I saw a program on TV, that dealt with such things. The consensus was that whenever a man pushes himself sexually on any female, in a forceful manner regularly for long periods of time—sometimes even for years duration—the resulting emotional impact on such women is severe. Surprisingly, I learned from this TV program, that this even has a name. It is referred to as "sexualization". Even wives enduring such as this, in their efforts to keep their marriages together, pay a price eventually in lower self-esteem, degradation and shame, which they keep to themselves so that the world does not see how badly they are hurting inside. In fact some of them, who later manage to get out of such relationships, carry with them through the rest of their lives the ridiculous belief that they must try harder with the next man in their lives. Thus, they open themselves up to being mistreated again and again—all because of their first damaging sexual relationship.

My last straw came in 1964, on one of those nights when my husband had been out drinking. At around 3:AM, my little 5 year old son came running into my dark bedroom where I was sleeping. He woke me, by pulling on my night grown sleeve, and he was giggling. Immediately, I switched on the bedside lamp and looked at him in alarm, thinking something was wrong with him. But his smiling face quickly dispelled that notion.

"Mommie.....Mommie....you have to see Daddy! I heard the car and looked out the window. The car is in the middle of the street, with the door open. And Daddy is walking like this."

He then proceeded to imitate the gait of a drunk man, as he laughed with glee. I watched in astonishment, as my son continued to walk around in circles at the foot of my bed, as he did his imitation, obviously feeling that it was so much fun. Little did he realize he was imitating the terrible condition of his own drunken father.

That was the moment, when I knew I had had enough! The next day, I took a good hard look at myself in the mirror, and realized that I was now into my 30s and nothing had changed with this man I married. If anything, he was getting worse, and his family was paying the price for his behavior. Now that my children were getting older and could see this for themselves, I had to do something. It was time to get them and myself out of this destructive atmosphere before it would leave a mark on them, and he drags us all down with him. At that moment, I decided that I had to divorce him.

Amazingly, days later when I asked him to move out, because I was divorcing him, he looked shocked and said. "Why? Why are you doing this?"

It was apparent that in his own mind, he really thought everything was all right. But I had come to realize—the hard way—that you can fall out of love with someone, and if there is still friendship left, you can go on. But if the friendship becomes depleted, and you no longer even have any respect for that person, there is no hope.

Because he refused to move out of our house, as he tried to call my bluff and was making it as hard as possible for me, I had to pack up the children and myself and go to my parent's home. Thank God for them! Without their help, until I could get through all of this and get a new start, I would have been truly trapped for the rest of my life.

Ah, but it was no easy feat to get him out of my life. Even though I had filed for divorce, I was into that infamous one year "waiting period", that the State of Louisiana (in those days) insisted all of us endure. For all, who applied to legally part company in those years, were subject to a full year before the final divorce decree would be granted. So, there was even more emotionally distressful months to get through.

Yes, my children and I were living at my parent's house, until I could get on my feet. I still had my hat and gift shop, that I tried to make a go of. But all the while, I had to endure his repeated telephone calls, imploring me to come back to him and try again.

"I'll change....you'll see," he would implore each time I took his call. But of course, I had heard that song before, and as the old song goes—"it had an old familiar ring"—denoting empty promises. One time, he even came over to my shop when I was closing for the day. My two children (ages 5 & 6) were in the back store room, where I kept a black and white TV, along with games and coloring books, for them to pass the time while I took care of the shop. It saved me baby sitting money.

When he came in, I knew at once he had been drinking heavily, and was in an obnoxious mood, as he began shouting at me. "This is ridiculous....you have to come back to me! This makes no sense, when we could be a family again."

I asked him to leave and walked toward the door, to open it so he could go out. But it was then that he lashed out at me, hitting me on the face with his hand. When the children heard his angry voice, they both came running out of the back room, crying and shouting at their Daddy to stop.

At that moment, as I held my hand to my face, that had just been struck, I witnessed a scene that I have never forgotten. Upon seeing his Dad strike his Mother, my little 5 year old son ran up to his father and started hitting him repeatedly on the legs with his small fists, with all his might, and at the same time screaming. "Stop hitting my mother!"

Just recalling that day still brings tears to my eyes, as I was so proud of the tenacity of my little son, in his efforts to protect his Mother. After that happened, my husband stormed out and never came back. I suppose he finally realized he had gone too far and there would be no hope of reconciliation ever again. Thereafter, this man accepted his plight, and apparently just gave up on life.

Throughout all of the marriage, I always knew that deep down there was a good person within this man. However, his alcohol addiction had for the most part subdued his good side. But, I do remember one time, when I came home from work. Upon opening the front door, I saw there in front of me a brand new stereo player with a vase of red roses set on top. The card read—"Thanks". It was not a special occasion, so I immediately, wondered what he had done now to make up for, by giving me this gift out of the blue. For in those days, I never knew what to expect.

It is a pity what excessive alcohol drinking can do to a person. This man ultimately lost his wife, his children, his business, his house and any self-respect he might have had for himself—all because of his uncontrolled habit. He would have literally gone down "into the gutter", had not it been for his sister and father, who took him into their house, where he lived for some time. Afterwards, it did take him several months, before he went out and got a job, because so far into depression had he slipped.

✿✿✿

After the end of this first marriage, I did indeed get a job and an apartment for myself and my children. Of course, it took two jobs to support us, because their father would not pay child support—even though his court ordered monthly amount was only $100. But I was willing to do everything I could to make a life for the three of us. After all, being away from that unhappy marriage was worth the price for me. For I had truly come to believe that it is far better for a woman to live without a man, than to live with one, who made her life miserable.

During the following years, the children and I went on with our lives. I began to have somewhat of a social life, whenever I could fit it in. After all, I was still a young woman, and maybe—just maybe—there might be a good man somewhere, who would appreciate me. Besides, I so wanted my kids to have a good life. Oh yes, there were lots of men out there, that was true. And a few of them became interested in me. But because I had two small children to support, mostly what I got were propositions—not marriage proposals.

But in late1969, there was one man, who appeared to not only be interested in me, but my kids as well. He made a fine living, was good to us, and appeared to be genuine. So, when he asked me to marry him, I said yes. What a mistake that was!

On our honeymoon in Mexico, he seemed to change overnight. We were having dinner in that hotel's impressive restaurant, and I remember relishing in the lovely atmosphere of the room, as I partook of some really good Mexican food. I could hear strains of music drifting into the room where we were dining, and I realized it was Mexican Mariachi music, which I dearly love. It was coming from the night club area where a band was playing. As I sat there, I couldn't keep my toes from tapping to the beat of that lively music. At that point, I was feeling pretty good, especially after partaking of a Marguerita. And all seemed right in my world at that moment, as I inquired of my new husband.

"After we finish eating dinner, let's go into the night club and listen to that wonderful music."

He looked at me with an authoritative air about him, which I had not seen before, as he answered. "We'll see, Beryl. We'll see."

I shall never forget that moment, when almost in a blink of an eye this man's attitude changed toward me—and on our honeymoon, would you believe? It was as if he was suddenly the boss of me, because I was now his wife and his possession. As it turned out, he did "allow" me to go in, sit awhile, and listen to that music, before we went back to our room. This was in 1970, and even though this was a first rate hotel in Mexico, there were no TVs in the rooms. So, he suggested that we sit in bed and read, to help pass the time. Read?!?

I knew then I had made another terrible mistake, marrying this man, who had changed so much in so short a time. But again, I was stuck, because admitting defeat again was something I didn't want to do. However, this was only the beginning of things to come, for there was so much reprehensible behavior, that this man exhibited toward me and my children, during our time with him, that space does not allow for the telling of it all.

However, it was something that happened on Mother's Day, the memory of which has stayed with me all of my life. At that point, he almost succeeded in breaking my spirit.

That day dawned bright and sunny, and I had been informed that he had invited his friend and new wife over that afternoon. She had just had a baby, only a few weeks before, so they brought this new child with them. It was a lovely baby (don't remember the sex), and they fawned over the new child all the time during that visit. The new Mother was quick to display the piece of obviously expensive jewelry, that her husband had given her for Mother's Day. To me, it seemed that this woman, who was much younger than him, was obviously the type who expected nice gifts to come her way—probably on a regular basis.

I endured that visit with this couple for a couple of hours that afternoon, and was glad to see them go, finally! You see, all the time they were there I was nursing a severe inner hurt—a hurtful sadness within my very soul at having been completely forgotten on this supposedly special day, that was set aside to honor Mothers.

After they left, my husband demanded to know why I was in such a bad mood. By then, I had come to the end of my emotional rope, and blurted out what should have been obvious to him.

"Why should that new Mother, who just left, be heaped with gifts and praise, when none of you even gave me a thought on this so-called Mother's Day? I have been a loving and caring Mother for over a decade, so why shouldn't I deserve some recognition, too?"

I understood that my kids were not to blame for this slight to their Mother, because they were still quite young and should have been guided by this step-father to at least buy a card for me. Also, I thought of my role as step-mother to his three kids, who lived in another state. Those were his kids, for whom I wrote his child support checks on time, and sent them gifts for appropriate occasions. That was always one of my jobs to do. Then, I thought of all the times since divorcing my kid's Dad, when I made sure to bring them with me to purchase gifts to be sent to him for his birthday, Christmas and Father's Day. Most ex-wives would never have done that, especially considering he was not sending any child support payments for his own children!

In my own mind, this did not compute. I was holding up my end of this marital union, as I always did—even under stressful circumstances. But I got little in return for what often felt like servitude. As all these things filled my mentality, he answered me with these hurtful words.

"Well Beryl, the way I see it is this. You are not my Mother, you are not the Mother of my children, so I have no duty toward you on this day."

I was so shocked at his hurtful words, that I ran into the bedroom and slammed the door, shouting at him all the way. "If you consider me so useless to you, then you fend for yourself for a while!"

It was hours before I came out of that room, as my very spirit was so damaged, that it took a while for me to pull myself together. But you better believe they all had to get their own supper that night. I must confess that this was behavior so unlike me, as I usually tried to keep my emotions in check, even under sometimes dire circumstances. But this time, it was too much.

However, I felt bad for my children, who had witnessed this. It certainly was not their fault, because they should have been guided for the Mother's Day ritual, from their so-called step father. Afterwards, I sat them down and explained, that they were not to blame.

This is just one example of the harshness of this man. But amazingly, I stuck it out for almost a year, enduring more misery, before throwing in another marital towel. However, he didn't go away easily. It was right before Christmas when I announced I was contemplating divorcing him, so one day when I wasn't home, he took all of my kid's Christmas presents from under the tree and hid them from me. I had to have my lawyer get an order for him to produce all those presents. It turned out that those gifts had been in the trunk of his car all the time.

What a guy, trying to get back at a disgruntled wife, in a way that would hurt her most—by hurting her children. However, it shouldn't have surprised me, because ever since the honeymoon, he was the self proclaimed boss of our home. During those months, there was such an under current of uneasiness in that house for both myself and my kids. So much so, that each day when I knew it was time for him to come home from his job, I would hurriedly take a couple of Midols, not because of PMS, but to give me a jolt of caffeine to see me through the evening with him.

Looking back, I should have taken heed to those, who tried to forewarn me about him. His second wife, who already owned her home before she married him, had to take her children and move out, because he wouldn't move. After she got an order to get him out of HER house, when she moved back in it was discovered that he had removed every light bulb out of every light fixture in the entire house—apparently just to get back at her.

The day, when this second marriage of mine was going to become history, dawned like any other day, and on that morning I didn't know I would be leaving then. It was a Saturday, and he was in the kitchen drinking coffee. This looked like a good opportunity to pin him down, for I had been pleading with him for us to sit down together alone and discuss the problems we were having, in an effort to save this marriage.

"This would be a good time for us to do some serious talking about our marriage," I said to him, to which he replied.

"No, I am going fishing with my good friend, who is coming to pick me up any minute now."

"Going fishing? Is going fishing more important than saving our relationship?" I asked.

"We can talk anytime.....I don't want to disappoint my friend," he replied. "So, I will be gone most of the day..... be back in time for supper."

As I watched him go out the door, to meet his all important "friend", that was the end for me. I had tried and tried to talk to him, about fixing this union. But he never had time for me, because to his way of thinking everything was just fine for him—and in his mind that was all that mattered.

It was then, that I picked up the local paper and scanned the "Apartments For Rent" column, and noted information about the apartment, which turned out to be the one destined for our new home. Luckily, the land lady was a former English teacher of mine, who always liked me. So, I took the kids and went over to see the place, and it was perfect for us. I wrote a check on the account, that we had opened just after we married, for half of what was in there, which was only fair. It covered the initial deposit and rent payment, with enough left over for us to start over. I knew only too well, that he would never allow me to have any money, if he knew I was leaving him.

Back at the house, I scanned the phone book to find someone to move us in a hurry. Luckily, a listing for two guys and a pickup truck filled the bill, and they were at our front door shortly, waiting to move our stuff. I had already instructed the kids to pack up their things in boxes as fast as possible. They were only too happy to do so, since they were anxious to move away from that man, too. I instructed the moving guys to only take certain things—only the things I came into this marriage with, which was most of the furniture. I left all of his things there. It took them three or four trips before they finished.

Unfortunately, the new apartment did not come with a stove and refrigerator, so we had to make do for a week with an ice chest and hot plate. There had not been time for a phone to be installed, so we were isolated for a few days—not letting anyone know where we were. This is in case he would try and find us and cause trouble. It was like another adventure for the three of us, and we happily all worked together to make a new home.

To this day, I often wonder how he must have felt, upon returning from his precious "fishing trip", when he entered that almost empty house. Oh, to have been a fly on the wall when he entered the door!

It was amazing how all the ingredients of that move came together in one day, as if predestined. But I knew without a doubt, that some unseen force was truly looking out for us, because during that offshore oil boom era in our towns, there were usually waiting lists for all the best apartments.

Ah yes, the three of us were so gloriously happy to get away from that man, we did not care that we had to start over again. In fact, years later both my children told me that after we left him, those almost five years spent in that apartment were some of the very best years of their lives.

✫✫✫

After that divorce, I did have some social life as a single woman. Through the Parents Without Partners (PWP) chapter, that I started in my home towns, I brought many divorced and widowed singles together, along with their children, for the numerous social events I organized. As a result, I also met a couple of guys, whom I dated.

There was one particular instance which comes to mind. I began seeing this one man regularly for a few months—long enough so that people thought of us as a couple. Then, because I was president of our local PWP chapter, I decided to take my two teenagers and myself to the international convention in Denver, Colorado. The date of this four day event was shortly before a Louisiana state convention of PWP, that was set for me to host at our local chapter in Morgan City. However, I made sure all the arrangements were made before leaving for Denver. Therefore, in my mind all the bases were covered.

So, my two teens and I did drive to Denver, to attend that convention, and we arrived back home in plenty of time for me to be there for our state event. On my return, I called the man, whom I had been seeing before I left four days previously, to let him know I was back. And of course, it was expected that he and I would go to the PWP banquet together. But I told him, since I had so many last minute things to take care of, he wouldn't have to pick me up. I would meet him at the auditorium where our event was being held.

In retrospect, I have to say that this ambitious event went off without a hitch, and we hosted PWP members from as far away as Alexandria, Shreveport, Lafayette, Louisiana—and town in between. The theme was "Come Have Jambalaya On The Bayou With Us", and of course that very tasty Cajun dish was served that night. There was a lively musical group, which kept the dance floor full for hours, and it was obvious that a good time was had by all. That is, until I discovered a reality of embarrassing, hurtful proportions for me.

As I recall, upon arriving for the event, the guy whom I had been dating came up to me to say welcome back. Then, he went over to one of the long tables to take a seat. After finishing my conversation with the caterer, I went over to the table and sat beside him. I noticed to his left was seated one of the women from our Chapter, whom I knew had a crush on him. So, I thought, lucky for her that she got to sit next to him. But I didn't give it another thought. That is until the end of the evening, when it was time to go home. Then, I saw him walking with that other gal toward the door—and it looked as if he was in a hurry to exit as quickly as possible.

I stared over at him, in disbelief, realizing then that he had taken her to this event—allowing me to assume that he would be there with me. My cousin came over to me, when he saw what was happening, and confirmed what I was thinking. According to him, it seems that they had made a connection at the one social event, that was scheduled while I was in Denver. And thereafter, he had been seeing her during those four days while I was out of town. Yet, he did not have the backbone to tell me this, when I called him upon my return. And the worse part was that everyone in my organization knew about this—everyone except for me! What a fool I must have appeared to everyone, being seated next to him all evening—dancing with him, talking with him as if nothing was wrong. And all the while his new gal was there on his opposite side—probably fuming that he was even paying any attention to me. In retrospect, it was apparent that he was trying to juggle both of us at the same time.

However, he chose to mislead me and ultimately humiliate me. And after the depth of this deception hit me, I took myself home, wanting only to get away from everyone as fast as I could. Later, so emotionally devastated was I, that I shut myself away for the rest of the weekend, staying in bed and crying most of that time. In was inconceivable for me to accept what had happened. How someone could have chosen to humiliate anyone like that was totally incomprehensible for me. What a coward he was! So, I thought, this was the end of another relationship in my life.

However, as an unimaginable footnote to this story, I am reluctant to relate, that after a one year war of angry alienation on our part, he dared to start getting in touch with me again. Apparently, he had tired of his new girl friend, and (as he said) regretted losing me. So, he wanted another chance. And what is so astounding, would you believe, I consented! Then a few months later, he became my third husband. Here is more evidence, of this lady's bad decisions when it comes to choosing men. What a glutton for punishment I was!

✫✫✫

Before I took this marital plunge, there had been almost five years of single life for me—years in which my children and I enjoyed life as much as financially possible for us. But then, I was pretty good at making money stretch a long way, if I do say so myself. Granted, I had to work at two jobs in order to support we three. But it mattered not then, because I relished in being so FREE—free from having to be under the thumb of another insensitive husband! Besides, I was still young enough to start over AGAIN ! I guess what kept me going was that indomitable strain of "pollyannaism", that was so much a part of my make up. Because for me, like that famous southern belle "Scarlet O'Hara", tomorrow is always another day. And I had found throughout all of these ups and downs of my life, that if one door closes, another one always opens. Sorry about the use of so many cliches here, but it all seems apropos to the telling of my story.

Of course, all of those apartment years were not exactly "a bed or roses" for me. Remember, the early 70s were years bearing much resemblance to those late 1960s, when drugs were prevalent everywhere—much of it among teenagers. Unhappily, my son was included in this scourge. Indeed, as a Mother it was a trying time, rearing a teen son, who participated in his share of that junior & high school drug scene, as did so many of his peers. But in time, he progressed and went on with his life, successfully becoming a professional artist. However, back then, I marveled at how a bright, happy young boy could suddenly undergo such a change, when he reached age 13—which marked the beginning of those dreaded teenage years. But in spite of the ups and downs of our life during those early 1970s, the three of us appreciated our years of freedom then.

However, after my "head of household" years, I did (as mentioned before) consent to marriage again in 1975. This time it was to that younger man—11 years younger, in fact. And he was the one, who had humiliated me so much at that banquet. Go figure? But since I always appeared more youthful than my actual age, the age difference between us was not at all obvious.

But upon reflection, it seems to me, that whenever I consented to marriage it was at a time when I was at a low ebb in my life. And these men seemed to come along at just such a time, when I was most vulnerable, and ready to throw in the towel of responsibility.

This third husband was a respected professional man and a former Navy flyer in Vietnam. We were both of compatible astrological fire signs, and had fun together. Besides, I thought at the time that my life and the lives of my children would not change that much, except that we would be moving into his house. After all, we would still be living in the same area; the kids would be going to the same schools; I would continue with my regular office manager and columnist jobs. However, it was not to be.

For just about a month after the nuptials, my new husband received a job offer that he did not want to refuse. It was in another state, and would result in the uprooting of us all to an unfamiliar region. I was devastated, because it was never my intention to cause such disruption for my children—much less myself. We were satisfied living where we were. And such a move would mean leaving my parents, extended family, my jobs and friends. And the children would be forced to go to new schools in a foreign (to them) place, where they had no friends or family.

But I had said "yes" once again to this husband, and felt an obligation toward him too. So again, I was trapped! And against my better judgment, I consented to the move. Looking back, had I known when he asked me to marry him, that it would mean a major move for us, I would have refused his proposal.

My daughter was in her Senior year at school, and I refused to uproot her from this important time in her life. So, I made arrangements for her to live with my parents, so she could graduate where she was supposed to. This meant that I would not be a part of this special time in her life. It also meant, that I would have to be parted from this wonderful girl, whom I had never been away from for more than a couple of weeks in her entire life. So once again, it was heart break time for me. Indeed, my life seemed to be a continuous journey beset with making sacrifices for others.

As for my teenage son, who was to relocate with us, well, that was another matter. My heart went out to him, having to move to a new school where he had no friends. And to add to this, my new husband was a very stern man and those two clashed repeatedly. Understandably, for a teen boy to accept a new step father into his life, is usually uphill all the way. But it was particularly bad in this case, because the two of them quite simply could not live in the same house. They literally came to hate each other. In fact, I feared violent altercations between the two of them.

Of course, I could see both sides of this situation. However, I was a Mother first, and wanted to look out for the best interests of my child. Needless to say, I was caught in the middle, and it finally came to the point where I had to make a decision. It was my reasoning, that I was the only common factor, in bringing these two males together, so I would quite simply have to take myself out of the picture. So, after almost five years into this marriage, we divorced.

✷✷✷

Again, I was alone. But this time I was really alone, because in those years my children had grown up and were getting on with their own lives. So, I entered into a really new chapter of my life—one where for the most part I became a successful career woman, managing editor of a company's resort newspapers. I had my own house on the Mississippi Gulf Coast, and my job allowed me to pay the mortgage and everything else I needed to get on with my life. Much travel was associated with this job, and I relished in this aspect, as I had always loved to travel. Amazingly, I was getting paid to do a job I love, travel, and was in a place where I came to have an active social life. I also wrote a couple of books during this time. What could have been better for me? I felt that I had finally arrived at a great point in my life.

Ironically, now that I was older (but still attractive), had my own house, a good job, with no children to support, my eligibility status amazingly changed. At that time, when it came to gentlemen callers, I was no longer getting propositions but marriage proposals instead! But I was content with my life the way it was then, and stayed single for almost five more years. However, I guess the next prospective husband came along when I was at one of my infamous "low points". And yes, I agreed to yet another marriage.

He was a twenty year retired Air Force man, who was still young enough to start a new career with Civil Service. For the most part, he was a good man, but like most retired military types he expected obedience from his family. He also had a hair trigger temper—a short fuse so to speak. Still, I managed to allow for his outbursts, and most of the time I learned how to handle these when such eruptions came. After all, I told myself, hadn't I been through so much ill treatment from those other guys? What does one more matter, when it comes to having to put up with another man's shortcomings?

But with this one, it was another case of my having become his possession—HIS wife! He had no concern about any accomplishments in my life before I met him. In fact, it was as if he looked upon my having started life when I married him.

Looking back, I remember when he showed me a photo of his deceased father, whom he loved very much. I noticed that the edge of the photo was ragged, as if it had been torn. When I asked why, he said he had cut his mother out of the photo. Of course, I was appalled that anyone would do such a thing, but I soon learned the extent of the disdain he held for that woman, who had given birth and reared him.

He also had disdain for fat women in general, and would tell me that he would divorce me if I ever got fat. I realized later, that his mother had been on the very plump side, so perhaps he was reminded of her when he saw fat ladies. But this union lasted some 17 years—through thick and thin, and longer than the others. The ultimate reason it fell apart will be covered in the chapter, entitled "The Worse Summer Of My Life".

✭✭✭

Now, I look back at those marriages, which were so disappointing, and probably doomed from the start, and wonder how I could have chosen so badly. I want to make it perfectly clear, that these particular husbands might have been right for some other women, but not for me. Certainly, I have my faults; I do not deny that. But I honestly gave my all toward the success of those unions, only to fail miserably.

Isn't it strange though, that I seem to have had such an affinity toward military background men? The first one had been a nine year National Guard member, the second a former Army man, the third was a Navy guy, and the fourth a twenty year Air Force retiree. I used to tell myself, that it was because military types were dependable and always on time—and they were for the most part. Of course, the National Guard one (mostly a weekend warrior back then) was apparently lacking in dependability. But I have come to realize that probably this interest in military types must have something to do with a previous life of mine, that I lived long ago.

But above and beyond this, my reasons for accepting four marriage proposals ran far deeper. In my day, most couples just did not co-habit unless they were married. If a woman did live with a man, without benefit of marriage, during certain of those decades in small towns, her reputation went down hill fast. After all, we were all subject to the dictates of church and society.

However, it is amazing to me, that for just about every product and endeavor in our lives, these come with instructions and hazardous warnings. Not so for marriage. Because all you have to do is get a license and a preacher/priest/civil official to say the words. And then you are married to that person for supposedly the rest of your life—or until that day when one chooses to get away from the other. Of course, there are marriage classes in some churches, where couples are supposed to become enlightened as to what lies ahead of them. But in the case of my own religion, no such class was expected back in my day. Even if it had been, how is one supposed to value any advice from a priest, who has never even been permitted to live with a woman?

In the case of young girls, going blindly into marriages that they are totally ill prepared to venture into, may God help them along the way. In my case, there was that inner voice telepathically warning me with those words, even back in 1952, on my wedding day—"What are you doing here?"

I have since come to realize that it was a dire warning, indeed. Pity, I did not take heed. But then my path in life was meant to be, I suppose. However, I do believe, that there are points in our life, when we have a choice—to go one way or the other.

As one example of what might have been for me, there was an event back when I was a teenager. I stood there, washing dishes at the sink of my family home during a lightning storm. There were double windows over the sink, and I watched the rain starting to come down on the hedges outside, while continuing with my chore. Suddenly, I sensed a bright light flash to my left side, between my left shoulder and the left window casing of the open window. It was an instantaneous brightness, that I experienced to the side of my line of sight, which struck the cast iron pot on the stove, just two feet from where I stood. It was over in an instant, but when I took a deep breathe and realized what had just happened, I was astounded. It had been a bolt of lightening, that came through the open window and struck that pot. Yet, it did not touch me, even though had it been a couple inches over, I would have been struck and killed—right there in my Mother's kitchen! This just goes to show how in an instant our lives can be altered—one way or the other. It is the same with automobile or plane accidents, where people are killed.

But such things are usually beyond our control. However, choosing a marriage partner is under our control. It is our choice to marry, and we have no one to blame but ourselves if we make a mistake in our choice of a partner.

There is much to say for "young love", "puppy love", and such, when couples are far too young to really know if a particular person is the one for them. At such times, too often for so many young people, it is difficult to know the difference between love and lust. But many are set on walking down that isle—no matter what. As I said before, countless numbers of young girls in past decades—and even today—are not prepared for marriage. In my time, we had our "hope chests", filled with embroidered sheets and pillow cases, table cloths and monogrammed towels, that we had been hand sewing for months. We also had all those beautiful wedding presents, that would go so well in the new home we would be making, together with our husbands. However, emotionally and sexually, many girls were at a loss to know what to expect.. It was just on-the-job training for us—like it or not.

However, those young guys in my era were not much better prepared either. Most of them had been foot loose and fancy free as young men just out of school. They had little to no experience in responsibility and how to handle their newly married roles. To them, life was still good. They would take us (good) girls out to proms, dances, movies and such. Then bring us home, kiss us goodnight, and get in the car with their buddies and drive out to that special place in another town some thirty miles away. Yes, I heard tell, that each of them would take their three dollars and visit a house of ill-repute, to do their thing. We girls knew what they were doing, and it was alright with us. Because it saved our virginity in the long run. So, everyone looked the other way, and it was accepted that "boys will be boys".

Yes, life was different in those days. Most people in my town married just once, and lived with that decision for the rest of their lives—right or wrong. But unfortunately, for some of us in subsequent generations, we went on to not only make one marriage mistake, but continue to marry again and find that we had made yet another mistake. It was because of our vain attempt to find someone, who was right for us.

Years ago, when a very famous movie actress was interviewed and asked the question of why she married so many times, she had this to say.

"When I was brought up from childhood, girls were expected to marry, and not just live with a man."

Thus, her eight marriages were obviously evidence of her ingrained up bringing. But no one should fault her for that. In my case, I was always searching for a better life for myself and my children, and with each marriage

I believed that this might be the one. Unfortunately, none of those afforded us the life I had struggled for during those many years. But these disastrous unions made me so much wiser. I know men may tend to think I am one sided in this epic. And I do realize, that there are many marriages that fall apart, as the fault of the wives in some unions. However, I cannot speak for those instances. I can only speak from my own experiences.

Being a 5 foot, 3 inch petite female, weighing about 115 (during most of those times), I knew how vulnerable a woman can be when faced with the physical power of a man. So, I learned fast never to argue with a drunk man, because alcohol tends to oftentimes change a man, whom you thought you knew, into someone else (a Dr. Jekyl-Mr. Hyde type). Thus, a small woman could be at risk of bodily harm. It is advisable to wait until the next day, when he has sobered up, to bring up any provocative subjects.

Also, NEVER hit a man in the face (or elsewhere), like is often shown in the movies. Should a woman do this, she risks being hit back by that man—with a force that could literally lay her out. After all, female physical strength is usually no match for the physical power of men.

Another bit of good advice, is to beware of a man, who has a big problem with his mother. I am no psychologist, but from my own experience I saw an example of this for myself, but neglected to take heed. For if a man has an on-going resentment of his mother, in some cases he may later aim this disdain toward his wife. When I was shown a beloved father's photo, with the image of that man's mother cut out of the picture, a warning light should have flashed on for me. Yes, I should have taken note of the emotional baggage he was bringing into this marriage.

Also, it is good to take note, when a man is a good bit younger than you. Some times, certain younger men are interested in women years older than themselves (not over the hill gals, but still attractive), who might (in his eyes) represent a maternal influence. This too, could make for an unhealthy relationship. Although, in some cases such age difference works for certain couples.

And then there are cases where offending husbands can't say they are sorry enough, in order to bring you back after you leave them. There are also many, who have a way of sweet talking you out of leaving, and many women fall for this—over and over again.

There are also those, who will promise you the moon if you will only come back. One of my husbands even promised me an all expense trip to France, if I would just come back. He knew that was one of the things, that I longed to do, so he thought this bribe would work. When I asked if he would be going with me, he said no. But he would pay for me to go. Go figure? Needless to say, I turned him down flat, in no uncertain terms, telling him that I could not be bought.

Another husband called to say he had just gotten $25,000, and would I come back to help him spend it? This too was just another bribe, which I refused. But most of all, they pelt you with empty promises of "whatever I've done....it will never happen again.... just come back!" And it is amazing to me, that so many times, they really do not know what it is that they have done to cause this split.

It has been my experience, that no matter how sincere their promises to change seemed to be, it was a facade. If women believe their husband's pledges to change so their wives will go back to them and try again—as I did on more than one occasion—it seldom works out. It never did for me. However, for a few weeks, things would go along smoother, but little by little those husbands reverted back to their real selves. After all, whether male or female, we are what we are. Our character and personality by a certain age is written in stone. And let's face it, some personalities just can't successfully live together.

Now, ladies, if all attempts at reconciliation fail and you find yourself on the brink of asking your husband for a divorce, be careful how you do it. It is best not to be alone at that time—especially when you begin to move your things out. For some men can get quite angry at such times. Also, never contemplate a separation without a plan of your own, where you have already made financial arrangements in your behalf. Because once many husbands know their wives are planning to divorce them, they will sometimes rush to the bank and close the account, leaving their spouse financially high and dry. In the case of one of my husbands, I got to the bank before him and took only my half of what was there. Because, knowing him, I knew he would have taken it all, if I hadn't gotten there first. You may think you know your husband, but when he is confronted with such an emotional and financial separation, you might just see a side of him, that you never saw before—and it is often times not pretty.

This advice is not meant in anyway to suggest, that separation and divorce is always the answer. Because if a marriage is worth saving, these couples should do their best to try and work things out. In my case, those unions could not be saved, and I learned the hard way how traumatic divorces can be. So, ladies take advice from one, who has been there more than once. Use your head before you act, and you can survive.

As I said before, I can only caution others by means of what I have learned the hard way from my marriages and divorces. These were four entirely different types of men—none of whom I now realize were right for me. No doubt, they went on to find other women, who could co-exist with them, and I wish them well. But I risked diminishing my very spirit had I stayed. And that was too high a price to pay. I cannot say it enough—my belief is that it is far better to go on alone, than to stay with someone, who brings you down.

Because far too often do some men view their female marriage partners as their possession, not realizing that many of today's women need more than just to be a wife—a shadow of the man. In modern times, more and more women are educated and professional in their own right, and should be recognized as such. A wise husband would do well, to afford his wife the respect she deserves.

My last husband did not even do me the honor of reading any of my published books. I can't tell you how much that hurt me. But I suffered this indignity in silence, realizing that anything I had done on my own would never be recognized as important in his eyes. For him, he only wanted to accept that my life began when I met him. So, none of my previous accomplishments were meaningful in his view. I was just his wife—his possession!

Therefore, I caution any girl or woman to be careful in choosing a husband or significant live-in other. Is he your friend and sensitive to your needs? Does he honor your accomplishments? Do you have fun together, without him getting jealous should you even speak to another guy? Does he have a violent temper, that has been turned on you on even one occasion? Does he look with disdain about your communications with family or friends? Does he insist on controlling all the money?

About an unreasonably violent temper, do be particularly aware of any man, with such. One of my former spouses had just such a temper, that could be set loose at the drop of a hat—and sometimes for the most ridiculous reasons. One time, one of my beloved dogs, that was adept at digging under the chain link fence to get out of the yard, after which I usually had to go chase her down in the neighborhood. On a particular day, my husband caught her digging again and I could see he was about to lose his temper. And he did. I saw him pick up a large piece of wood, and hurry over to my dog at the fence. The dog cowered and whimpered, as she saw him approaching. I ran there as fast as I could before he got there, and threw my body over the dog, to protect her from him, just as he had raised that threatening piece of wood to hit her.

I screamed at him, as I lay there on the ground over her. "Hit me.....why don't you hit me!"

At that moment, as he held that board up about to strike, it was as if the realization of what he was doing became apparent for him. Then, he dropped the board and walked away from us.

Usually, when couples are supposedly so "in love"— or a reasonable facsimile thereof—they are blind to the faults of their beloved. They usually see what they want to see, and none of the bad things are deemed important. Because, for the woman, she usually believes that she can change him for the better—no matter what his faults are. Well, don't you believe it! Because what you see, hear and experience from him or her is what you will be getting. Few ever change such ingrained behavior. And there might even be some previously unknown, additional, bad traits to deal with—not long after the nuptials.

Indeed, a woman's choice of a husband is right up there as one of the most important decisions she will ever make. And if she chooses badly.....there could be detrimental, unanticipated repercussions in store for the rest of her life.

☆☆☆

CHAPTER - 7
Working For And Against Oil Companies

"Oil feeds My Family", was the motto of a bumper sticker at the end of the 1960s in coastal south Louisiana. Back then, it was seen on the bumpers of countless pickup trucks and cars (including mine). This was because it was an era of great offshore oil production— in a region where many oil companies were represented, and thousands of people were employed in numerous capacities by big oil.

In some of those last years of that 1960s decade, this writer was also employed in certain of those oil company land office & supply depot locations, which supplied the needs of countless offshore rigs way out in the Gulf of Mexico. I worked first in an office of Shell Oil, and later in a Texaco office.

For those, who know little of the history of offshore Gulf drilling, allow me to elaborate. Following the seismograph findings of oil along that continental shelf, just after World War II, the subsequent years saw numerous oil companies staking their claims in that region. Then, the rush was on with people moving in from many places! This boom was made even easier for the big oil companies, because Louisiana's powers-that-be back in those days looked the other way— legislatively speaking—when it came to environmental concerns. All that was important then was that big oil was bringing in jobs and money.

As a result, the coastal marshes, swamps and lowlands—so rich in salt water and fresh water seafood—were detrimentally impacted. For the oil companies had a free hand, to crisscross that coastal area with dredged canals anywhere they pleased, in order to get to their drilling rig sites, many of which were situated in that delicate eco system. There were apparently few to no rules and regulations in place, to prevent harm to the land, water and it's species. Offshore rig personnel were dumping toxic polluted fluids off of their platforms straight into the marsh and Gulf waters, at will. This was accepted as standard operational procedure for years, as those big companies literally had a free hand, to do whatever they needed to do, in order to keep that oil and gas production flowing!

Few voices were heard to object, because we had those good paychecks coming in regularly, and life was prosperous. Unfortunately, little did many of us realize what a price our beloved coastal Louisiana environment was paying for those paychecks.

Then, on earth Day in 1970, something remarkable happened! It was a wake-up call about the environment of this planet, when 20 million Americans marched in defense of Mother Earth. It was reported to be the largest mass demonstration to that date in US history.

After that day, things began to change. The conscience of our legislators seemed to wake up, and more environmentally protective laws began to be passed and then implemented. I know, because it was during that time when this former oil company employee switched sides, and took employment with one of the newly implemented testing laboratories. This particular laboratory industry came into being, for the express purpose of pulling in the reins of those polluting oil companies. The United States Geological Survey was mandating that all drilling by-product water (usually dumped into the Gulf with no oversight) would now have to be tested regularly, before being thrown overboard. That was to make sure that this water did not contain pollutants.

So, as it turned out, I became employed by the "enemy" of big oil—a thorn in the side of oil companies, if you will. But these testing labs were much needed ingredients in helping to finally rein in the free will polluting activities, that had been going on for so long. I saw for myself in the lab, those mandated samples of that horribly polluted water. Had I not seen with my own eyes how gross those water samples were, I would not have believed it. And to think, that such polluted water had been thrown freely in the Gulf waters for so many years. This was indeed quite an "eye opener" for me.

But thankfully, the new USGS rulings became the law of the land. Each drilling location was federally mandated to send in (usually by helicopter) sample bottles of that suspect drilling water, earmarked for dumping. It is still appalling for me, to realize the preponderance of watery pollution, that these companies had been throwing into our beautiful Golf of Mexico for so many years. The contents of each sample bottle had to be tested, and the amount of pollution noted, with the results being sent to the various oil companies and the USGS. If pollution was found (and it almost always was BIG TIME), the USGS fined each and every offending drilling location so many thousands of dollars per day, until they cleaned it up.

So, this lady has been involved with both sides of this environmental oil company issue. But, in retrospect, I can see it for what it was—oil company opportunistic ravishing of the land and water, to get what they wanted. Then, when through, they would leave a trampled environment in their wake. Pity, but coastal Louisiana is still paying a damaged environmental price for what those companies did to the land and water. But apparently, in those days it appeared, that big oil just didn't care!

However, even today, there are still countless big corporations that seem to have little regard for the ecology of this planet. And that is so scary! For some such companies, if there is ore there, let's dig for it, they demand! If oil and gas are under already protected land, let's drill! Let's cut down those ancient mighty redwood trees; we need the lumber, they say. If it means a better profit bottom line, let's release those fumes into the air and dump pollutants into the waterways! To heck with the environment seems to be the mantra of many. Anything for the almighty dollar. And to think that this attitude still exists for some people, in this environmentally enlightened era—unfortunately even among many in the Bush administration.

Through those employment experiences then, I saw for myself both sides of this issue. And as a result, this really invigorated my drive to speak out in behalf of the ecological well being of our world. As a result, among other things, I wrote several newspaper columns, elaborating on the obvious rape of our land and water by those big companies. One column in particular is being shared here.

ON OIL AND THE ECOLOGISTS
(A Parable of Our Times in 1970)

Some giants of industry, gathering unto them great wealth and resources, and went in search of black gold. A goodly sum was spent and they had much pride in their accomplishments of erecting towers on the waters, with which to obtain the black substance.

And it came to pass that they called together their workers and went in search of the prize. Rig floors were filled with the activity of many, and the motors of vessels roared, while going back and forth over the wide water to their destinations, bringing men and materials to support the busy industry.

Oil was there, hidden beneath the vast depths, and great was the drilling of it. And the companies said to themselves. "Thou hast much money invested in this venture, so take thine chances. Drill and be daring."

And they thought within themselves. "This is important. This is good! The sky is the limit." Then the citizens of the country were happy and all rejoiced at such prosperity.

Alas, polluted spills became the norm, despoiling the waters. The black substance spoiled the waters and killed birds and fishes. The citizens became outraged and great was the roar of it.

Then it came to pass that a great lesson was learned from this dilemma. For those of ye, who spoileth Nature and her creations, the price to pay is great, and much anguish will be the result in the end.

The multitudes became more learned as a result of this awakening, and were perhaps saved from a more terrible fate. The great leaders of the land placed restrictions on the oil companies, and the ecologists in the land smiled and said. "This is good; this is just!"

Verily I say to you, that great was the wisdom learned from this judgment, and great will be the rejoicing when preventative measures, inspections and good judgment are successfully used, when taking from the earth's bounty.

Even though years have passed since the great judgment, future-wise the people of the land are far better off than before. But constant diligence is required to protect Mother Earth. So, be it known Bretheren, that there is a moral to this tale.

For ye, who haveth much, must preserveth much. Then and only then, will ye be worthy to have thine cake and eat it to.

✸✸✸

CHAPTER - 8
Standing Up For My Beliefs

Speaking out and voicing an opinion is one thing. But doing so in news print is something else all together! Because it could become dangerous business for the writer.

During my lifetime, I have seen a lot of injustice—and I always wanted to fight against such things. So, since I was granted this God given gift as a scribe, the written word became my means of fighting against what I considered unjust.

When the case for war was being made by the G.W. Bush administration, it was as if every fiber of my being was screaming from within—"No...No! They had nothing to do with 9-11."

Afghanistan, I could understand, but not Iraq! I just could not comprehend how so many of the American people could be so fooled by those hawkish leaders, in their unrelenting push toward an unnecessary war. And I expressed these opinions in my newspaper columns—at my own peril as it turned out.

Being called "unpatriotic" is a terrible thing for someone like myself, who can trace ancestry before the Revolutionary War—and every war in between—when so many of my ancestors fought for this country. How dare those people, who did not agree with me on the Iraq War, try to demean me ,(as well as literally millions of Americans, who thought as I did then). Their behavior was indeed disgracefully abominable to all of us. In my case they did so, over and over again, in their cruel

"Letters To The Editor" and insulting phone calls to the editor, trying to get me fired from my columnist job. Why at one time, I even feared that certain of these disgruntled people might try to do me bodily harm, so filled with hatred were they.

So much for freedom of the press, and feeling comfortable when expressing my views. But there was even more personal repercussions for me.

Yes, even more heart breaking than those repercussions from strangers, was the attitudes of several of my extended family members. Certain of them even told me, that they did not wish to hear from me anymore, if I continued to voice my political and anti-war stands. It amazed me that even people, whom I thought cared about me, were willing to accept me— only with those strings attached.

Now, my case was just one of probably millions, who were being persecuted all over our nation, merely for standing up for our beliefs. This state of affairs made me realize how divided my beloved country had become. I had never seen such an extensive division of attitudes, as evidenced in regard to where the Bush administration was taking us in this decade. Certainly, there was no such wide divide during the Great Depression years, nor during WW-II, when Americans worked together toward a worthy cause. Of course, during the Vietnam War era, there was much unrest, as to where that leadership was taking this nation. Here again, what caused this? Why, another ill-conceived disastrous war, of course.

But all of this did not deter me from continuing on with my crusade against that unjust Iraq War. For I felt it my duty to do so. Amazingly, some misguided people regarded this as "treason and unpatriotic", to speak out against the administration, that led us into that war on trumped up evidence. But I chose to agree with Abraham Lincoln.

"Allow the president to invade a neighboring nation, whenever he shall deem it necessary to repel an invasion, and you allow him to do so whenever he may choose to say he deems it necessary for such purposes, and you allow him to make war at pleasure."

Along these lines, here are some other great words. "To announce that there must be NO criticism of the president, right or wrong, is not only unpatriotic and servile, but it is morally treasonable to the American people." President Theodore Roosevelt said that, and he was a Republican!

Pity, that mankind never seems to learn from the mistakes of the past. It is quite obvious to those of us, who have taken the time to read and research similarly chaotic events throughout history. In this case, the G.W. Bush administration apparently learned nothing from the debacles of both Hitler and Napoleon. If they had taken any of those historic accounts seriously, the administration would have learned a lesson from them—that the actions of those driven leaders represented two of the most disastrous military blunders in history.

During the Napoleonic & Nazi German wars, when those leaders directed devastating invasions of their neighboring countries, they both made fatal military mistakes. Feeling unbeatable at that time, each of those leaders chose to split their armed forces, redirecting much of their military strength to invade Russia. A reading of the history of those eras reflects how their misguided decisions turned out. Indeed, it spelled disaster—and the beginning of the end for them both.

In the case of the Iraq War, a similar decision was made—with disastrous repercussions that will be felt for generations. George W. also split his country's military forces, from what appeared to be a successful righteous campaign in Afghanistan, only to invade another country at the same time. Thus another war was created in Iraq, at the expense of the first one. It would seem that the American people would have seen this action for what it was. And it is still amazing that so many people backed that war—with some continuing to back it, still following leadership that has misled us all. We do not have to be military geniuses to see what an unwise move that was. In the future, history may very well list G.W. Bush's leadership in the instigation of the Iraq War, as another of the worse military blunders in history.

But again, they should have learned from the past. History has always shown that invading and occupying Middle Eastern nations has meant defeat for several European countries, that have tried (as far back as the Crusades). For the cards are usually stacked against the attackers of those ancient lands. Many western nations failed (and are still failing, along with our nation), to take into account the multitudes of religious sects and tribes, and their conflicting allegiances—not to mention all the fanatical fringe groups. After all, how can people in a young country like the USA possibly understand such cultures, that go back many thousands of years?

Now that time has passed, after the beginning of this useless Iraq War, most people have seen the truth— that they were fooled and sold a bogus bill of goods. As it turns out, it is now fashionable to be against that war. So, those countless people, who had previously heaped so much abuse on those of us, who knew from the beginning that this war was wrong, can go on their merry way. Yes, they are now going on with their lives, and not giving a second thought to all the hurt and insults they heaped on those of us, who were merely exercising our American right to free speech.

☆☆☆

Over the years, I have fought for several causes for which I now know, that I was spiritually urged to champion. But a particular one, that was a favorite of mine, was the fight for women's rights back in 1972. It was another struggle against injustice.

The Equal Rights Amendment (ERA) in 1972 read as follows: "Equality of rights under the law shall not be denied or abridged by the United States or by any state on account of sex." That should have seemed pretty straight forward in the eyes of the multitudes.

So, the ERA passed the U.S. Senate and House of Representatives, and was then sent to the states to be ratified. But only 35 states voted yes, and 38 were needed. I am sorry to say most of the southern states were against the ERA and would not vote to ratify. Even my own home state said no to ERA passage.

As an excuse for this denial, several of those so-called "southern gentlemen" were quoted as saying this. "We, men in the south, like to put our women up on pedestals."

My reply to that nonsense was voiced in news print, in one of my newspaper columns. "We women (and our children) could die of starvation up there on those pedestals!"

Then there was that hard core, right wing, religious lobby, which voiced their opinions against passage of the ERA thusly. "We are against the ERA, because it would deny women to be supported by their husbands, and there would be no privacy rights. Girls and women would be sent into combat, homosexual marriages would happen and abortion rights would be upheld."

Well, guess what! Most of those things have come to be—even without ERA passage. For the life of me, I could never understand why so many people came out against this proposition. A concept that would allow women to hold up their heads, and take pride in being regarded as more than second class citizens. As heads of households, supporting their children, they should always be paid the same salaries for the same work, as men. But that was not the case then.

The struggle for women's rights began back in 1848. But it wasn't until August 26, 1920, that the 19th Amendment was ratified, giving women the right to vote—72 years later. And it only happened because of the courageous women who marched, lobbied, picketed, even went to jail for that cause. We women should all salute those earlier ladies, who wouldn't give up.

But even back then there were those macho male voices resounding with disdain, when women were granted the vote. "Voting women would bring down families, because it would require more of women than their female sex could handle."

Baloney! How ridiculous were such arguments. We women know only too well how strong we are, and how we have to work oftentimes twice as hard, just to be thought of as on a par with men.

But we American women have always had many strikes against us. However, our plight was not as horrendous as the African slaves, who helped to make this country great. However, the rights of those in these categories of people were left out of the early Constitution, which was written by white males.....for the benefit of white males.

Even in 1776, Abigail Adams, wife of John Adams, realized this existing inequity toward women. She asked of her husband then. "In the new code of laws," she pleaded. "Remember the ladies and do not put such unlimited power into the hands of the husbands."

Of course, this no doubt went in one of his ears and out the other, as no such thing was written into our Constitution back then. In fact, in that era white males held all the cards. Women could not vote, nor own property, or keep custody of their children in separation cases. Women were truly at the mercy of their husbands in those days.

It was not until my divorce, when I was faced with rearing two children alone, that the depth of this unequal treatment of head-of-household women hit me like a ton of bricks. So, again I used the power of my newspaper column in an effort to educate people, as to such inequities. I even wrote many letter to our Congress people, in support of the ERA, and also became a member of the National Organization For Women (NOW).

When the ERA came up for a ratification vote at the Baton Rouge capitol building, I drove there, accompanied by my friend Lacy and my teenage daughter, to be in attendance and lend our support to this historic cause. The chamber was packed with many for passage and many against passage. But the greater majority appeared to be against, and I could see why when buses pulled up to unload countless women, wearing "NO ERA" buttons. Apparently, that organized group of what appeared to be "church lady" types had been bused in from north and central Louisiana.

So, the rest is history. Those Louisiana so-called "southern gentlemen" congressmen, who were intent on "protecting" the flower of southern womanhood, voted against ERA. But no one can say, that we women who lobbied for ERA passage did not try. We tried...and we tried....and we tried—failing again to get justice for women.

But the beat goes on!

✫✫✫

Well, I am here to tell you, that expressing my opinion and backing certain causes that were close to my heart, was a hard road to travel. But I was so driven for so many years in this regard, by what I often thought in those times was my feminine intuition. However, I learned later that it was really my Spirit Guides struggling to direct me in the direction I was supposed to go. And that certainly succeeded in saving me from some bad decisions—not all, but some.

Remembering years back, I had a distinctive nagging feeling that it was time to trade in my car for a newer one, and I did. A week later, the man at the dealership, who took my old car as a trade, called to ask a question. "Were you having any trouble with the car when you traded it in?"

"No," I honestly replied. "The car was working fine. I just needed to get a newer one with air conditioning." To this he replied.

"Well, just to let you know, a week after you traded it, the transmission went out."

Certainly, that was not my fault, because I had just heeded my "inner voice", which was directing me, as it did again not long afterwards. At that time, I had an unrelentingly strong feeling, that I should look for another job—even though I was happy with my present one. So, I took heed and did get another job. Shortly after I left the previous job, that company laid off a large number of employees. Now, whether or not I would have been one of those, I will never know. But obviously some force was looking out for me. I was convinced of that!

As to my strong backing of certain important issues, I believe that it was not just my opinion at work here. Quite simply, I was directed to take such controversial stands, in order to help bring about change for the good. A man once told me, that I was "too opinionated". Duh?!? How could I be a life long columnist if I did not have strong opinions? It comes with that career's territory.

To sum it all up, I concur with that old adage— "If you don't stand for something, you will fall for anything."

✰✰✰

All we have to do is look back in history, to find many people, who were obviously driven to back their own particular cause. Their paths were difficult, but they never gave up. Just thinking about all those strong willed people, who pursued their cause for the betterment of others and their country, is mind boggling! We all owe debts of gratitude to those folks, who came before us, and whose paths were so difficult. For many of them, in spite of real danger, they persevered. But in the end, several were gunned down by assassins.

Consider Mahatma Gandhi, that driven man, who would not stop in his efforts to gain independence from the great British Empire, that had occupied his country for so long a time. Then, soon after he could see his goal being reached for the independence of his country—the sub continent of India, and subsequently the more northern nation of Pakistan—life ended for him. For just after this goal was reached, in 1948, he was shot.

Also, I dare say there are few Americans, living then and now, who have not heard of the assassination of President John F. Kennedy in Dallas, Texas in 1963. He apparently was destined to ascend to the leadership of his country, for the purpose of inspiring a new generation with hope, and to set the stage for those famous visits to the moon by the end of that decade. He too, was stopped by assassin's bullets.

Later, in that same decade, another great leader met his demise in April of 1968. It was Martin Luther King, Jr., who was apparently sent at that pivotal time in history, to lead his African-American people toward the equality, that they so deserved. Yet, he too was stopped by yet another assassin's bullet.

And amazingly, also in June of that same year of 1968, another potentially great leader was killed by an assassin. It was Democratic Presidential candidate, Robert Kennedy, who was becoming a symbol of hope for that generation—much like his brother had.

Also, how can any American ever fail to take note of Abraham Lincoln, who was responsible for keeping this nation from being divided. Probably, few leaders ever endured such adversity and overwhelming responsibility than he did, trying to keep this country from tearing itself apart from that infamous Civil War.

But just about the time of that conflict's end, he was downed by an assassin's bullet in 1865.

So, what are we to make of so many noteworthy leaders, who were cut down seemingly before their time of natural death? It is my belief, that in certain generations there are leaders, who are literally heaven sent, in order to do much good for others. But once their job was well on it's way, sometimes even before we believed their job was done, and in spite of our belief that they still had more to do, their time on this planet was at an end. Their exit point had been reached.

I set forth these examples of notable leaders, because each of them had unbelievably strong drives. Yet, in their efforts to make the world better, they all met a violent demise. But our gratitude toward those great ones must never wane.

Unfortunately for us, there are also dark force leaders, who emerge throughout the world from time to time—leaders who do so much harm to others. Their evil is always sent to challenge the good in people. And we, individually and collectively, have to be up to the task of successfully dealing with those dark forces. Hopefully, as long as there are good souls on earth, who are not afraid to speak out and address injustice, our lives can get better.

However, the dark forces sometimes can be devious and difficult to recognize as such. But with God's help, we can see them for what they are and steer clear of their evil.

✦✦✦

CHAPTER - 9
Hard Times For
Divorcees & Widows

Getting a divorce in 1965 (and before) was a far different experience, than it came to be in modern times. Back then, no matter how terrible a marriage had become, the wife was expected to "stand by her man".

The Church expected it, society expected it, and even those who were previously thought of as "friends" expected it. Even in cases where the man would beat his wife and kids, she was expected to endure. Indeed, at such times a woman soon found out who her true friends really were. For no mater how badly a man had treated his wife and kids, despite the fact that this reality was known by many, it mattered not. Because when that woman finally had had enough and separated from the man, most of those so-called "friends", amazingly, took his side against her.

Of course, in the cases of an ex-wife's former women friends, there was sometimes another reason for this. It was because they no longer wanted the divorced woman anywhere around their husbands, fearing that he might take an interest in this newly freed lady. I personally felt repercussions from this attitude myself—as if I would ever have been interested in their husbands! That was certainly insecurity on the part of those women.

Then, for me there was terrible gossip, which was spread about a year after my separation, the gist of which was—"Have you heard about Beryl....she is pregnant!"

It goes without saying, that I was appalled when I heard this awful lie in a beauty shop. As it turned out, this cruel untrue gossip had been spread by a woman from my ex-husband's extended family, who apparently took offense at my divorcing her relative. This is in spite of the fact, that she well knew what a terrible husband & father he was. I was so furious by this, that I nipped it in the bud, by phoning her husband and demanding that he put a stop to his wife, spreading such a lie about me. Thankfully, he was a man of honor, and he did stop his wife from spreading any further lies. I shall always be grateful to him for his consideration.

Pity, that newly separated/divorced women, when we are at our lowest ebb, sometimes have to find out who means to do us harm. However, there were so many more rude awakenings yet to come, after I became emancipated.

In those days, there were very few credit cards owned by people. We only had one, for a big department store in New Orleans. But of course, it was on my husband's name, as single women rarely had one, and divorced women were probably never issued one. So after the divorce, I kept that card in order to outfit my kids with clothes and shoes for school each year. I made sure I received the bill at my new address, and paid for those purchases on time. For I knew if they sent the bill to my ex, he would not pay, and the card would get cancelled. So, I saw to it, that he never saw the bill, even though no child support was coming from him.

But there was one exception to this situation. When my daughter took band in school and had to have a musical instrument—a clarinet—I knew I could not afford to pay for that. So, I got in touch with her father and told him of my problem. I asked if he would please pay for this instrument, which we would go to New Orleans and buy at that same big store, where I had the credit card? He begrudgingly said to let him know how much, and he would pay for it.

So, my daughter and I went to New Orleans and shopped for a clarinet. We looked at many brands, and when the clerk showed us the finest quality one she had to offer in the clarinet line they carried, I made my decision. That's the one we'll take, I told the clerk. It was the most expensive one offered, and I decided then that money would be no object in this case. After all, he had stiffed his kids long enough, and in at least this case he would pay.

I tried to see what could be done, to make my ex-husband live up to his obligations toward his children, of paying the $100 monthly court ordered child support. This was even to the point of driving to the Parish seat, to plead my case and lodge a complaint. I was told that unless a warrant was issued for his arrest, for defying a court order, there was nothing else they could do. But if I would lodge a complaint, he would be arrested and sent to jail.

How would that help, I wondered? What then? He would just languish in a jail cell for an unspecified time? How could this punishment succeed in getting any child support money from him? Indeed, how could he be expected to pay anything, if he is locked up?

Yes indeed, the cards were really stacked against women and children back then—with no allowances available to make men pay what they owed. So, I decided against that course of action, as I just couldn't put the father of my children in jail. This was just more evidence, that for us to go on I had to rely on myself and my ability to support my son and daughter. Because there would be little—if anything—coming from their father.

In years to come, I did well at my jobs and managed to provide a decent life style for the three of us. But even as a head-of-household woman, with a good reputation, I still had to have a man sign for me if I wanted to get a bank loan! At one time, my dear Daddy had signed on my behalf for a $500 bank loan. After I paid that one off, I requested a $1000 loan from that same bank. The young man, who took my application noted that I had diligently paid off the former loan, so he told me there should not be a problem for a new loan. However, he had to check with his boss before he could approve it.

Well, when he came back to where I was waiting, I could see by the expression on his face that it wasn't good news.

"I'm sorry....but we cannot approve this new loan," he stammered.

"But you said it would be all right....I was never late with my payments before....and now suddenly I am a bad risk? What is the reason for this denial?" I anxiously inquired as he struggled to answer.

"Well......we could renew it if your father would come in and co-sign for you, like for the other loan. But we can't approve this loan on just your signature.... because.....you are a woman, you know."

Upon hearing this outrageous excuse, I could no longer keep my composure. "Yes, I have known for a long time, that I am a woman! Let's get this straight, this bank is discriminating against me, simply because I am a woman?"

At that point, the young clerk shamefully nodded his head, and couldn't look me in the eye, as I continued my tirade in a rather loud voice, that was heard by everyone in that bank.

"I am a 35 year old head-of-household, with a good job and children to support. I'll bet that if I were a man requesting the same thing, there would be no problem. Let me tell you something, this is not over! I will report this to the National Organization For Women in Washington, D.C., and trust me, you do not want those women on your bank's case!"

After my emotional tirade, I stormed out of that bank and went back to my job. But I couldn't resume my office duties, because I was so upset. Just then, I could not hold it in any more, so I laid my head on my arms on the desk, and an eruption of tears came like a torrent.

My boss came over and asked what was wrong. I proceeded to tell him that sorry bank story, after which the surprise on his face became evident. Then, his expression changed to one of anger, as he said.

"I can't believe this! I am going to go down to that same bank, where I have an account, and take my money out of that place.....and let them know why I am doing it!"

When my boss left, I called my Daddy, who had done business with that bank for decades. I repeated my story again, after which he replied.

"How dare they do this to you! I have done business with those people for a long time, and they would treat my daughter like that? I'm going over there to give them a piece of my mind!"

About an hour later, the phone on my desk rang. "Hello," the male voice on the other end said haltingly. "I understand you came by today to get another loan. Well....we have reconsidered....and as president of this bank, if you will come back by.....I will personally authorize the new loan you requested."

In that moment, I felt such vindication, that it is difficult to put it all into words. No doubt by that time, I figured not only my boss, but my Daddy had gone over there and given them hell. So, now they were trying to placate these men, by reaching out to me.

"Thanks, but no thanks," I replied. "I will never set foot in your bank again, as I am going to find another bank, that will treat me with more respect just because I am a reputable person....one that will not judge me detrimentally because I am a woman. In addition, I will never encourage anyone to do business with your bank, because of your sorry discrimination. Also, I intend to write letters to the appropriate federal agencies that over see such things, as well as letters to the NOW organization, from whom you just might get repercussions. Last, but not least, as a newspaper columnist, I intend to write an account of this distressing event—leaving out your bank's name, of course. But you will know who you are!"

I guess the word got around our small towns, because I never ever had any trouble getting future loans. However, this is but one area of difficulty that divorced women had to endure. Getting automobile insurance on my own name was a hassle of huge proportions, too, in the 1960s. In spite of the fact, that I had a good driving record, suddenly after my divorce my name was added to a long list of suspect drivers. Because divorced women were considered by some companies then as unreliable drivers. Isn't it strange, that one day before my divorce, I was considered a good risk as a married woman? But one day later as a divorcee, I was a bad risk?

So, no matter how many insurance agencies I applied to for car insurance, it all seemed to be in vain. Even my own dear Uncle, who had his own insurance agency, was not allowed to sell me car insurance, because that was the stipulation against female divorced drivers at most home offices. He apologized to me about this, because he knew I was a good risk and should not have been lumped in with every emotionally distraught, erratic, female driver—which was apparently how the insurance industry regarded all divorced women. So, I had to go to great lengths to prevail.

As I struggled with this problem, my brother, who lived near Washington D.C., suggested to me that I apply for a little known (to me) insurance company up there, which was known to insure clerical office workers, regardless of male or female status. So, this shows the length this lady had to go, in order to become insured as a single divorced woman in the middle 1960s.

But even though there were these seemingly endless troubles I had to go through, just to get on with my new status in single life, one thing was sure. No matter how much trouble all of this was, it was worth it—just to be my own person and free from hurtful marital male dominance.

I often marveled at the actions of several women, who were divorcing around the same time as I was. In Louisiana, the divorce couldn't be finalized, until after a mandated one year of separation. But it mattered not to me, because I had no plans that included another man. However, I personally saw one woman, at the time of my final decree at the courthouse, come out of court with her divorce paper in hand. Then, she met her new man in the hall, and the two of them proceeded to go into another courthouse door, where couples were married. Amazing, I thought upon seeing this. She just could not wait to jump into marriage again.

Not me, that was for sure! I needed time to find myself again after enduring so much heartache. Of course, I eventually married more than once, but never were any of my divorces because of "another man". I had no desire to start that over, before I could learn to cope with my own life again.

For we women, who chose (or were forced) to make our own way by working to support our children, the going was often made many times more difficult.—even on the job. Yes, in addition to the economical and social obstacles put in our way, there was also the existence of sexual harassment on the job, that often reared it's ugly head.

Back in 1968, I worked as a secretary in the marketing department of a large boat building company near my home town. Now, that was back in the days when working women in offices dressed up each day. It was expected that we were always attractively attired in skirts, heels, hosiery, and looking our best every day in flattering hair styles, as well. I suppose this gave the appearance of class and reflected well on the prosperity of the company. I was also expected to converse with prospective boat buyers, who sometimes sat in my office while awaiting their appointment with the sales team. At such times, it was expected that I be adept at intelligent conversation, to keep the customer happy.

However, sometimes I was really put to the test of keeping certain of these prospective customers contained. For here is one lady, who knows what it was like to have been literally chased around my desk, trying to get away from an amorous client. Let me tell you, it was really difficult to smile all the while, during the pursuit, so as not to alienate this male. But such as this became a part of life for this divorced mother, who became adept at not upsetting such men, all the while getting my point across that I was not interested—in as nice a way as possible.

Back then, it didn't seem to matter how degrading this was for working women, as it was all part of the job. Today, this would be "sexual harassment", and against the law. However, I continued to work for my pay, well knowing if I did not keep my job, I was just one paycheck away from a serious financial setback.

Then there came a day, when I could perhaps see a bit of financial sunshine on the horizon for me. A local church was having an auction for a brand new Cadillac automobile, and each raffle ticket cost $100. Nine guys in my office had contributed $10 each, and they asked if I wanted to get in on this by contributing the final $10. So I did, and we all anxiously awaited the big day when the winning ticket would be pulled.

Now, we had considered the very unlikely event, of our ticket possibly being pulled. This would mean, all ten of us would have a share of that car. So, in such an eventuality, what should we do? It was decided that we would have a playing card dealt to each of us, and the high card would get the car. But the winner would have to pay the other nine $100 each, before taking possession of the Cadillac.

Well, the anxiously awaited day finally came, and guess what? Our ticket was picked! So, the president of our company said that we ten could all meet in the conference room, stand around the table, and he would deal the cards to us. There we all were standing in place, awaiting the big deal. Only one man was late; one of the sales department guys, who was not know for being on time, anyway. But finally, in he came and squeezed into a spot to the right of me, commenting thusly.

"I'm going to stand next to Beryl, so she can bring me luck!"

I shall never forget the intense feeling of anxiety that seemed to envelope us in that room. All of the office employees had come to observe this momentous event, and you could have heard a pin drop when the dealing began.

Needless to say, I was so nervous at that moment, as I awaited my all important card. For I well knew what a great thing this would be, should I get the high card. There would be no riding around town in that new luxurious car, for me. No! I had already decided that I would sell the car and use the money for me and the children to get ahead financially. So, a lot was riding on this for me personally, and all the girls in the office (I was told later) were rooting for me to win.

Well, the high card went to the guy, who had come in late and who had squeezed in to the right of me. If he had not done that, the high card would have been dealt to me. Alas, I cannot express in words the disappointment I felt at that moment, as I literally had to hold back the tears that welled up in my eyes. But then, I told myself that this was just another in a long line of missed rewards, that always seemed to be just beyond my reach. However, I comforted myself with the fact that at least I would be gaining an extra $90.

So, it was back to the daily grind for me, trying to succeed in a man's world. But I always kept up appearances, and everyone thought I had more than I actually had. After all, as Mother always told me, looking prosperous is a key to being perceived as being successful. Besides, it was not my intention to have to depend on a man again for a long time—if ever. For as hard as my single status was, I still relished in my freedom.

During my life, I noticed how so many married women literally appeared to have become just a shadow of their husbands. Everything these women did was geared toward the husband and family. Most of them, whom I observed seemed to be bowing to their husband's wills in just about every instance. It appeared that they had no time for themselves; they were just put in that situation to take care of a man and kids. Of course, in a male dominated society, this is the way it was designed to be—much to the benefit of husbands. But it appeared to me, that many of those women had lost their personal identities, and had become only a "Mrs.", which seemed so sad to me. And it was easy to see many of these suppressed women becoming old before their time.

Thinking back, I recalled hearing the story of my Daddy's Mother—Grandma Oceania, who had been married when a young teenager. In her day, the fathers usually picked a particular man for their daughter to marry. In Grandma's case, she once related to me that she really was partial to a certain young man. But her father had dismissed that. This was because her choice for a husband was still too young and had not made a name for himself as yet. On the other hand, her father had picked an older man for her to marry—one who had already established himself somewhat, and had some money set aside with which to marry. This was a man, whom she hardly knew. But she was pushed into this marriage, against her will.

I often look at her wedding day picture, hanging on my wall. There she appears, all dressed up in a fashionable dress of 1905—with a bustle and wide lacy hat, grinning somewhat at the camera. She looks so innocent, and of course she was just that, being a protected teenager at the time. The body language in that photo is evident, with them both just standing there, not even holding hands. There was obviously not even any affection between them. It was as if they were there to merely play a part—a part that had been orchestrated by others, geared toward bringing them together. Indeed, it is apparent in that picture, that they knew little about each other. Yet, they were expected to suddenly become husband and wife. However, I must say that her new husband (my Grandpa Lafayette), in that picture appears to be a handsome man, but with a very stern expression on his face.

And so it was, that they went on into married life from this dubious beginning. Thereafter, within subsequent years, six children were born—one after the other. Grandma was such a small boned petite lady, barely standing about 5 feet tall, that we can only surmise how difficult it must have been for her to suddenly become a baby producer, before she even had time to get to know her own husband. After all, farm life was always so demanding, back then—with little time for the niceties of life.

Grandpa Lafayette was a sugar cane farmer at that time—a crop that was very labor intensive. During harvest season, cane stalks were cut by hand, with much help from hired field labor. The stalks were then hoisted onto a barge and transported by sternwheeler river boats to the nearest sugar cane mill, five miles up river. Their farm was located across the river from a Navy Shipyard, where, in those years, ships were built during World War- I, and was quite a few miles from the nearest town.

It is interesting to note, that the 1917 site of this very same WW-I shipyard also became the site of a

1942 WW-II shipyard, where huge dry docks, to be used for the repairs of war time damaged military vessels, were built. These dry docks, destined to be transported to Great Britain, played a big part in the war effort.

I have always heard, that Grandpa was a strong man, descended from some interesting ancestors. In fact, there are several provocative tales about his grandfather, who (reportedly) knew Jean Lafitte the pirate. Also, stories are told about another ancestor, who contracted to make knives for the Bowies, and also sold land to Jim Bowie, of "Bowie Knife" fame.

Others in Grandpa Lafayette's ancestry were equally interesting. Records show that an ancestor of his became the third wife of William C. Claiborne, the first Governor of Louisiana. Among that governor's many achievements, which are well documented, was his backing that helped to get Thomas Jefferson elected President. As a result, Jefferson held him in high esteem.

But it mattered not, who my Grandpa's ancestors were, when it came to the reality in his era of making a go of the farm. And as for Grandma, such interesting ancestors of her husband's meant little to her. On the contrary, she was probably overwhelmed with household and farm chores, as well as bearing and taking care of so many babies—one after the other. We, in these modern times, can only marvel at how such women of earlier eras accomplished what they did. Because certainly they did not get much help with child rearing from their husbands. It was the woman's job, because in those days, the man worked hard to provide for his family, but was not expected to do much in the way of what they considered "woman's work". Also, I had heard tales that her husband, (my Grandpa, whom I never knew) was indeed a stern man, and a harsh man, who certainly never held back from severely punishing his own children.

However, that family's way of life underwent an extreme change on a hot south Louisiana day in August of 1917. His young boys were outside playing under a tree. He and Grandma, and her parents, were on the front porch, scanning a newspaper list, searching for names of the young men, who were being drafted into the Army for WW-I. This is because they wanted to make sure, that Grandma's sister's husband was not listed there.

Satisfied, that his brother-in-law's name was not listed, Grandpa Lafayette walked over to the barn where two men were working on the roof. Then, Grandpa climbed up there to help them, so they could get the work done before any afternoon rain shower came their way. Although it was still a clear day and the sun was shining where they were, there was a hint of dark clouds on the horizon—evidence of an approaching shower.

Suddenly, there came a blinding bolt of lightning. Those, who witnessed this, said that at first they couldn't quite comprehend what had happened in that instant. But after the brightness receded, they looked toward that barn roof, where the three men had been working, only to see that two of the men had apparently been shoved off and were falling to the ground. Amazingly, it seemed that neither of them were badly hurt. They appeared only to be stunned. But apparently, so strong was that lightning bolt, it had knocked cattle, grazing nearby, to their knees.

However, the other man, who had been in the middle of the three on that roof when that bolt struck, had been directly hit. And from reports, he had been turned into what appeared to be a blackened hulk, as his body rolled off the roof onto the ground, where he lay as smoke emanated from what was left of his body. That man was my 37 year old Grandpa. And all of this happened in sight of most of his family, who were nearby.

It was reported, that this one direct hit bolt was the only one that day, but it only took one to take the life of that man. Grandma used to say, that Grandpa had an extreme fear of lightning all his life. This was so much so, that at times of ordinary heat lightning, during a hot day, he would cover his head with a pillow.

After this tragic happening, Grandma found herself a widow at age 29, with six children to rear alone. Her sons then were age 11, 10, 8, 5, 4 and there was a baby girl, too. Now, becoming a widow with six young kids to support in 1917 was something that should not have been wished on any woman. Of course, everyone expected that my Grandma would re-marry, as did most widows of that time did. Otherwise, they and their children had no other alternative—unless they were independently wealthy. And of course, that was not the case for my Grandma. As a young widow, who could still bear more children, she had a couple of marriage proposals. Now, most women of that time would have accepted one, if only for self-preservation. But not Grandma, She had had enough of men and the struggle that came with them.

Grandpa had been a tenant sugar cane plantation farmer, on Bateman Island at Bayou Bouef, where it was necessary to use a boat to get to town several miles away. At first, with the help of her husband's brothers on the farm, the family survived. Then she opened a boarding house in her home, to provide noon meals for the WW-I shipyard workers nearby. Of course, that was in the days when everything was made from scratch—bread making, parching the coffee beans, you name it. Her sister helped with these chores, and she also had the much needed assistance of a colored lady, who looked after the smaller children, while Grandma cooked and served.

The two oldest boys had been attending a one room school at Rock Bayou, where it was necessary for them to go by row boat. But as her younger children became of age to attend that school, it was decided that the distance for those little ones to travel would be too far and too difficult for them. So, with the help of her brothers-in-law, the family moved to Berwick, which at the time was quite a prosperous town, with the surrounding lumber mills, seafood and fur businesses, as well as the adjoining plantations and sugar cane mills. With the $400 from her share of the sugar cane crop, harvested after the death of her husband, the sale of their boat and some farm equipment, she was able to buy two properties in town—one for a home and the other for renting.

At first, she did washing and ironing to bring in money for her family. But then she decided to use the front room of her home for a grocery store. She would send her two oldest boys, who had been taken out of school, to get grocery orders from people in town. Now, grocery stores of that era had to purchase everything in bulk—sugar, rice, lard, butter, kerosene and such. So, after the orders had been obtained, back at their front room store, the family had to package the amounts ordered into individual containers, so that the next day, the boys could deliver these orders by means of a wheel barrow, all over town. It could be said, that their order and delivery grocery business was probably the first of it's kind anywhere in that area. But there were lean times, when trappers were unable to pay their yearly grocery bills, because of a bad trapping season. So, the two oldest boys also delivered newspapers, to make sure there was enough money coming in for the family.

No doubt about it, Grandma's oldest boys—my Dad Howard and his brother Moise—really gave up a lot, having to leave school to take on such responsibility, when they were still just boys. And they both went on to work hard most of their lives. This reminds me of how many times Daddy used to say this to my brother and me.

"You kids don't know what hard times are!"

In this way, the family went on and prospered. But I wonder sometimes if Grandma had re-married and had to go on into the seemingly unending child bearing culture in those days, how many more children she would have had to bring into this world. However, apparently, she had had enough of that life. No more child birth pangs for her, and no more having to be under the domination of another man. So, that petite little lady persevered, against terrible odds. And from my point of view, she had more "get up and go", than most people (male or female), whom I have known in my lifetime. As an early lady entrepreneur, she ran that grocery store out of her house for over ten years, closing the business in 1930.

When Grandma was in her 80s, she told me a bit about her teen years. She said that girls where she lived were not allowed to go higher than the eighth grade. Because young women then were not expected to need any more "school learning", as the term was used back then. For the men in those times figured further learning would be wasted on girls, who were meant for one destiny—that of wife and mother. None of these men even considered how a woman and her children were supposed to survive, in cases of the male bread winner's death. Yes, as widows, previous higher learning for such women could have made all the difference for a better life.

I thank God, that I was allowed to be descended from such a strong woman, who had endured so much, yet chose to make her own decisions and be her own person.

✦✦✦

Pity, that more women of today do not stand up for themselves when they need to. But then, most are obviously content to live their status quo lives. And this works for many women, particularly so, for those who have chosen a good husband the first time around. But for certain women, who were married so young, that their own real identities had not even had time to blossom before they became some man's wife, such females often feel cheated.

For those of us, after we found ourselves in the divorced category, it was expected that we would still carry our married names, since we had been known by that last name for several years. Besides, it was easier for our school age children, to have their mother have their same last name.

But later on, for this former wife, that last name by marriage no longer reflected who I am. And considering that I was married more than once, I sometimes wondered about my own identity. For men, it is easy, as they get to keep their own last name throughout their entire life—no matter how many times they marry. But we gals, as usual, are expected to sacrifice even our own identities, because after all men have called the shots from the beginning. Do you detect a little bitterness here? Understandably so!

Consider, if you will, having to change your last name on your card at the Social Security office four times! But then this is a woman's burden to accept, since from the beginning women were supposed to be some man's wife for life. Even these days, many men have not completely accepted the fact that one person does not have the right to own another human being (even in his own mind). A wife is not a possession, but a person in her own right, and should be considered respectfully as such.

After my three last husbands and I parted company, I knew then that there was no longer any bond between any of us. We had no children together. However, the third husband's last name was used as my pen name for a couple of my books. The fourth one's name was also used (in part) for one previous book. But other than that, none of us had anything left in common.

I finally realized after the last divorce, who I really am! I am my parent's little girl—the one whose name was written on that birth certificate, as my maiden name. That is who I have always been, even though for some fifty-three years there were many people, who have tried to change me into someone, whom I was never meant to be.

But no matter how many names I have had to tack on, there was one thing I have never lost as a result of those divorces—something that to this day has been a source of gratification for me. It was the respect and affection of the parents and (later) the step children from those former husbands. During the years when I had been the wife of these men, their families and I had come to care deeply for each other. This is probably because those families realized that I always took good care of their son and/or father. So, the parting from these dear family people was most distressing for me, as well as for them.

Notwithstanding these aspects, life goes on after such partings. And the struggle to make ends meet financially continued to be a constant for this mother. Let's face it, for the most part, women have never been paid equally with men. Although it has gotten somewhat better, it is not where it should be. Even today, working women earn only 75 cents of every dollar that is earned by men. This continues to be so unfair.

Sometimes the rat race of such seemingly unjust struggle can overcome the most positive of thinkers. It often did in the cases of some of the other divorced women I knew. For they would latch on to any man they met, just to get financial help for themselves and their children. Distressingly, many of these new unions turned out to be cases of "out of the frying pan and into the fire". And then there were others, who just wanted it all to end. They wanted out of this life of hardship and struggle.

Unfortunately, I have to say that I was one of those, who had entertained the idea of suicide in 1969. I am ashamed to even confess to this, but it is the truth. In my depressed state of mind, I figured that my two children would be better off if my parents reared them. So, by taking myself out of the picture, I would indeed be giving them a better life after all. Such is the irrational thinking of a seriously depressed person on the verge of giving up. In considering this prospect, I had even gone so far as to map out in my mind how to go about it. By stock piling a couple of bottles of strong, prescription, sleeping pills, I rationalized that this would be an easy way to go. But where would I do this terrible deed? I could not do it at home, where my children and parents would find me. That would be too hard on all of them. So, I decided to drive over to the Mississippi Gulf Coast and rent a motel room. I would do it there, far away from the town where I lived—where no one knew me.

I arrived in late afternoon, and went into the room I had booked. Then, I sat down in the semi-darkness for a while, thinking about what I was planning to do. But then I realized that I was hungry, and decided to go out for my "last supper", before taking the pills. This, I did. In fact, I partook of a lavish meal in the motel dining room. After all, I deserved it, didn't I? This would be my "going away" celebratory dinner, before checking out of this cold, cruel world.

After finishing my fine dinner, I walked out by the little lounge where a great band was playing. There was no hurry, I thought, so why not have a final drink before checking out of this life? The lounge was quite crowded, and people were dancing on the little "postage stamp" size dance floor, and generally having a good time. I sat at the crowded bar, ordered myself a drink, and continued to listen to the music.

Soon after my second sip of bourbon and ginger ale, the man sitting next to me started to talk to me. I figured that he was just another guy, trying to hit on me. But he seemed nice, so we began to chat. Well, our conversation went on for a couple of hours and my previous troubles seem to fade into the back of my conscious mind. We spoke of many things, as he was very knowledgeable and a great conversationalist.

When the lounge closed, he walked me to my room. I thanked him for being so nice to me, and he in turn said much the same thing. After we said goodnight and he left, I went into my room, where I was again left alone with those two prescription bottles of strong sleeping pills, that I had previously placed on the lavatory counter. In fact, those were the first things I saw when I entered—those intimidating bottles appeared like sentinels, sitting there, awaiting what my next move would be.

But something had changed from before. I no longer had any desire to take those pills. What had happened, I wondered? Before, I had it all planned out, and now it no longer was a priority for me. Something had changed within me, something that made me see my life as not such a total loss, as I had previously viewed it.

Remembering back to that night, I have often wondered whether that very nice man, who talked to me for so long that evening, had been sent from God to deter me from making such a fatal mistake. That man had made me feel like a special lady—above and beyond average and a person of worth.

Was something unseen at work here? Just hours before, I had every intention of going through with this deed. That is, before I encountered this strange man, who talked to me for such a long time. Was he an Angel, who was transformed into human form, in order to save me from myself? I suppose I will never know the answer to this.

Recollecting that time, had I really been at such a low ebb, that I would have even contemplated suicide—much less mapped out a plan as to how to go about it? True, during those years, it seemed to me that everything had failed for me—with the exception of my dear parents. I could not turn to the Catholic Church. They were no help. If anything, they would have told me to go back to my husband. Besides, that church had already destroyed my faith in that religion, bringing my spirit down further after the birth of my son.

True, some in society tended to look down on me, because I was divorced. Most of the men I dated then—those men in tarnished armor, carrying their own personal baggage—only looked upon me with propositions in mind. There was little hope for me to get a better job in my small home towns—a job that would pay a better salary. There was no prospect of financial help, coming from my children's father. So, in my depressed state of mind, I guess there appeared to be no light at the end of this tunnel of despair. Thus suicide, at that time, seemed the only way out for me.

When I recall back to that time, I realize the extent of my severe depression—this depression that had invaded me. Pity, that I had no one to talk to then, or anyone who would remotely take me seriously, about my dangerous inner turmoil. For my role in life up to that time seemed to have always been designated as the "strong one", who had to overcome all adversity— someone to be depended on. But as a result of having been in—and successfully come out of—such a void of inner emotional devastation, I am able to relate to those, who for one reason or another can see no other way out, except to take their own lives. In other words, I now know what it is like to walk in the shoes of others, who have given up.

Since that time, I have learned also, that no matter what any depressed person may use as their excuse to end it all, it is never acceptable to take one's own life. To refute the words in that theme song from the 1969 MASH movie, suicide is NOT painless! This is because of the hurt and suffering suicide perpetrators leave behind, for their loved ones to bear.

Yes indeed, it is our destiny to live the number of years, that our life's path and God has allocated for each of us in this lifetime. And no matter the difficulty of our paths, we do not get to decide when to bow out of here. For taking our own life is never the answer. However, severe depression can do strange things to people.

This reminds me of something that happened to a cousin of mine. We had gone to high school together, and back then she was seriously dating a particular boy. It appeared that the two of them might just have marriage in their future. But after graduation, he went on to play football at college, and she stayed in her town and got a job. With the passage of a few years, they drifted apart. And he met someone at college and married her.

I heard that my cousin was devastated by this, because I do believe he was her one true love. Later, she also married someone and went on to have three children. But apparently she never forgot her first love, because she even named her first born boy after her high school sweetheart.

As time passed and her children grew up, her husband had an affair with a younger woman. He then asked my cousin for a divorce, so he could marry this new woman. Thus, this former wife was left all alone, after devoting her life to that husband. But most who knew her realized that she had never gotten over her first true love—even after all those years of never seeing him again. It appeared that her husband's betrayal by divorce, along with all those memories of "what might have been" for her, all culminated into a state of despair—causing her to drift into severe depression.

She no longer cared how she looked, nor did she care about even eating any more. She spent many hours in bed, refusing to get up. Her house was falling into disrepair, because it was no longer a priority for her—nothing was. At that point, her health began to fail, and she wouldn't go to a doctor. She just couldn't shake that severe depression, which was the culprit here—nor did she appear to even want to.

Finally one day, she was found dead on her kitchen floor. Some said she passed away from an untreated ailment. But I say, she died of a broken heart. To put it simply, she just gave up.

In such cases as this, no one could possibly understand unless they have walked in similar shoes. People are fast to judge, but so slow to try and understand. And absolutely no one could hope to relate, about the road divorced women walked then—no, not even widows! For most women, who were left single again after the deaths of their husbands, many of them thought of themselves as special ladies—worthy of sympathy and respect.

I recollect sometime after 1965, being a part of a study group for single women—both widowed and divorced. We each shared our thoughts in regard to our singleness. But what I most remember was the obvious difference in attitudes between those two groups. The widowed ladies, for the most part, related tales about how wonderful their dearly beloved departed husbands were. But of course, for those of us who had known some of these men, we knew better. Because many of those husbands were certainly no prizes when still alive.

However, that was the way those widows chose to remember them—no matter how far from the truth their recollections were. Do understand, there were some deceased husbands from this group, who were worthy of praise—some good men, who were credits to their families and society. But obviously among this gathering, all of those widows chose to see each of their husbands in the light of perfection, rather than to remember them for whom they really were—imperfections and all.

One of the questions that was put to this group of ladies was this. "Finding yourself alone, to rear your children on a budget, how would you handle it if your young daughter came to you and asked for a special pair of new shoes? These would be shoes that she needed for a school play—new shoes for which there was no allowance in your budget."

A widow raised her hand and answered. "I would pray to the Lord, so I could be sent the money with which to buy those shoes."

Upon hearing this, which to me represented a lame reply, I spoke up right away. "If my daughter needed such new shoes, I would do everything I could to get the money to buy those. I can't see myself just sitting there praying, merely hoping that my prayer would be heard, and those shoes would just miraculously drop out of the sky. I believe that God helps those, who help themselves!"

That has always been my attitude—how I thought about life in general. As for the widows I encountered, during my divorced years, I always felt that they looked down on us divorced gals. From their standpoint, it seemed obvious that they thought of themselves as on a higher strata than we divorced women. After all, in their eyes, the Lord had taken their beloved husbands in death. Whereas, we divorced types had chosen of our own accord to discard our husbands, inferring that we didn't have what it took to keep a husband. It didn't matter to them how, in some cases, many divorced women left their husbands for the self-preservation of themselves and their children. Also, those widows failed to consider that many divorced ladies did not do the leaving, but were left by their husbands—even deserted, so those men could be with other women.

Little did they know, that divorced gals often had to have much more stamina than widows, because our road was a harder one to travel. Most of us did not get financial help from our ex-husbands and had to support our children alone. Widows, on the other hand, usually had insurance money to help them go on with their lives. Many of them received Social Security payments for their dependent children, because their father had passed. But children of divorced women were never afforded such financial government help, and most were cheated by what amounted to totally oblivious "dead beat dads".

Another detriment for divorced women was the very fact that their husbands were, in fact, still alive. Yes, they were alive and still kicking, and showing up from time to time to cause more trouble for their former families.

But between those times when many of us ladies wondered if there would be enough money to pay the rent—not to mention buy groceries and new coats for the children—some of us did manage to have a bit of social life. However, respectable places to go and things to do as mature, single women were few and far between.— especially in small towns. Let's face it, the world is geared for couples—not singles. That phrase, "prices listed are for double occupancy" are everywhere from hotel rooms, cruise cabins, tours, etc. Indeed, singles are often financially penalized just for being single.

After I realized how little there was for single people to do in the early 1970s where I lived, I decided to do something about it. I knew there was a large "Parents Without Partners" organization in New Orleans. So, I went there and attended some of their events. Then, I applied to start a Chapter in my towns. Afterwards, PWP (through my organizational efforts) was off and running. As a newspaper person, I wrote articles publicizing this new organization. The word spread, and it worked. Many formerly lonely single adults (parents of children) came out and joined. We all met new people, whom we never would have met otherwise. Our Chapter scheduled events for the parents, as well as our children. So, this turned out well for us all.

It is said that "loneliness is a terrible thing", and I certainly concur. Sometimes loneliness can turn to depression, and that is something we all should avoid. So, such clubs for singles often times bring bits and pieces of happiness to many.

After the children were older, during my years between marriages, I started yet other organizations that promised social events for "Over Thirty Singles". Yes, in 1973 and again in 1981, I started two of these organizations, which also turned out to be successes.

But above and beyond the social planning and bulletin writing I did then, sometimes young women members would seek me out—I guess because I gave them the impression that I cared. And I did care about so many of those distressed divorced gals, who seemed so lost after their husbands dumped them. There was one in particular, who sought me out to talk about her situation. She was so upset, trying to find her way in her newly divorced status, and she gave the appearance of being really beaten down by it all.

"My dear," I said to her. "Have you looked in the mirror lately? Do you not see the reflection of that lovely young woman staring back at you? So what, if your husband left you for another gal. You are probably better off, away from someone so untrustworthy. You are a kind, caring person and it is his loss. There is probably a more special life awaiting you in the future. But you have to pull yourself together and know that you are a wonderful soul in God's eyes....and in the eyes of those, who care about you. Don't let your ex win!"

She started to cry, and I truly believed that no one had ever taken the time to say such things of support to her. After that, she and I spoke often and I could see as the weeks went on, that she had indeed started to believe in herself, as her newly emerging confidence became evident. After a while, I didn't see her as much. But one day a package arrived in my mailbox. It was from her. When I opened it, there was a beautiful little music box that played a special refrain. It was "You light up my life".

I have said several times, that I wasn't ever trained in psychology, other than a couple of rudimentary courses in college. But it doesn't take a PHD to counsel those, whom you can relate to—especially when you have walked in similar shoes.

Indeed, I was so happy that I succeeded in making some people's lives just a little bit better. And they helped me, too, just by thinking so well of me, to the point that they sought me out for advice. Yes, these organizations that I started did a lot for us all in many way. Why even some of the members met others, and eventually they got married. Now, I do not know if today they might either thank me for making this possible, or curse me because it possibly didn't work out.

Notwithstanding, the merit of some of those social outlets that had been made available to us, for some ladies there still remained situations when certain ex-husbands popped us from time to time. And they had to be dealt with, even decades after the split. For there is no statute of limitations with ex spouse appearances in one's life, as long as both in a couple are still alive.

One particular case in point for me was in regard to the father of my children—my first husband—whom I drove hundreds of miles to see, when he was gravely ill from a serious stroke. Even though we had been divorced for 42 years then, he still held power over me and my grown children. When I arrived at the hospital where he was, there he sat, propped up in that bed, barely able to speak. But while I was there, he still managed to be his old caustic self, as he looked at me through his pained eyes, which still showed such disdain for me. At that moment, I realized what some say is true—that a woman (even after a divorce of many years) is never free of the father of her children, until death finally parts them.

Yes, an ex-husband will, on occasion, be heard from in a woman's life when she least expects it. My last husband, who has been gone almost eight years at this writing, sent me a Christmas card with a photo of him and his new woman thereon. Inside, he had written a note in his own handwriting, asking—"How are you doing, are you all right?"

This irked me no end. How dare he ask if I am all right after all that time, and while flaunting a photo of himself with his current woman! So, I got out one of my Christmas cards to send to him, but not before writing my reply thereon.

"Yes, I am just fine. In recent years, I have gone on cruises to foreign countries for four years in a row. I have done so much more—a trip to Niagra Falls, South Beach Miami, Florida. I bought a piano and re-taught myself to play, had another book published and am now writing still another, and I have been active in politics. All of these things I would not have been allowed to do, had we stayed together. I am now my own person again, and do not have to ask your permission for anything. So, I want to thank you for having divorced me....my life is so much better without you!"

Ah yes, through my divorced status I have become enlightened as to some good things in life. But unfortunately, the bad experiences have remained in my psyche. So, this has tended to harden me somewhat. But how could it fail to do so? Bad experiences can't help but leave detrimental marks on a person. However, it is a pity that this unpleasantness I endured has instilled in me a general distrust of a lot of men. Yet, there are certain men, such as my Daddy, several Uncles, my brother and a few notable special male friends I have been privileged to know in this life, do occupy a special place in my esteem. I wish I could say, that my ex-husbands occupy a special, hallowed place in my memory bank, but I cannot. However, I am thankful to my first husband, for being the biological sperm donor, so that I could give birth to my two great children.

Most women sell themselves short, believing that they have to have a man in order to feel complete. Ladies should understand that if a woman does not feel complete in her own right, no man is going to do it for her. No man will make her happy, unless she is already content with herself.

I've heard that silly phrase—"He completes me.....
and I can't make it without him!"

What a bunch of baloney! If a woman has faith in
herself and is willing to endure the adversity necessary
in order to get to that reputed "better life" for herself
and her children, she can succeed. The road is hard, but
women do it everyday.

But anyone on the verge of walking down that aisle,
toward marriage, should take heed ahead of time—be
they man or woman—before making a possible mistake.
For the many habits and idiosyncrasies of a potential
spouse should be carefully considered, in order to
ascertain whether or not you will be able to tolerate such
in a marriage.

Personally, I now realize the warnings I should have
taken heed of before my marriages—warnings from
which I should have learned lessons in better judgment.
I was not serious enough when making certain choices,
as I overlooked some important traits, that I should have
known would cause problems in the marriage. The very
fact that I was marrying a "drinking man" in my first
marriage should have set off alarms for me. But it did
not, because I truly believed that I could help him stop
drinking. Wrong!

In the case of the second husband, I had heard of his
vindictive cruelty in his previous marriage. But little old
"Pollyanna" me believed this time would be different,
and I so wanted to believe his slick promises of a better
life for me and my children. Wrong again!

As to my third marriage, I knew going in, that he
never ever wanted any children, because if the truth be
known he really did not like kids. Of course, I certainly
did not want any more children either, but he was
marrying a woman with two teenagers—his dislike for

whom soon became evident. My children did not like him from the beginning, and sometimes we should take heed to the incite of kids—incite which oftentimes, we adults do not have.

In regard to the fourth husband, a week before our wedding ceremony was set, we attended a formal ball, that we had been invited to by friends of mine. Having become a social butterfly of sorts in the singles social club I operated long before I met him, I was used to dancing with different guys at any given dance. This is something, that dancing people do. So, this time didn't seem any different for me, when I was asked to dance with an old friend. We danced onto the crowded dance floor, to the far side of the dance floor. Then another song started up. So, we danced to that one too, ending up back at our table where my friends and potential husband were seated.

Well, you would have thought I had committed the worse offense ever, for the anger in his eyes said it all. I knew he would be making a scene if I did not get him out of there fast. So, I made excuses that he wasn't feeling well, and we left to go to the car, all the while he was fuming with rage. Outside, he opened up the car door and literally pushed me onto the passenger seat. Then he eased behind the wheel and began driving in an erratic manner. At that point, I was in tears when I asked him what was wrong. He shouted at me.

"How dare you dance two dances with another man, when you are about to be married?"

It was then, that I saw the face of his untamed illogical jealousy, and knew how dangerous this could be. Indeed, I literally thought he was going to hit me. After he brought me home, I cried for hours about this man's violent anger at me for so ridiculous a reason.

And here I was about to marry him? At that point, I contemplated calling the next Saturday's wedding off. But then, I realized that this would be my admitting failure again. Besides all the plans had been made, newspaper announcements had run, a place and caterer were set, invitations were out and people were coming from out of town. Therefore, against my better judgment, I went through with it.

Here are four examples of my being forewarned each time, about the difficult traits of these men, whom I married. Yet I chose to ignore those warning signs—much to my detriment. Therefore, I say this to anyone contemplating marriage. Should you see signs, habits or traits (before the nuptials), about your potential spouse—things that make you wonder whether or not you can cope with, do not take the marital plunge. Yes, if you have strong misgivings about this person or what he/she may expect of you in the future, think before you act. No matter how much inconvenience you may cause for potential wedding guests, better to be safe than sorry, and call the event off. Or at least delay it so you can weigh your options. Otherwise, you could become a candidate for divorce court, sooner than you think—once again to make an unexpected entrance back into single life, and that ever expanding realm of the previously married.

However, getting to that new life takes a heap of doing. Because divorce can be likened to a death of sorts. It is the death of a relationship. It is a parting of the ways for two souls, who had agreed to join in matrimony and experience a spiritual bond. Of course, when that bond is discarded by divorce, some individuals feel as if a tremendous burden has been lifted from their shoulders. This is especially so in cases where negativity has permeated a union. For me, there was such a sense of freedom from an individual, who was bringing my spirit down—every time. It was as if I had shed a terrible burden, opening the door to a new lease on life for me. But there was also a sense of sadness, that I felt—sadness at the prospect of another failed endeavor.

Indeed, as with the death of a spouse, so should the finality of a divorce be mourned. Recipients of divorce papers should take time afterwards, to literally pull themselves together and seek a cleansing of their spirit, before beginning their new lives. Coming to terms about being single again takes time. It is like finding one's self all over again. So, a period of at least three months should be devoted to this process, before a newly divorced person can feel comfortable enough to enter their new social life. Even then, many will find that some people will tend to look at them in a different light, so they might feel ill at ease for quite a while. Because some people can be terribly vindictive and judgmental, it is at just such times, when divorcees find out who is really there for them.

For the most part, I have noticed that it is usually the divorced men, who afterwards are quick to get out and find themselves another woman. Whereas, more divorced women tend to stay clear of getting into a fast relationship after that decree is granted. From this evidence, it would appear that more women are far better suited to living on their own, while such men seem to need another partner as soon as possible.

But it is good advice for all divorced folks to take their time, before jumping into another relationship so fast. Because there are the adjustments to deal with, in regard to a different financial situation, as well as perhaps a changed residential location. Then too, having to find ways of living on perhaps a different income, have to be dealt with.

Most of all, divorced persons are now in another category, again. No longer are they a partner, who is subject to checking with a spouse before they can spend money or make many other decisions for themselves. Not anymore. The ball is now personally in their court, and they either sink or swim in the real world.

But it never ceases to amaze me, that so many unhappily married people continue to stay together for decades. In recent years, I have met several still married (obviously in name only) people, who fill this description. They are usually middle aged or early "Seniors". These couples have grown children and are many times grandparents. Most of them still live in the same house, but occupy separate bedrooms. But some such couples even live in separate houses. At this stage of their lives, they oftentimes have different life pursuits and interests, and rarely even go anywhere together. Some only share each other's company at family events, where they are expected to show up together. And yet, they remain married.

In some such cases, they believe that a legal separation is out of the question for them, because they fear a division of assets in a property settlement, should they divorce. Some have become comfortable in their homes, and do not want to risk having anything they value taken away from then. Also, many fear the prospect of having to struggle on alone, after so many decades with their spouse—even though they have nothing left in common, except for their children and grandchildren. So, each of them has accepted that they must continue these arrangements indefinitely, patiently awaiting the day when one or the other of them passes over.

From my point of view, I believe that two people are either a devoted couple, or they are not. And to go on living separate existences while still legally bound to each other is selling both of them short. As for me, I found out the hard way how a lack of proper final divorce papers could come back to haunt me financially.

Back in 1965, I had to adhere to the state of Louisiana's law mandating a one year waiting period before the final decree. This was a throwback from another time, since 1803 when the French Napoleonic Code was the law of that land. So, along with the backing and influence of the Catholic Church, which was all powerful back then, laws regarding divorce were very stringent, and that was still the case in 1965. I suppose the Church believed that mandating a one year waiting period would be enough time for divorcing couples to change their minds.

In my case, during that one year waiting period, I proceeded to go on and attempt to build a new life for me and my kids, while we lived at my parent's house. At that time, I had a hat and gift shop, and our family car had been awarded to me, during the property settlement. But it was during those waiting months, that my soon-to-be first ex-husband lost his business and filed for bankruptcy. And would you believe, they came after me, to take my business and anything else, that I owned, which the bankruptcy court could attach, because I was still legally his wife. Thankfully, I had my furniture stored in one of Daddy's storage buildings on his property, so they couldn't attach that.

Words cannot express what a distressing time that was for me. Here I was, trying to get on my feet and start over, only to have the rug pulled out from under me, once again! To say that I was angry, would be an understatement! Because I felt that this should not be my fault. However, since he filed for bankruptcy, I was taken down with him. Thus, I became a part of those sad proceedings, too, and this meant I had to go to court, as well.

For those you, who have ever been in a bankruptcy court, you have seen how all the different people appear in such cases. I drove myself there alone, I wouldn't even ride with my soon-to-be ex, so mad was I at him. But when I walked into that courtroom, all I could see (with the exception of lawyers, judges, court room employees) were fellow participants in other bankruptcy cases, who looked so down and out. Most of them were dressed shabbily, and were just sitting there, looking down at the floor in shame—appearing so beaten.

But not this lady! For I had anticipated such a sad event. And I had no intention of adding to such a depressing tableau. So, that morning when I dressed to go to the parish seat courthouse, I made sure to look my very best, as attractively attired as possible. And when I looked around and saw all those defeated looking folks there that day, I felt rejuvenated. Because I appeared to be the best dressed woman there. And I took some satisfaction in that.

It was as if I wanted to show everyone, that I did not belong there, and that this mantel of bankruptcy had been unjustly heaped on me. I felt this to my very core. After all, I had done nothing wrong and should not be to blame. So, why should I have to suffer the humiliation of appearing there that day? Indeed, I would be darned if any of those court proceedings would succeed in pulling down my spirit that day, and I told them so when I took the stand. Of course, it mattered not, because it was my ex and his partner, who filed for bankruptcy. I just had the misfortune of still being legally married to him—albeit separated at the time.

And so it went. Later that week, they came and took all the stock and fixtures out of my store, and I could do nothing to stop them. Then, there was absolutely nothing left for me to do, but get out and look for a job. Thankfully, I did have the paid for car for transportation. But alas, even that was not to be for me.

This is because one Sunday morning, not long after that court appearance, at my parent's home we were all getting ready to go to church, when the door bell rang. Surprisingly, it was my ex. I asked him what in the world was he doing there at such an odd time? He told me that I had better sit down, for he had something to tell me.

"I haven't time to listen to any more of your excuses." I told him. "Just say what you came to say and leave, because we are going to be late for church."

He stammered and looked away from me, but finally hesitantly said. "I wrecked the car, and it is totaled."

"What? The car is parked out front where I always park it!" I anxiously shouted at him as I hurriedly walked to the front windows to peer outside. And what I saw confirmed what he was telling me. The car was indeed gone.

"I came by last night," he tried to explain, "and since I still had my set of keys, I just wanted to borrow it for a few hours. I planned to get it back before you missed it."

Upon hearing this, I was stunned! How could he do such a thing, I thought. But I had to accept that this man, who had already caused me and his children so much harm, was continuing to hurt us. Such behavior should have been incomprehensible to any rationally thinking person. But it shouldn't have surprised me, that during his stolen joy ride in my car, because he was so drunk, he ran into the back of another vehicle. The sad part was that this car was just about all I was awarded from the twelve years in that hellish marriage. Once again, it came crashing down on me, even worse, that I truly had to start from scratch. Thank God for the goodness of my parents, or I would never have survived.

This story is related, to show that as long as a spouse is still legally married in the eyes of the law, either can become responsible for the unwise actions of the other. So, I made sure, that in my subsequent divorces I would not rest until those were finalized. There would absolutely be no living separately, but still legally married, for me! I valued my peace of mind too much.

But here's a word of warning. For most women, who never thought they would find themselves single again, it takes much strength to continue on. Indeed, only strong women should embark on such a perilous journey. But then I have come to believe this. There are certain people, who should not be married in the first place. Because many of us accomplish more while single, than when we are married. And sometimes, the effort it takes trying to make a man happy is in vain. I discovered how many more worthwhile things I could accomplish without a man. Now, I regret that so much of my life has been wasted in my efforts to please them.

✵✵✵

CHAPTER - 10
About Organized Religion

Once upon a time, way back in 1959, this so-called "good little Catholic girl" had a rude awakening, when she went for help through Confession.

It had been six weeks since I gave birth to my second child, and I wanted to know what to do about prevention from another pregnancy. You see, this had been a very difficult second birth, at which time both my baby son and I came as close to dying as we could get. This is because my first child and second child had been only ten months apart, and were both born by Caesarian Section. After my son and I survived, I was told by my doctor, that I should never get pregnant for at least five years, because I would probably not survive.

So, what was I to do? I well knew the Catholic Church's stand on birth prevention, but thought there might be something they would approve of. It was worth a try, so I went to confession to plead my case. I proceeded to tell the priest in the confessional my problem, and asked if there were any preventative measures I could use, that would be O.K. with my religion.

This visiting Jesuit priest told me something I already knew—that adhering to a woman's monthly cycle was the only accepted manner of birth control. The church called this the "rhythm method". I called it "Catholic Roulette"! Because my periods were so irregular, this would never work for me, nor would it work for probably many other women, as well.

"Does this mean," I asked, "that I should go on in my marriage without prevention and risk getting pregnant again.....a pregnancy that might well kill me and the baby?"

"Yes," he replied. "It is your duty to bring more children into this world, even at the risk of your own life."

"But I already have two babies to care for," I implored. "Are you saying that the Catholic Church suggests that it is all right to leave these two children without a mother, if I do this and die?"

"God will provide for them," he answered. "And if it becomes a doctor's choice between saving your life or the life of your new born baby, that baby must be saved, even if you die."

By now, I was in such distress emotionally, that it was difficult to comprehend what this man was telling me. How could this be, I wondered, that some man who is supposed to bring comfort to parishioners could sit there so calmly and pronounce such a dire death sentence on me? This man held such power, but his only credentials were that he studied and took courses to become a Catholic priest. Yet, he sits in judgment of those, who come for help. Such male priests have never been married. They know nothing about what it is like to face the trials and tribulations that women face in their lives. Those priests have never even lived with a woman (other than their mothers). And most of all, they have never ever (supposedly) been with a woman in the Biblical sense. Yet such as these men are given full rein to pronounce the devastating demands of that church's dogma on emotionally distraught women?

After hearing his pronouncement of doom for me, I pulled myself together and told him this. "I am only

27 years old, yet you suggest that I knowingly seek to risk my life, in order to bring another life into this world—another life which might also die in the process? Sorry, but I do not accept this. I do not want to die. I want to be a mother to my two babies, who are already born. So, I refuse to accept your words, because I see no merit in taking their Mother from children, who are already living."

I left that confessional and never ever went back to confession in the Catholic Church again. After this experience, my entire outlook on religion was changed, and my former belief in that church had been shattered.

We are born into the Catholic religion—those of us from Catholic parents. Perhaps some adults choose to become Catholics later in life. But for most of us, we are literally born into that faith, and have no say in the matter. Thus we go on throughout our lives, following the dictates of that church, and no other.

As good little Catholic girls and boys, we start with Baptism when a baby and then go on into childhood with First Communion, Confirmation, and as adults it is expected that we also be wed in this church. Later, we have our own children baptized after their birth into this faith. Thus, the cycle goes on—over and over again with each generation.

But in more recent years, more and more formerly life long Catholics have been questioning this Church's stand on many issues. No longer does every one of we disillusioned Catholics simply accept without question many of this church's stands on certain social issues. I refer to such issues, that this church says we must blindly accept, without reservation. So, to ever more spiritually thinking people, many of this religion's rules have become unacceptable.

After my terrible experience with the Catholic Church, I lost faith in that religion. Of course, I took my two children to Sunday Mass over the years, so they could have some back ground in religion, until they could reach adulthood and make up their own minds.

Many decades later, I was still searching for some possible religion, where I could go and pray with others. I tried a few protestant churches—and even a couple denominations where, quite frankly, I could not endure the screaming preachers there. For they shouted at the congregation about the wages of sin and hell—to the point of giving me a headache. Wow, were those ever downers! If you were depressed when you went into those services, when you came out you certainly would have been a basket case. This was absolutely not what I was looking for.

It was always my understanding, that a church should be a place of comfort and spiritual healing, where one could go to seek the presence of an all loving God—not a place where we are screamed at and warned of a vengeful god, who would punish us all horribly for even our smallest sins.

Later, I attended an on the fringes Christian church, where the music and singing was so elevating and the sermons were good. I attended there for a while—that is until election year hit. Then the preacher begin to imply to us from the pulpit, that we should consider voting for this (in his words) "Godly man.....George W. Bush."

Did that ever infuriate me, being told in a church how to vote! I well knew, that we have separation of church and state. So, how can some preachers get away with that, I wondered? Needless to say, this was the end of that church for me.

So, after searching for several years, I have failed to find any man-made, Christian denominations, that are free from politics, social demands and money grabbing attitudes. And then there are all those giant mega churches, that seem to be so popular these days. For it appears that these are run more like big corporations than houses of worship. I sometimes wonder what Jesus thinks about those ministries.

It is true, that most of this earth's people have historically believed in some kind of god—their own version of a supreme being. Why even primitive mankind worshiped their own gods, or a particular god. But after Judaism/Christian beliefs came on the scene, a great deal of the world's troubles could be laid at the feet of religion. Then later, there emerged so many different religious splinter groups, that formed their own sects, and believed their way was the only way. Ever since then, the world has become an even more violent place. History has shown that more horrors have been committed in the name of religion, than for any other reason. So, we shouldn't be surprised that this still goes on, even in modern times.

As a result of my futile search, I have certainly not given up on finding what is right for me—and I never will. And anyone, who dares to question my devotion to God will be treading on volatile ground. It is just that I do not believe a particular building or structure is necessary for such worship. Now, I pray from my home at an altar I had built. My crucifix stands there, along with my white candles at the ready to be lit for prayer time. In fact, I dare say that considering both my evening and morning prayers each day, I probably pray much more than the majority of those who attend church.

Not so long ago, while discussing my search for spiritual answers, the person I was conversing with told me in no uncertain words—"I am a Christian and will always be!"

I wondered then if he thought that because I had given up on organized religious denominations, that I was no longer a Christian? How insulting for me, that was!

It is this kind of channel vision that I usually get from most people, who are so into their own particular religion—to the exclusion of other ways to worship God. They refuse to believe that any other way—besides the teachings they belong to—is really viable.

But in truth, there are ever more people these days, who are questioning—looking for answers that organized religions cannot give them. These searchers are regarded by so many self-proclaimed religious authorities as probably candidates for a psychiatrist's couch, or in their opinions destined for damnation.

However, such judgmental folks should get real and realize that searchers for spiritual truth can never be understood by any psychiatrist or psychologist. So, to subject such sincere people, who are looking for the real truth, to scientific clinical trials about their beliefs and attitudes would quite simply be an effort in futility. After all, science and spirituality are usually always at odds with each other.

The Bible says—"Judge not, lest ye be judged." So, this is good advice for those holier than thou types, who believe that their religion is the only way.

Even since childhood, I have felt as though I was a spiritual searcher out here in the world mostly by myself. Because I dared to question. But in more recent times, I have been fortunate to be in touch with many other people, who are out there searching as well. And it is so wonderful to have finally found others, with whom I can share my thoughts and continue to seek a credible relationship with Almighty God—without having to follow all that pomp and ceremony, man-made dogma and accept the monetary rules of so many organized religions.

In spite of the debunkers, who look down on our search for real truth, those of us who believe we are on the right path are motivated to continue our search for the truth we seek. We believe in this pursuit, and our numbers are increasing, with countless others, who are seeking answers that organized religion and society can never supply. And having become acquainted with many such special people, who do not judge me and put my beliefs down, is so gratifying.

Our numbers are far less, than those of the status quo, who are content with their style of religion. For most have known nothing else, nor do they wish to risk being put down by society for even voicing any questions. But the fellow searchers of my acquaintance and I, along with probably millions of others like us, accept that we should reach out to our fellow searching souls, as a source of comfort for each other. And upon finding similar people, who are seeking truth like us, we rejoice with an inner feeling of such joy, that mere words cannot define. At such times, we know what it is like to be in the presence of our authentic fellow kindred spirits. So, together, we become closer to God.

I have not come to this point lightly, at this time in my life. For religion played a big part in forming my character from childhood—good and bad. As a result, I have done much research in regard to the origins of some religions, and the origins of the Roman Bible. I found, that many things have been kept from the majority of we Christians, all of our lives. In my generation, as well as hundreds of years before, it was never accepted that we Catholics were ever to read the Bible. What I learned about this holy book, from the time I was a child, were certain stories told to us, during Catechism classes. Otherwise, any other references from the Books of the Bible came sparingly to us, but mostly from the orations of priests during the Mass. It is supposed, that this all started way back in history, when most people were illiterate. So, the Priests, many times being the only educated persons, were designated to interpret the Bible for the multitudes. Thus, this manner of worship was carried on for centuries, and still today most Catholic worshipers still do not read the Bible—in spite of the fact that almost everyone is able to read and write, and most of all, to think for themselves.

But it appears that old ways die hard. Because for so long religious man-made rules and regulations were the norm. In this regard, I often wonder about all those folks, who went to their graves still believing that they had sinned grievously, because they slipped up a couple of time and ate meat on Friday—something forbidden in that church for so long. And ironically for many years, the Catholic Church now says it is all right to do so, with no fear of sin attached. This is what I mean about some man-made religious laws, that are ridiculous and have gone so far in hurting the very spirit of many people.

I have learned that the compilation of the Holy Roman Bible, which church hierarchy put together, took many years to become complete. In fact, it did not entirely come to be until years after the Council of Nicea in 325 AD, when Emperor Constantine gathered together some 318 Bishops in that country, which is now known as Turkey. That gathering was for the purpose of unifying all the people of Christian faith. But it was not until centuries after Jesus walked this earth, that the first acceptable Bible was compiled. Thereafter, it was hand copied by countless scribes—from Aramaic, into Hebrew, to Greek, to Latin and finally into all the languages of the world.

Now, we might ask this question. What are the chances, with all that copying going on over millennia, and in so many languages, by so many writers, that mistakes could not have been made, and personal interpretations added? So, how can anyone living today be absolutely certain that all of those writings are exactly the real thing from centuries ago? No doubt, in the beginning the included writings were probably valid. But only if we had a way to go back in time to check this out, could we be entirely sure of the validity of that complete text. So, without time travel, we can only wonder about this.

Ever since those early days of the Christian church, every religious denomination has been operated as a patriarchal hierarchy, entirely ruled by men—to the exclusion of women. This is the opposite position, that Jesus Christ took when He walked this earth. For He was reported to have looked upon the women in His day with great respect and consideration.

To bolster this point, an astounding discovery was made in 1945. In a Middle Eastern cave was found, what we now refer to in modern times, as the Dead Sea Scrolls. These ancient writings have contributed added ingredients to the biblical controversy, and it continues to this day. This is particularly in regard to which texts were kept out of the holy book, especially with reference to the importance of women, back then.

After the writings found, in those earthenware centuries old jars in that cave, were revived and deciphered, some interesting surprises were revealed. Reportedly, among those writings were several long lost texts, that included gospels of Mary and Sophia from Jesus' era. In addition to this, there were also many other texts discovered there, that quite possibly should have been included when the early Bible was compiled.

Indeed, to discover that there were probably several over looked written texts by and for women, that should have been included as part of that holy book, reveals the unfair mind set of most men, who succeeded in excluding women in ancient times. And this still goes on today, albeit to a much lesser degree. Case in point, I refer to the many religious denominations nowadays, that still refuse to allow women to become priests and preachers.

However, above and beyond these prejudiced leadership attitudes in so many churches, I have found that there is a belief that supercedes all of this unfairness. It is the belief that if we humans on this planet do not accept Jesus Christ personally, we forfeit salvation for our immortal souls.

Certainly, Lord Jesus should always be revered by us, and long ago even as a child I realized His importance in the hierarchy. I was taught to acknowledge Jesus Christ, back then when a "good little Catholic girl"— and I certainly did! But what I could never accept was a premise, which did not seem logical or fair to me. And as I grew up into adulthood and later into older age, this still hangs heavy on my belief system.

Why? Well, I reasoned that Christians represented only a minority, when we consider all of this Earth's people. However, Christianity preaches that without acceptance of Jesus Christ as a personal savior, souls are forfeited. So, I wondered about all the people, who did not choose any Christian denomination, but were nevertheless good people. And what about all those far northern people near the North Pole? What about those native people in inner Africa and the primitive people deep in the Amazon Basin of South America? This is not even to mention the mind boggling numbers of Middle Eastern and Far Eastern people, who know little or nothing about the teachings of Christianity? What about those, who follow no religion, or who follow other religions—many of which are thousands of years old? What about all of those folks, I wondered? Are we to believe, because Christian churches tell us so—through their interpretation of the Bible—that all of these vast numbers of souls have no right to salvation? This question has always bothered me.

Are not all of we humans supposed to be part of Almighty God—a spark of the divine, if you will—no matter what belief system each of us adheres to? After all, we are taught that we are all God's creation—His children! So, as such shouldn't everyone's soul be valued and not excluded?

What about souls on distant planets? Are they not valued as much? I wondered about them, long before it was acceptable to do so. As a young girl before World War II, I can recall standing in the driveway of my family home on a clear night, just to look up at all those sparkling stars in the night sky. The magnitude of that sight often left me with awe, as I marveled at God's creations. I knew, even then, that our little planet was but one tiny blip in this entire creation. For I could accept, that countless planets far, far away existed in distant galaxies, where other inhabitants there were also gazing up at that same night sky—but from different vantage points. And like all of us, they are also God's children with their own immortal souls.

Of course, there is one particular long lasting residual, that my religious background imbued in me, and that was the infamous "guilt trip". No doubt, in the staid small town society in which many of us lived, those feelings of guilt kept us young folks on the straight and narrow. But for so many, it also succeeded in diminishing our spirit, causing some of us to spend much of our life, trying to become the person we were expected to be, rather than the person whom we truly were meant to be.

Because of my seemingly never-ending search for true spirituality, I now realize that most organized religions do not offer strictly the word of a "loving God" within their church walls. On the contrary, many churches have learned long ago, that the word of a god, who evokes fear and guilt from the masses will more readily fill their pews, and enrich their weekly collections.

Fear keeps church goers coming back each Sunday. And guilt bombards people with the need to give money until it hurts—in an effort to ward off possible repercussions from what they believe to be a vengeful almighty—damnation from which people were warned about in sermons.

Yes, religious guilt was ever with me, most of my Catholic life. Whenever I would enjoy a bit of joy, the thought always lurked in the back of mind, that there would be a price to pay for it. But many of us dealt with the memories of guilt and fear, of some kind of retribution, by keeping it to ourselves. I recall, back in the late 1930s, when my family and I always attended Mass every Sunday. There I was, a little Catholic girl sitting sometimes in the second or third row of St. Stephens church. Hovering above the altar was that large wooden cross, upon which hung an almost life size statue of a man, who was depicted as being nailed to that cross. And throughout the service, this constituted what I had to stare at for an hour at a time.

My impressionable young mind had difficulty coming to terms with what I had to observe each Sunday. I would try to shut my eyes, to avoid looking at the pained face of this man on the cross—that face which was shown in such excruciating pain. So often, I tried not to see such obvious suffering, depicted with blood running down from his wrists, feet and side, as well as red trickles dripping on his forehead, from that crown of thorns that was shoved on his head.

And in addition to such a distressing vision, in sermons we were told that we caused him to die such a horrible death, because of our sins. How could this be, I thought? For I would never want to be responsible for such suffering to befall anyone, because of me. But yet, this was what we were bombarded with throughout my youthful years. And how traumatic was that for young children to endure—fear and guilt early on?

Nevertheless, that was the way it was—and still is to this day in some places. But it is my belief that most of earth's people always believed in a supreme being—even primitive man. However, the conflict resulted in regard to the differences, as to how each culture worshiped this almighty being. Thus, Planet Earth's people have endured war after war, because of religion.

In ancient writings and legends of Native Americans, Mayans, Hopis, Aztecs, Aborigines, Tibetans and several other early cultures (even as evidenced in the Dead Sea Scrolls), God occupied a special place of reference for them all. And whether the world's people referred to Him as the Great Spirit, Allah, Yahvey, etc., He was still God.

Pity, that so many early Christian missionaries were sent to save the Indian races from what the Europeans deemed as paganism. If the truth be known, those early native people were probably more in touch with God, as the caretakers of the land, than any of those so-called Christians from across the ocean. Indeed, earlier cultures probably prayed more to God than the uninvited invaders to their lands, who brought all their "holier than thou" monks and missionaries, to look down on those simple people.

Granted, certain of the Indian societies practiced terrible sacrifices, as their misguided way of pleasing their god. But there is little good to be said about the Europeans, who came in search of gold, and along the way succeeded in decimating entire cultures—even to the point of destroying written records of those people.

We have only to look at historical accounts of the horrors the Catholic Spaniards inflicted on the Aztecs, and the suffering of the early Hawaiian natives at the hands of north American Protestant missionaries. Yet, we are taught that all of the world's people are God's children. So, it is difficult to comprehend how all of the horrendous treatment of other cultures—throughout history—could in any way be deemed appropriate in order to spread the word of Jesus Christ.

But then all of this seems to have been glossed over in modern times. However, if you want to get in an argument fast, just bring up the subject of religion, and everyone has an opinion. Amazingly in these modern times, there are even those who are trying to re-write the historical origins of our planet to suit their religious views. A TV segment was run, about a Christian museum, that has opened in a middle state. And it features exhibits and (slanted) Biblical explanations, that show the age of this planet at only 6,000 years! Exhibits at this museum were shown, with figures of early mankind, attired in home spun cloth and looking pretty much like Caucasian people do today. And amazingly, they were shown co-existing with the likes of Tyrannosaurs Rex and his fellow species. Considering that such dinosaurs lived in the Jurassic and Cretaceous periods—168 million to 60 million years ago—how does this compute with the true reality of Earth's history?

And where does this museum depiction fit in with what has been related about the great continent of Atlantis, which is believed by many to have been a viable land mass over 10,000 years ago? Even in some of the writings of the great "sleeping prophet" Edgar Cayce are found references to this land mass, having existed in portions of the Atlantic Ocean—including the island of Bimini and all the Bahamas Islands region and beyond. Indeed, it has been revealed from several sources, that Atlantis suffered terrible destruction as far back as approximately 50,000 BC, then again around 28,000, with the last horrific event occurring about 10,000 BC, when that land went beneath the sea.

But it is said, that during and between those several upheavals inflicted on that land mass, did many of it's residents escape to other lands, bringing their exceptional advanced knowledge and experience with them. Foremost among their destinations ranged from

Egypt, India, Pyrenees, Gobi, Peru, Yucatan and sectors of North America.

There was even another great civilized land mass, that is said to have existed in the Pacific Ocean. It was Lemuria, which pre-dated Atlantis. Both were reported to have been remarkable civilizations. However, it is surmised, that both probably misused their great technology and abused Mother Nature, to the point where they helped to cause their lands to sink beneath the sea.

Therefore, how can this new Christian museum version of our planet be considered as anything but figments of some people's imaginations? But sadly, there will always be some folks, who will accept—blindly and without question—such a misguided version of Planet Earth, inspite of historical and geological evidence to the contrary.

Personally, I particularly believe in the lost continent of Atlantis, because of what I saw on a flight over that sector of the Atlantic Ocean almost twenty years ago. It was a clear, blue sky day on that flight out of Miami, Florida. I was on my way for a week's vacation on the island of Barbados in the Caribbean, when I looked down at that beautiful, clear blue/green water below. It was then that I saw something, that I figured really shouldn't be there. It was a line of square white blocks, laid side by side as if on a road, deep under that water. I knew it was not a natural formation, because those blocks were squared on all sides, as if by a stone mason. It was certainly no natural formation. So I am convinced, below that sea exists the remains of a great civilization.

Unfortunately, many choose to use the Bible as their only point of reference, and final authority.

However, there are many contradictions in this book, and sometimes one person's selected version is not the same as another's view. A particular case in point is this. There are many religious believers, who are convinced that they will be "taken up" with Jesus when He comes again. So, for them there is no need to take care of this planet or it's species. Because these people believe they will be leaving Mother Earth, they see no need to take care of the planet. What's the use, they ask? What they fail to realize is that God has given mankind His mandate, to take care of our beautiful sphere and it's species, for as long as we all shall live here. To do less, is to fail in our efforts toward the good health of this planet, which God has entrusted to us.

Since that March day in 1994, and into the following years—as a result of the knowledge I have received from my Guide, along with the realization of ancient texts and my research into little known aspects of organized religion—it is as if a light of revelation has been turned on for me. No longer do I look at my life the same as before. No longer do I see the entire concept of life, and what happens after we pass over, in the same light. I now know, why I have asked "why", about so many things throughout my life—particularly about man-made religion. For I have learned, that what I had suspected for a long time is true. No organized religion has the answers we need. And what is sometimes so intolerable, is that many churches even change the rules of their faith at the whims of the home office.

For hundreds of years, the Catholic Church was fairly predictable. That was before the Ecumenical Counsel in the 1960s, when the church hierarchy in Rome decided to change the rules. I believe it was because so many Catholics were falling away from the church. So, in an effort to come more into the modern main stream, many rules were all of a sudden changed. Before that date, we could not eat meat on Fridays, women had to cover their heads in church, and wear skirts & dresses. After that Counsel, when a bunch of men in the Roman Vatican changed the rules, all of the world's Catholic congregations were affected. Afterwards, women were allowed to wear pant suits at Mass. The altar was turned around, so the priest could face the congregation, instead of having his back to us during Mass. In addition, after countless hundreds of years of saying the Mass in Latin, now English (or whatever country's language) was to be used in the celebration of the Mass.

But old habits die hard sometimes, especially for most Catholics, for whom it was difficult to accept those drastic changes, in the way they were to worship from then on. It was such a departure from the norm. At that time, it was even suggested that Catholics could now read the Holy Bible, if they chose to. Always before, the only Bible I ever saw was the one my Mother bought, through a fund raiser at her church. It was the Catholic Church version of that holy book. So thick was it, filled with full page beautiful color pictures of Jesus and the saints, it was just too heavy to hold for reading. As a result, even though one of these fine books graced my Mother's house, I do not recall even one of us ever reading it. I do believe it was mostly for show. So, to say that we life ling Catholics were confused, is putting it mildly.

To add more fuel to this fire of change, another amazing alteration to this religion's doctrine was revealed at the end of the 1960s. It was done with not much fanfare, so most of us never heard about this at the time. But reports have it, that Mary Magdalene, whom we were brought up to believe was a prostitute in Jesus' era, no longer was to be referred to as such. Instead, she was from there on, to be referred to as a disciple. Finally, after hundreds of years of her reputation being tarnished, this notable woman who played such an important role in Jesus' life, was redeemed. But doesn't this seem like too little, too late on the part of the Church?

However, certain protestant religious doctrine has, for a long time, also reflected suspect ideas. Ruled by their own strict man-made dogma, certain of these are sometimes less than comforting to their congregations. Some protestant religions even teach, that dancing is sinful, because it leads to sexual activity. And anyone who participates in this is bound to burn in hell. No wonder so many people carried terrible guilt most of their lives. For they were fooled into believing, that they were surely meant for damnation, if they did not accept church man-made doctrine.

I remember a girl friend of mine when we were teens, who told me how she enjoyed herself so much at a particular Saturday night dance. But she related to me, how her feeling of joy was cut to shreds when she attended her Baptist Church the next day, when the preacher's sermon admonished anyone, who participated in dancing as on the road to damnation!

Now, many have come to realize that so much of this was only man-made rules—not God's word. But looking back, I marvel at how so many of us were held captive to a way of religious life, the rules of which could be changed at the whims of the patriarchal leaders in charge. This only goes to prove that so many of these dictates, which filled us with guilt if we did not adhere, were nothing more than fearful church laws, that had nothing to do with the worship of God.

How misguiding all of this is, when what we believers in God are really looking for is a place of comfort—a place to pray—where we are not condemned for our every human failing. We seek also, to be in the presence of others, who are looking for the same thing. To put it quite simply, we are seeking a place where our spirit can be elevated and celebrated, rather than diminished.

Fortunately, in addition to the literally millions of spiritual "searchers" all over the world, I have found my own special group. Yes, I have found others, who believe as I do, and will not judge me or put me down for my beliefs. I am especially grateful to Robin G., Carlee, Nicky, Patricia, Robin C., Bethany, Ali, Fay, Myrtle G., as well as other kindred spirits, who are yet to come into my life.

May God continue to bless you all!

✲✲✲

CHAPTER - 11
The Worse Summer Of My Life

Mother almost dropped the phone, as she slumped down onto one of her kitchen chairs. I took the receiver from her and asked what was wrong. My 89 year old Mother, who had been suffering from some heart problems, started to cry as she replied.

"The doctor wants me to check into the hospital..... he says I am anemic and wants to give me a blood transfusion."

I considered her words and tried to encourage her. "Well, Mom, that doesn't sound so bad..... maybe it will help you to feel better."

"No.....no....if I go into the hospital, I just know I will never come out alive!" She shouted, as the tears ran down her cheeks.

This event happened on the eve of the day we were supposed to leave my home town, in summer 2000, to drive the hundreds of miles back to where I lived. After my Daddy passed away in 1998, I told Mother she couldn't continue to live alone in her weakened condition. But she wanted nothing more than to reside in her beloved home, that had been built in 1938, until it was time for God to take her. This was not feasible. So, I made a deal with her, that we would temporarily close up her house, and she would come up to my home, 650 miles away, to live there for a month or two. After that time, I would bring her back to her own house, where we would stay for a few weeks, so she could see her friends and sisters for a while. So, this we did—back and forth for several months.

I was doing what I could to honor the promise I had made to my Daddy, years before he passed. Back then, he asked me to promise that I would never put Mother in a nursing home, after he was gone. Of course, I agreed. But I knew then he was asking a lot of me. Yet, how could I refuse him—this man, who had always been such a good Daddy?

Yes, I had indeed been blessed with good parents, who had been married at the time of his death for some 68 years, which was even considered amazing by standards in that generation. For usually one or the other in a married couple passed over long before that milestone. And as far as attitudes about similar marital longevity in these modern times, such an accomplishment is considered to be astounding—if not impossible.

As I pondered those things, in my Mother's kitchen on that fateful day in June 2000, my memory went back to a similar time, just a couple of years before in 1998, when I was called upon to be strong for my Daddy, too. It was a time, when he was living his last weeks.

Indeed, my parents had always been there for me— through thick and thin, as they say. That is why I chose to be at his bedside to take care of him, after he had a stroke at age 90 and could no longer speak. His mind was still good then, but it was trapped in a debilitated body. When they could no longer do anything for him at the hospital, we took him home to his house, where we had a hospital bed put into the dining room after removing all the furniture. I spent weeks there, because Mother was in no shape to take care of him. My daughter was there, too, to help out some of that time. Of course, we had a visiting nurse come in every morning, to see to his personal hygiene needs. Thank God for that wonderful service.

I slept on the couch each night, just a few feet from his bed, so I would wake up should he need help. A "Living Will" was in place for him, accompanied by a specified DNR notation. So, that meant no heroic measures would be taken, in an effort to revive him should his heart stop.

My heart ached so much for him, this life long independent, dependable husband, father, brother and son—a man of the "Greatest Generation"—who was always there when his loved ones needed him throughout his entire life. As far back as age nine, he had to work to help his mother and siblings. So, his life of doing for others started much earlier than most men.

Now for him (the independent man whom he always was), to have to depend on others to do everything for him, had to be almost unbearable. One only had to look into his pained eyes to see how distressed he felt, being trapped in that sickly body, which was going downhill fast. It was my chore to tie his wrists to the side of the hospital bed each night when it was time to retire. Even though he couldn't speak, I shall never forget the look in his eyes, as he watched me do this, every night. Usually, at such times, I couldn't look him straight in his eyes—those eyes of his, that seemed to be imploring me to stop, and silently asking me, WHY?

Such restraints were necessary, because he had become disoriented the first night back at his house, when he managed to crawl out of his bed in the dark of night. He had struggled for a few feet, before collapsing on the floor. An ambulance was called to take him to the hospital, to make sure he had not broken any bones in that fall. Luckily, he had not. But after that, the doctor suggested we use restraints on his wrists to keep him from doing that again.

I certainly learned how difficult it is to be a care-giver for someone you love. With the dawning of each day, one thought would take hold—is today the day when he breathes his last? This thought was followed by asking myself another personal question. Was I ready to lose my Daddy?

The answer to that question was a resounding NO! But watching him go further down hill with each day, was like watching a person in a seemingly never ending state of torture. Finally, he started to give up. He stopped eating and drinking, on his own. We could not make him take nourishment, because he wouldn't cooperate. It wasn't long after, when he gave up that struggle. So, I saw for myself how a person can literally will themselves to die, in an effort to be free from a debilitated body. And I must confess, it was a relief when that time came, to know that his soul had passed over to that "better place", and he was finally out of pain.

Of course, the death of someone, whom I truly loved so much, was a blow—to say the least! Knowing that I had to go on with my life, yet at the same time having to accept the fact that he would no longer be in this world, was emotional devastation for me. After all, I had been given the gift of my Daddy being in this world with me for some 66 years—more years than most people have with a parent. And the bond between us had grown considerably in his later years. But along the way, while taking care of him near the end, I also came to realize how hard it is to be an around-the-clock caregiver. Indeed, few people realize how hard that is, unless they have walked in the shoes of a care-giver for a terminal loved one.

But that was then, and this was now on that June 2000 day. However, at that moment in my Mother's kitchen, when I was trying to comfort her, my fear returned with the prospect of possibility having to do much the same all over again for my frail Mother.

On that day, we drove Mother to the hospital, for that blood transfusion. She had to be checked in for this and after the transfusion, something went terribly wrong. To this day, we never found out whether it was because of her frail body not being able to tolerate all that fresh new blood, that they put into her veins, or if she was already so weak that any procedure would have worked against her. Whatever the cause, her prediction was to come true shortly. Because she would never leave that hospital alive.

She spent some weeks there, and passed over in middle July of 2000. During those weeks, I would go to sit with her everyday in her hospital room, and try to cheer her up. My brother was there with me, during some of that time, at his Mother's side. But there was no cheering her up, as she had become so depressed over the situation she now found herself in. Of course, her mind was still good, but her emotional state was failing. And so it went, day after day, not knowing when she would pass. It was not until a couple of weeks after she went into the hospital, that things took a drastic change......for me!

For a few days, I had experienced a slight nagging pain in my right side, but figured it would pass. But one morning, after going to sit with Mother, the pain became much worse. So, after telling Mother that I would be right back, I went down to the ER, so they could check me out. Those were famous last words, that did not pan out quite like I had hoped—to put it mildly.

The culprit was a big kidney stone, that had become lodged in the exit channel of my right kidney and would not move out. Thus, the terrible pain escalated— pain that was hard to bear. For anyone, who has ever had such a stuck kidney stone, there are no words to express the discomfort this causes. Even for those, who endure moving kidney stones, which eventually pass through their urine, the pain is bad enough. But for a stone, that refuses to pass on into the ureter tube and eventually down that channel to the bladder, the pain can be excruciating. This is especially so, when the only movement it does exert is caused by the stone's jagged edges rubbing back and forth against sensitive tissue around the kidney's outlet, in a vain attempt to become unstuck.

The only Urologist on staff there was a doctor, whom I knew little about. But this was an emergency, so he was called. And it became his considered opinion, that they could do a "simple procedure", which would involve no surgery. But they would go in through my bottom along the urinary tract, by means of a long extension with a small "basket" attached. This basket was supposed to capture the offending kidney stone and bring it out.

By that time, I was almost out of it from the medication they had given me to ease the pain, so this whole episode is remembered by me as a hazy experience. I do remember my brother being there. And also as I was being wheeled into the procedure room, I had the presence of mind to alert the Anesthesiologist, before he put me under, that I had not included a copy of my "living will" amid the paper work when checking in. And I needed for them to know, in case anything went wrong. He smiled down at me, and said these words.

"Don't worry about that. This is only a simple procedure. Besides, you won't be needing that.....you have me."

So, after hearing those words, it was lights out for me. And it was several hours later that I woke up. However, I learned later, that something went drastically wrong with this so-called "simple procedure". Apparently, the Urologist had inserted the basket, but he pulled too hard. Thus, it broke the right ureter tube, resulting in it becoming much like a severed rubber band, of no use anymore. At that point, apparently when the Urologist realized what he had done, the medical team was instructed to hurriedly move me out of that procedure room and into the hall, on the way to the big surgical room.

It was then that my daughter—I was told later—who had been waiting patiently for this procedure to be over, was approached and told what had happened. She was also told that they had to now cut me open, to try and correct the damage that had been done. And as my next of kin, who was there at that moment, her O.K. had to be given for this serious surgery, because I was out of it. My poor dear daughter had no choice, but to hurriedly give her approval, as there appeared to be no alternative.

All I actually knew, many hours later after being in intensive care, was very little. I awoke in a private room, which was filled with people all around my bedside. Some of those people were nurses and the doctor, but others were members of my family, who had been waiting for me to come to. Upon becoming conscious, I immediately was aware of all those eyes on me. And it was difficult to get any comprehension of what had happened to me. It was like having been locked in a dark place with absolutely no light, and then suddenly having a spotlight shine directly on me. My mind seemed to be whirling in circles, in it's effort to ascertain what had happened. Finally, when he saw that I was awake, the doctor leaned over and spoke softly to me.

"Mrs. Beryl....the procedure did not go like we expected. There were complications and we had to do major surgery on you."

It was then, as I looked down under the sheet covered sides of my body, that I realized I had two urine tubes coming out of me. One, I reasoned had probably been inserted into my bottom, to drain urine, allowing me not to have to get up and go to the bathroom. But what about that other one, coming directly out of my right side? What was that one attached to, I wondered? As if almost reading my mind, the doctor elaborated further.

"We had to go in and attach a tube to the outlet of your right kidney, because during the procedure your right ureter broke and is no longer viable. The plastic tube we put in comes out of a hole in the side of your body, and will serve to drain the urine from your right kidney into a bag, that you will attach to your leg when you leave the hospital. But your life can go on. I have one patient, who has carried just such a bag on his side for over fifteen years."

Can you imagine, waking up to those words, that your life as you knew it before will never come back? That your physical well being has been altered for all time? That you will not even be able to dress as before, because of a urine bag you will always carry strapped to your leg?

Upon hearing his words, all of these thoughts bombarded my mind. And as the seriousness of this situation became more evident, it was then that I cried out to him.

"I can't live like that! I am only in my sixties and before this I was in good health....I didn't even take any prescription medicines. And now, I am a basket case, with a bag of urine to deal with the rest of my life! There must be another way.....please!"

"There is one thing you might consider," he answered. "But it will take a really good surgeon to reverse this. When you get back home in north Georgia, maybe you can find such a surgeon, who would agree to such a serious operation. But I have to advise you, not many doctors will take this on. But it is your choice to try."

Do understand, that all the while this surgical fiasco for me was going on, my Mother lay dying in another section of this same hometown hospital. Before that day, when I was whisked away into surgery, I had previously promised my Mother that I would be with her always until the end of her life. Now, in my present plight, the prognosis seemed dim for me to keep my promise to her. Already, I had been away from her for days.

Almost a week later, on the morning when I was to be discharged from the hospital, I remember getting ready from my hospital bed to go home (with my urine bag attached to my right leg). I was going to my Mother's house, to spend the weeks it would take until I was well enough to travel back to my own home. It was on that morning that a strange thing occurred. Originally, my daughter (as next of kin present) had given her permission for my surgery. My husband was hundreds of miles away at the time of my emergency surgery, but had since driven down to be there. They and my son, as well as several other relatives and friends were in my room on that morning.

The nurse came in and asked who would sign me out to go home. My daughter pointed to my husband to do so. But he became obviously perturbed with her, and remarked as he pointed to her. "She signed her in, so she should sign her out!"

"I only did so," replied my daughter, "because you were not here at the time. Now you are here, and as her husband you should do this."

"No....no, if I wasn't required to do so in the beginning, why should I do so now?" My husband shot back at her, raising his voice in anger. And so it went, with neither one of them wanting to take this responsibility.

"I'll do it.....I'll check my own self out," I finally said above the fray, as I attempted to sit up in my hospital bed. "Nurse, bring the paperwork to me and I will sign for myself!"

At that point, because my husband stood firm and made no effort to sign his name to my hospital release papers, my daughter stepped forward and signed me out. I have played that scene over in my mind during these past years, seeing it for what it was—shameful behavior on his part.

He had also not been present, when I was originally rushed into that procedure room at the beginning of this event. My daughter and son had not been there either at that time. So, it fell to my brother Sonny, to sign the papers for my original, so-called "simple procedure. And I shall always be thankful that he was there, to help me.

Before I forget, let me interject this word of caution. NEVER believe any doctor, when they try to make you feel better by saying, "It's only a simple procedure". Because any procedure in a hospital should never be considered "simple". Always remember what happened to this lady!

But I digress, so I will get back on course. My husband should have behaved better through all of this. But he did not. I already knew that he was jealous of my affection and love for my grown children—especially my daughter, because of the close bond we have. However, how could he have acted so abominably at such a critical time? What is it about some of these macho males of our species? Does it always have to be their way, or the highway in all things? Pity, that with so many men, it always has to be about them—their feelings. He should have been thankful to not only my daughter, but to my brother as well, for coming to my aid when I was so incapacitated.

Why couldn't he face the fact, that he had not arrived there in time, and someone else had to step in for this emergency situation? How could he ever justify his inexcusable behavior toward my daughter, merely for helping her own Mother? I thank God, that she was there for me, when I was so in need of a next-of-kin, who truly cared about me, after they had butchered me in that procedure! Considering that she was already under stress, with her grandmother dying in that same hospital at the same time, as she bounced back and forth from Grandma's bedside to her Mother's room for days, she certainly did not need any more stress heaped upon her, by him.

But instead of my husband being grateful, in his jealous anger about her taking precedence over him, he berated her and caused an embarrassing scene. How often had I seen that hair trigger temper of his let loose, over the most ridiculous things. But this time took the cake. His behavior was abominable, and the damage was done.

Then, there was the aftermath yet to come. After being discharged from the hospital, I was brought back to Mother's house, to begin my six week healing period. But Mother was left in the hospital, where she passed over several days after I was discharged.

Her funeral was well done, if I do say so, and I do believe she would have approved of those proceedings. Even though still not able to walk or stand very long, during this recuperation period, I was helped up to the podium at the funeral, to give a eulogy (one I had previously written) in her behalf. Although she was sometimes hard to please in life, I do believe that in spirit Mother approved of our efforts. And there is no doubt in my mind, that she was present there that day.

Then, as Executor of her estate, I had to see to so much unfinished business after she was laid to rest. It was an awesome responsibility to dispose of all my parent's possessions, which had been accumulated in that house during their long marriage. Of course, my brother and I set aside things we wanted to take back home with us. After this, Mother's grandchildren were allowed to select items they wished to have from their grandparents. When this was done, there was still so much more to dispose of. So, we held a big estate/yard sale, which turned out to be a successful way of getting paid for much of what was left. The things remaining were donated to charity.

During that hectic day, I was up and down from my sick bed, over seeing this event. But Mother and Daddy would have been proud to see how their kids and grand kids worked together, to get all of this done. When I think of so many instances when families bicker and fight over what is left behind by their parents at death, it makes me proud that there was none of that with our family.

A couple of days later, my brother had returned to his home in Florida, my niece and nephew returned to Maryland, my son returned to Philadelphia, my daughter and family returned to north Georgia, and my husband left for our home too. They had taken so much time away from their jobs and life already, that it was necessary for them to return. It couldn't be helped.

So, I was left behind all alone with my best friend doggie in my parent's house, still continuing to recuperate further. There was left a bed, a couch and a TV, along with the refrigerator, stove and washer in the house, so I could continue to live alone there until that six week healing mark was reached. After that, it would be all right for me to drive my car back home. A visiting nurse came every other day, to take my vitals and assess my progress. But for the most part I was there alone for weeks. Thankfully, there were those in my extended family, who lived in that town—especially those wonderful souls—Aunt Hazel, Cousin Bobby, Aunt Ada, Aunt Corinne and Aunt Margaret—who checked on me every day and came by to visit with me. Also, several of my relatives, who lived elsewhere, telephoned often to check on me—Cousin Betty from Harahan, Louisiana, my dear Aunt Jeanne in northeast Texas, and my Niece Kim from Maryland.. And I also want to interject a special thank you here, to Cousin Jane, who has always been in my corner. Of course, there were others also, who came to offer their help should I need it. I shall always remember their kindness toward me, those good people, like Rick, Debbie and their son, who came over to load my car on the day before it was time for me to drive back. All of those good people have a special place in my heart.

However, through it all, everything went smoothly for me, during those days of waiting. That is until the day after my car had been loaded the night before. It was the morning when I was to start driving north, when my emotions overflowed. After making sure that everything that could fit into my parent's Buick, which was now my car, had been packed solidly in the trunk and throughout the width and breath of every conceivable space in the back seat area, I was ready to start. With my ever faithful doggie friend "Ronnie Bonnie" sitting in the passenger seat, I got behind the wheel to begin that long journey. It was then that I broke down!

As I looked around the carport and backyard of my parent's home, the tears suddenly came in torrents. I could not stop crying! But then, it was understandable, because amid all of those weeks of activity, after my botched surgery, when mother passed over, and the estate had to be settled, I had not yet been able to properly mourn the loss of my Mother. It had been a time when I had been so busy, seeing to her funeral, making sure the estate was settled and trying to heal. It was a time when I had to be strong, to make sure everything was done. So now, at that moment, it suddenly all came down on me like a ton of bricks. The realization hit me, that no longer would I be visiting this house and expect to see my parents coming out to welcome me. No longer could I look forward to all those yearly Thanksgiving gatherings at this house, when all of my bother's and my children would get together to celebrate. I had to face it! No longer would this house, that had seen so many happy gatherings for decades, ever be there for any of us anymore. No, this house that I always thought of as that special place, which I referred to as "back home", would never be my place of refuge anymore. What was even worse to accept was this house was now on the market to be sold.

So, I sat there on that departure day, and cried until there were no tears left. Then I hugged my loyal dog, said a silent "goodbye" to that special place, attached my seat belt, turned the key in the ignition and backed out of the driveway, to begin that long trip north.

This would be my first long outing, carrying that urine bag attached to my leg. I could no longer wear long pants, jeans, shorts or above the knee skirts anymore. There would be only ankle length loose fitting skirts and dresses for me in the future. I suddenly felt old before my time!

☆☆☆

After returning back to my home in north Georgia, as advised, I made an appointment with a local Urologist for on-going care about my condition. Since coming home, I must confess that I had fallen into a dismal funk, bordering on serious depression. However, when my husband came with me for my first local checkup at the Urologist's office, I was given some hope.

Following an examination of me, and reading through my medial reports from that doctor and hospital, where the botched procedure had transpired, I saw him shake his head. It was then, that he said he would not have done that particular procedure on me, as there were so many other alternatives that could have been used.

As I began to cry in dismay, I uttered these words of despair. "My life is ruined.....I will never have my good health back again!"

Then this doctor gave me the hope, that I was praying for. He informed me, that there was a surgery, that could be done in rare cases such as mine. But it was not one, that most doctors would attempt. However, he assured me, that he would call around to every hospital in north Georgia, to try and find a surgeon, who would take my case to fix what had been done to me. And he did just that. He did so for days after I left his office, just as he promised. But he was unable to refer me to one, who would take my case.

Finally, one day he called me with good news. He had found a surgeon in an Atlanta hospital, where they did state of the art surgery, and he had agreed to see me. Needless to say, I went to that appointment with this new surgeon, with so much hope. And my hope was not in vain. For this remarkable, wonderful (in my eyes) surgeon said he would help me. But he wanted me to know, that this was a very serious operation, and not to be taken lightly.

It would involve cutting me open again, to retrieve inches of my intestine on my left side, to be brought over to my right side, where my ureter had been. Then that piece of intestine would be fashioned into a tube, to replace the destroyed one. Of course, the intestinal tube material was never intended to carry urine, so it would have to be made smaller and would probably cause my urine to appear hazy sometimes afterwards. But this would prove to be no problem, the doctor advised, as I would be expected to wear a Medic Alert bracelet, with these words on it. "RT Uretero-Plasty Repaired With Ileum". This would advise any Emergency Room personnel, whom I might have to seek aid from in years to come (should I not be in condition to speak for myself), that if the urine is hazy it was no cause for alarm.

I was so excited. Immediately, I wanted to know when could he schedule this surgery? He informed me, that since I had only just had major surgery, it could not be done until three months had passed from that time. So, I asked him to set my surgery date for the middle of September, so anxious was I to get this show on the road. After all, I feared no surgery, that had any hope of putting me back together in workable condition again. For me, any improvement was preferable if it meant I would no long have to wear that detestable, outside attached urine bag anymore. So, now all I had to do was finish healing, and look forward to that much anticipated surgery date.

But while waiting, for the time of this new surgery, another blow befell me—something that I had no clue was coming. It all started after my parent's estate was settled and a monetary inheritance came to me.

After Mother's demise, I inherited some money and my parent's car. Her two houses were yet to be sold, the proceeds of which would be divided between my brother and me, later. After I returned home, my husband became upset again, when I registered that car in my name, because he wanted his name on it, too. He then vowed never to drive that car.

But he did drive me to my local Urologist visit in our other vehicle, on occasion. On one such visit, while driving home from town, sometime after I had met with the surgeon in Atlanta, who would take my case, I dared to ask a question of my husband.

I explained to him, that I just wanted to be as stress free as possible, in light of this coming surgery. So, I wanted to know if it would be all right with him, if I deposited my inheritance money in a special account under my own name, as well as my daughter's name, in case I did not survive this coming surgery? After all, I explained to him, this is my children's grandparents' money. And I had come into this marriage with a paid for car, a house and a career. Now, I had nothing in my own name, but this inheritance money, to leave exclusively to my kids. Besides, I told him, if all went well with the surgery, he would share in whatever I chose to spend my inheritance on, in times to come. However, for now I just wanted a bit of personal security in my own name—so I could rest assured, that my children would inherit that money from me .

I pointed out to him, that should he expire, he had insurance policy money to leave to his children by a previous marriage. But I had no such thing for my children, in case of my death. Besides, this was their grandparent's hard earned money, and should be left to them.

"In light of this coming surgery, I just want to have some peace of mind," I told him, "knowing my financial affairs would be in order, should I not survive. The way it stands now, if I put this money in our joint account and I don't make it through the operation, that inheritance money would go to you. And thereafter, if you expired, it would go to your children—depriving my kids of their rightful Grandparent's legacy."

Well, almost before I had gotten these last words out, my husband exploded in anger. He forcefully slammed down the palm of his hand on the steering wheel of the car, so hard I cringed. Because at that moment, I thought he had, indeed, broken the steering wheel. Then, he shouted at me in his raised voice, forcibly voicing his ultimatum.

"Oh no.....that does it! I want a divorce!"

I reeled in shock, upon hearing this, as he continued. "If you do not consider me an equal partner in this marriage, then it is time for me to go! Any money you get....I should share in equally with you. Your kids should have no claim to your parent's money. It was left to you!"

Upon grasping his angry words, I was astonished at this outburst! In fact, I do believe I was dumbfounded! But I struggled to pull myself together and calm my emotions long enough to attempt an answer to the terrible ultimatum I had just heard.

"You want a divorce....over this? How can you dare ask such a thing?" I implored, "especially at such a time when I am about to undergo serious surgery....and a time when I am supposed to be as stress free as possible! How in the world am I supposed to deal with this now? Have you no compassion for me? We have been married for almost seventeen years....and something like this is your breaking point? What are you thinking? If you leave me now, how will I keep up the mortgage payments on the house? I haven't enough money to pay it off.....I have no job....and I am still a physical basket case!"

And so it went, our arguing back and forth, until we got back to our house. Even though I had pointed out the obvious to him, that this coming surgery would be no small thing. I had even impressed on him, that I might die. So, all I wanted was to have a little peace of mind. All of this did not seem to matter to him. It was so hard, for me, to accept that he had little compassion for me, asking for a divorce at such a terrible time. And after all, I had been through, during this summer of 2000. I was still mourning the loss of my Mother, and still healing from that botched procedure and uneasy about the coming fix-it major surgery. So, I was trying to keep my stress level as low as possible. But none of this mattered to him.

In fact, my problems seemed to be of no interest to him. Only his hurt, over the disposition of my inheritance money from my parents, mattered to him. But he did condescend, as his way of throwing me a crumb of compassion, which he probably thought was a magnanimous gesture on his part, when he said this.

"I will stay with you through this coming surgery..... after all, you deserve that much from me."

And so our lives went on from that point. We continued to live in the same house, but it was an extremely strained existence, as the days passed slowly before my fateful surgical appointment at the Atlanta hospital. But, true to his word, he continued to live at the house (albeit in a separate bedroom), before and during my operation, as well as for a few weeks afterwards.

As for that surgery, I could not have imagined beforehand—even though the doctor had warned me— how difficult it would be to get through this serious physical interior reconstruction. And little did I realize how the weeks would turn into months afterwards, in the healing process.

So it was, on September 14, 2000, the operation began about 9:30AM, and it went on for 4 hours and 15 minutes. I was later told, that the surgeon came out to the waiting room, to tell my daughter and husband that all had gone well, and the surgical team was now closing me up. But it was another few hours, before I was awake in recovery. Amazingly, my daughter told me later, that my husband had sat on the opposite side of the waiting room from her through all that time, and he did not speak one word to her—still holding his personal grudge against her.

As for me, all I can remember as the anesthesia began to slowly wear off in the recovery room (in my state of semi-consciousness), was the intense pain I was suddenly plunged into. So intense was it, that I have a memory of screaming out. "God.......Jesus.....please make it stop! I have done everything you asked me to do....please don't desert me now!"

So, because of the distressing state I was in, the attending nurses and doctor apparently administered some heavy duty pain meds, to put me back under. It was as if my conscious mind quite simply could not deal with that level of agonizing pain. Thus, more hours were added to the length of this already very long day. But then next day, my daughter returned to find me in my room, even though in a shocking state.

Apparently, I was on oxygen, and a tube was in my nose going down to the stomach. There was a vacuum of sorts to suck out whatever fluids were therein. Three bags were attached to my body. Both legs were wrapped in something like large ace bandages, hooked to a machine, that was supposed to massage the muscles. There was an IV and a morphine pump, which I could administer as needed for pain. And you better believe, there was a lot of morphine pumping going on by me, during those first days.

But I have to say, that the level of care and professionalism I received from the staff of that notable Atlanta hospital, was great. I was on the floor, where they did state of the art surgery, such as liver transplants and such. That is how serious my surgery was.

After many days in the hospital, it was finally time to go home. True to his word, my husband did stay with me through the surgery and for some weeks afterwards. Of course, for the first weeks, I was mostly bed ridden. But a visiting nurse came to the house regularly to tend to my needs. Also, my dear daughter was in and out, making sure I was all right. But my husband was of little use. For throughout this time, he went back and forth to work, and the rest of the time he sat in his easy chair in the living room, watching TV, and mostly just getting up to eat and feed the dogs. But he would let my daughter and the nurse in when they rang the door bell. However, he spoke little to the nurse, and absolutely nothing to my daughter, when she came to the house. By this time, he resented her so much, that he would not even acknowledge her presence.

After I was able to be up on my feet for a time, he took me to the lawyer's office in town to finalize the business of this divorce. It was a simple legal effort, as there was no fighting over possessions. I agreed to pay him, with some of my inheritance money, his share of the house equity. And I asked that he agree to send me half of the mortgage payment each month for a specified time, so that I could keep the house. Then, it was time to sign the papers, and time to pay the lawyer. We had used the same lawyer, since there was no property settlement dispute. When the lawyer announced his fee, in that instant, my husband looked at me and I looked back at him—both of us questioningly. Then my husband had the nerve to say this.

"I thought we were going to split the lawyer's fee— you pay half and I pay half."

At that point, I could no longer hold back my frustration at his ridiculous suggestion. "Oh no! You wanted this divorce......I didn't! Now, you pay for it all."

✡✡✡

After the dust had settled, from this terrible year of 2000, I went on to live alone with my best friend dog. Though still a basket case, I managed to push myself to do the things necessary to take care of me, my house and my beloved dog. It was kind of an adventure in "mind over matter", but all things are possible with God in our corner.

However, looking back at those horrendous months, I marvel at how I got through it all. Seeing my mother dying each day, and then when she needed me most, I had all that emergency surgery, which left me a shell of myself for so long. Then, she died, and though far from well, I had to take care of funeral arrangements and help with the disposition of her estate. Following this, I arranged and went through a risky "fix-it" surgery. And in between those operations, my husband announced he wanted a divorce. Any one of those things could break a person's spirit. Yet, because of God's grace, I was allowed to survive all of this somewhat intact.

So, obviously my work in this lifetime was not yet done.

✡✡✡

CHAPTER - 12
Getting Old Can Be Hell !

Yes indeed, reaching Senior Citizen status can certainly turn out to be hell for many people. It was so for my dear Daddy, especially as he approached age 90. In his case, this statement would have read more like this. "Getting old IS hell !" That is what he used to tell me every time I phoned him.

For people, who have been hard working, contributing members of society all their lives, to suddenly enter another phase of life when they retire— a time when to them, they seem no longer valued as much as they once were—this is hard to take. Indeed, this realization is difficult for such folks to accept. Personally, in my older age, I have found that our children still value us, and they need us to a degree. But they are so caught up in their busy lives of rearing children and trying to make ends meet financially, that it is difficult for them to find enough time to spend with their aging parents. And this is as it should be. This is the order of things. But we know, who they still call, when times get tough for them. And it is comforting for our kids to know, that we are still available to listen to their problems, as my parents listened to me for so many years.

In the olden days, when Grandma and Grandpa got old, they still lived in the house with one or more of their married children and their children. In this way, the old people could help with the kids and do chores around the house, as long as their health lasted. As a result, those aging people could still feel a sense of worth, and were an asset to the family. Not so these days, when so many older folks are mostly out of sight, and in the case of many, they are also out of the minds of their kids.

I remember when I was a young girl, my parents took my brother and I to visit some relatives, whom I had not met before. They lived on a nearby island, where there was high enough land to farm, but it was surrounded by much swampland in that coastal region of Louisiana. I believe this was the farm of my Daddy's Uncle and his family. This Uncle, wife and family lived in the larger farm house on this property. But there was a smaller Cajun style house next door, where a rustic front porch ran the length of the entrance side of this two room structure. This, we soon learned, was where my Daddy's Grandma lived. I remember going inside and seeing how sparingly it was furnished. There was no running water, except for cistern water outside, and of course no electricity, because there was no such hookup on that island.

But what I most remembered was this great Grandma's bed. It was a rustic four poster, but with connecting beams along the tops of the posts. From those beams hung thin white curtains, that draped all around the bed. When I asked why the bed was encircled with this white filmy material, I soon learned that this was called a "mosquito bar". It was to keep mosquitoes away from the bed at night, when great Grandma was sleeping.

So, here was an example of how aged folks used to be treated way back when. By the way, as far as I could see, that lady was treated with much respect and reverence. And she lived right next door to her son and family on the same property. In this way, she would participate in the family life, but would also be allowed her own privacy too. Also, her family was always close at hand to assist her, should she need help. This is probably the very best of all worlds for aged folks. Great Grandma lived there until the day she passed on, at what was reported to be age 97.

In days of old, it used to be that aged folks were revered for their wisdom and life-earned good advice, as well as for the experience they gleamed from the school of hard knocks. Again, not so much these days. This is because many younger people today seldom want to hear what Senior Citizens have to say. Because many of the younger ones put little to no value on their elder's advice. It appears, that due to the fact we now live in a world of so many technological inventions, younger people quite simply believe they have no need for any advice from older folks.

As a result of these attitudes on the part of the younger generation, there seems to be few places where Seniors fit—and even less places where we are valued. We certainly do not fit with those youngsters, from whom many times we feel that we are merely being tolerated. And for those of us, who are getting up in age, but still have a vibrant mentality, a will to accomplish things and tolerable health for independent living, there are even fewer places where we can fit in, and be productive.

Some of us try the Senior Centers, where many activities are offered for older people. But for this lady, I found nothing offered there that would suit me. Most of the good folks at the Center have health issues, that limit their getting around. Sadly, I noticed so many were even in wheel chairs. But the Senior Centers do offer much help to many people. There is no denying that.

However, I found the activities offered, although sufficient for some, were most unappealing for a life long, active, independent career woman, like myself. Playing cards, games, bowling and such simply hold little interest for me. My mind still wants to accomplish creative things, and to be valued for what I can continue to contribute in this world. I am not dead yet! I still have more years left to live, and I want more. So, just passing time idly has little appeal for me. And certainly spending hours sitting in a rocking chair and rocking away, should rank at the top of the list as the most non-productive way of wasting time.

After checking the list of recreational things, offered for retired Senior Citizens, I found nothing where I would fit. So, now at age 75, I have chosen to become a recluse. This is also due to all the distressing things I have been through in years past. So many betrayals in my past have left me with trust issues. Much of my stamina and health was taken from me, by that inept doctor in 2000, and since then I have had recurring bouts of PTSD (Post Traumatic Stress Disorder), that comes upon me from time to time. In such instances, so many bad memories that I still harbor, come crashing down onto my mind, and I am often unable to control my emotions of despair. The pity of it all is that I never know what will trigger such an emotional trauma. I just have to live with this, and try to make end runs around certain people, things and places, that tend to cause recurrences. To this day, I do not want to ever go back to my home towns, because for me the sad memories that permeate the atmosphere there are too hard to relive.

Now, even though getting up each morning has become a more difficult accomplishment for my weakened body, I refuse to give into just lying around all day. That would be a cop out, and I am not that kind of person. On the contrary, when I know that I have some where to go on a particular day, or yard work to do, that will take more energy on my part, I resort to drinking one of those protein drinks, which gives me such an energy boost every time.

For most Seniors, part of our nightly problem is that many of us never get what is called a really good night's sleep anymore. After all, having to get up a couple of times a night for a potty visit, is not conducive to restfulness. However, I suppose this is all part of our container body's aging process, which we must endure.

But there is an "up" side to this. For those of us, who do not have to get up every day and go to a job, we can sleep until 10AM or later, and stay up as late as we wish in the evening. This somewhat makes up for the sleep time we lose each night. Besides, who cares? After all, it is nobody's business but our own what schedule we keep.

For those of us of the "green thumb" variety of human, we have this drive to "grow something". And in order to keep on keeping on, we must have stamina to occasionally push on that shovel, use those hedge clippers, pot those plants, and such. And I do believe that we gardener types would all agree, that we never feel closer to God, than when we are working in the soil, planting something. Yep, my Spirit Guide agrees with me, that we are truly doing God's work when we plant trees, bushes and flowers—literally replenishing Mother Nature's realm. In fact, I sometimes find myself, while doing yard work and planting, speaking out loud to the universe—praying and giving thanks for allowing me to live in such a lovely region.

Personally, I come from a long line of "green thumb" folks. My Mother grew beautiful flowers, my Grandpa Lafayette was a sugar cane farmer, and my Grandpa Ben Landry was a great vegetable gardener. In fact, I believe that if Grandpa Ben lived today, he would be considered a "master gardener". But back in his day, growing a garden was not a hobby, but a necessity. My Mother used to tell me about the productive gardens he planted each year. But then, he had ten children and a wife to feed, and those long rows of sweet corn, field peas, cucumbers, okra, tomatoes, onions, squash, potatoes and such were necessary for the well being of his family. And he always planted by the phases of the moon, to insure maximum produce. So, I guess some of those genes drifted down into this lady. For the very thought of living in a high rise apartment or condominium, where one never sets foot on grass and soil, is repugnant to me.

In my lifetime, I have had the privilege of visiting grand cathedrals, with altars aglitter in gold gilt, which I suppose is meant to remind us of the reported opulence of heaven. And I have also worshiped at humble country churches, with sparse interiors. But for me, nowhere is there any man-made structure—either humble or grand—where I have ever felt the presence of God more than I do when planting a seed or a tree.

Indeed, for Seniors, who can still garden, live alone and do for themselves, this is a blessing. And it is essential for us "green thumb" types. Because we can still call the shots and set our own schedules. And not have to ask permission to do anything. No wonder most such Seniors dread the prospect of ever having to be in a nursing home, where they would be told when to get up, when to eat, when to turn off the TV, when to bathe—you name it! For most independent older adults, such regimentation is to be avoided like the plague.

As for this lady, whom some might say has become somewhat eccentric in her older age, well I figure that is my business. One of the things, that might be referred to as an idiosyncrasy of mine in recent times, is the fact that I have stopped answering the telephone after 8:PM. This is because that time (between 8 & 11:PM), is when I want to be entertained and not interrupted, from a good movie or TV show. Such a time is when my answering machine comes in handy.

However, certain idiosyncrasies attributed to Seniors should not be looked upon as detrimental by younger people. On the contrary, it should merely be regarded as older folks just quite simply asserting ourselves. After all, haven't we earned the privilege of living our own life, after decades of having worked and sacrificed for others? Generally, some eccentric behavior should not reflect detrimentally on our mental capability. Personally, I give thanks every day for being allowed to retain my good, mental cognition, and tolerable physical health. Ah yes, to be blessed with a good, sharp mind throughout a lifetime, is a priceless thing.

My Spirit Guide tells me, when the end of my days comes, my mind will still be viable, but my body will have given up. After all, she reminds me, my body has been subjected to so many serious surgeries, not to mention having had serious illness during my lifetime, that these things have weakened my physical container. So I suppose, this is understandable. However, I do take comfort in knowing my brain will still be active on the day of my demise. But then I am reminded of those, who have retained their mental capability, only to become trapped in a debilitated body at the end. So, I guess we had all better be careful what we wish for.

I used to hear my aged Aunts, when they reached into age 90. They would talk about how they wanted to die—how they wished to die. Everyone used to try and make them feel better, so that they could drop such thoughts. But now, I am realizing what they meant. Because it can feel futile in older age, when there seems to be no logical reason why life should go on, with no beneficial goal in sight. On occasion, I have entertained such thoughts about myself, and at this point I am a decade and a half younger than those two dear Aunts, who ended their days in a nursing home. However, what saves me from such dismal thoughts, is the knowledge I have been given by my Spirit Guide, that there are still important things for me to accomplish before my end comes.

But older folks just have to blindly struggle on through old age, still looking for that illusive meaning of life. And most never find the meaning of it all. But our "exit points" are determined by a higher power, and we are not permitted to hurry that date.

For the most part, I am thankful for what God has allowed me to have at this point. But most of us Seniors have to live with maladies, that we knew nothing about in earlier life—things like weak painful knees and/or ankles, arthritis, eye problems, Osteoporosis, and worse. In my case, I did not learn, that I had Osteoporosis until age 71. I was pulling weeds in my backyard, when I fell over and reached out with my right arm to break my fall. The palm of my hand hit that hard Georgia red clay, and I just knew I had done it. Yes, I knew in that moment, that I had broken a bone. As I lay there on the ground, I considered my options. My neighbors were not close, and my backyard could not be seen from the street, where there was little to no traffic in this part of my subdivision. So, I knew it would do no good to scream out for help. Then it struck me, that it was left up to me—which has been usually the case throughout most of my entire life—to pick myself up and go get help the best way I could.

So, I went into my house, with my useless broken arm hanging loosely at my side. Since I was in my old yard work clothes, and didn't want to take myself to the ER looking like that, I decided to take a shower. I always remembered that old adage, that most Mothers used to say to their children—"always wear clean underpants, because if you're taken to the hospital you don't want to embarrass your Mother with dirty underwear."

Well, by the hardest, I showered and put on fresh clothes. Have you ever tried to hook a bra with a broken right arm? It can't be done, so I discovered. Anyway, after dressing I went out to the garage and got into the car, to drive the eight miles to the Emergency Room at the nearest hospital. Then I discovered how difficult it was going to be to do the shifting with my left hand, as the lever was on the right hand side. Luckily, my trusty Buick LeSabre was of the automatic transmission type. Otherwise, had it been a shift type auto, I could not have accomplished this at all. But by threading my left arm through the steering wheel, to allow my left hand to use the lever, I could drive my car.

Finally, I got to the ER and was taken care of. Then I called my daughter, who lived some 30 miles away, to tell her what had happened. She was quite upset with me, for not calling her immediately. I told her that she was at least a half hour away and as long as I was able to drive, why should I bother her? Besides, I was never of the "shrinking violet, clinging vine" type woman, as she well knew by now. So, whenever there is any way possible for me to accomplish something—perhaps something that most other women would never even attempt—I was going to try and fend for myself.

Of course, my dear departed Mother would also have been upset with me, for doing all that on my own. She always thought I attempted to do too much—to do things that she considered not meant for a lady to do. But then, my Mother was from that other generation where the attitude was "men are men and ladies are ladies"....and they should each play the parts intended for them. I always remember her telling me to "always be a lady", and for the most part this has held me in good staid throughout life—especially when dealing with some men. For I have found that most men really appreciate a woman, who conducts herself in a lady-like fashion.

But my Mother never had to deal with the things I have had to deal with in my life. She always had my Daddy, to do things for her. He was always there for her. To put it bluntly, he spoiled her. Personally, it was my experience as an adult woman, that the only times any men in my life really attempted to "spoil me", was when they were "courting" me. It was then, that they showed mostly their good side, and they couldn't do enough for me. But this behavior was so deceiving, because soon after the "I do" ceremony was done, certain of them reverted to their true behavior. So, I guess this only goes to show that you really never know another person, unless you live with them. And sometimes even after years of co-habitation, there are still some undesirable surprises down the road.

To this day, I think of myself as a "Southern Belle-Steel Magnolia" type. This simply means that I have all the soft feminine attributes of what was expected of a southern belle. Yet, there is still that side of me, which is strong of character and resolve—with the kind of strength that has been tested by my school of hard knocks' difficult curriculum. And amazingly, I have found that these qualities do not disappear with age. On the contrary, my strength of character and resolve seem stronger than ever.

But there is no denying that for many older folks, each day can become a struggle of it's own. During the past seven years, I must confess that there have been some mornings when I simply had no drive to even get out of bed. But at such times, my trusty doggie would come to my bedside and nudge me with her cold nose, reminding me that she was waiting for her morning brunch treat. It was then that I would realize, that there was another soul in my house, who was depending on me. And that would make me feel needed, every time.

However, for the most part, the reasons in the affirmative for continuing on with each day became less. After all, it was not as if anyone would be coming to visit me. And I certainly had no schedule to keep. In fact, many times I have gone days without venturing out of my house or yard, or even speaking with another human being, except for my loyal daughter's daily phone call. Other than going out to shop or meet my Daughter for lunch some times, that had become my life. Of course, I realize that so much alone time can become emotionally debilitating, because this life style necessitates a daily struggle to ward off dangerous depression, that could rear it's ugly head at any time. But there are special event times, like Christmas, Easter, birthdays and such, when I gather with my daughter's family for a celebratory dinner—and a chance to intermingle with my teenage grandchildren. That is always so refreshing mentally and emotionally for me.

Many years ago, I listened when someone was complaining about his elderly Aunt. This person said that his Aunt was always ordering items (mail order), that she really did not need. At that time, I had no answer to this, because I was just middle aged and quite active. Now, I understand why his Aunt did that. It was for the excitement she got out of having UPS or Fed Ex or the mail trucks come to her house so often, to deliver all those packages. Personally, I can relate. Because just going to the mail box everyday, to see if there is any good mail there, is a treat for me. I anxiously scan the envelopes in the box, hoping to see a personal letter or card addressed to me from a friend or family member. And when a package arrives, wow, that is really an upper! Let's face it, when one gets old, it is the little things that really mean a lot.

But there is a particular light in my life as a Senior. It is my "Ronnie Bonnie" doggie, who was indeed a gift from God for this lady. This wonderful dog is ever at my side. She even senses my distress when I am sad, and she reacts with glee when I dance around the living room by myself. But most of all, this tan colored "best friend of mine", who was rescued from an animal shelter almost twelve years ago, has a way of looking up at me with those golden brown eyes, that so warms my heart. There is no question in my mind, that she was sent at an important time in my life, to keep me company in anticipation of the sorrow, betrayal and depression, that would descend on me in times to come. Truly, she is my gift from God, and a priceless treasure.

One of my Uncles, in his late 80s, lived alone with his beloved little dog for many years. And almost never did we see one without the other. When his dog became old and ill, he told the Vet he didn't care how much it cost—"just save my dog." Yes, such valued pets are indeed God-sent gifts, that make our lives better, especially us Seniors. It is such a pity, that when some folks become old and have to go into assisted living facilities or nursing homes, where their beloved pets cannot be included, this is so devastating for them. I personally saw an elderly, white haired little old lady at the dog pound, who was turning in her little poodle, because she was being forced to go into an assisted living place, and she couldn't take her dog. She was there, to beg that they find a good home for her beloved pet. And this lady was crying so hard, as she hugged that dog to her chest, that it was difficult to stand there and watch this, and not be personally affected.

That is why I so dread the thought of life without my "Ronnie Bonnie", as she is getting on in years and will probably go long before me. In fact, for a while, this thought would come into my mind almost daily, thinking about what I will do if she expires. Then, I will be truly alone. But such thoughts laid heavily on my mind. Then, amazingly, a few months ago when out on my front walk, this spunky little beagle-terrier mix, with her wagging tail came right up to me, wanting to be petted. She had no collar, so I knew not where she came from. But I put her in the backyard, and called the pound to see if anyone was looking for such a dog. I put a "found dog" ad in the newspaper. I even had them put up a note at the pound's bulletin board about her being found. But no one ever called about her. She is a younger dog, so she will no doubt outlive "Ronnie Bonnie" by many years. So, this appears to be another of God's gifts, sent especially for me, to soothe the devastation I will feel whenever my "Ronnie" expires.

But I have concluded long ago that our pets—especially dogs and cats—are sent to be of comfort for us, during some years of our lives. Pity, they do no live longer. For surely, these magnanimous creations of God certainly have souls. Personally, I have long ago come to the conclusion that I value the company of my dog more than being around most people I have known in this lifetime. Those devoted pets do not judge us. They do not expect much from us—above and beyond food, a warm place to sleep and a petting as often as possible from us. But most of all, they consider us the light of their lives, and they love us no matter what we do. Seldom can we ever find such devotion from human beings. I pity anyone, who has gone through their lifetime without having known the comfort, that these creatures of God bring to us. For such people have missed so much.

However, over many decades of my life, I have come to value many of God's species. At one time, I even had a portion of my backyard fenced in and a shallow pond dug within, to make a home for several Muskogee and Mallard ducks. Each day, I would go out and feed them, and even talk to them, too. For I found that each of them had a personality of their own. To this day, I will not eat a duck I knew. Of course, I have eaten Long Island Ducklings on occasion—the ones you buy already frozen in the super market. But I am still attracted to ducks in ponds, or petting zoos. Why, I even like the AFLAC duck in TV commercials.

This love of ducks at one time became so entrenched in my psyche, that a while back, I told my daughter something I wanted inscribed on my tombstone. I explained to her, that I was unlike that favorite folksy commentator (from the 1920s and 1930s)—Will Rogers—who proclaimed that he "never met a man he didn't like". On the contrary for me. I have met a number of men, whom I didn't like. So, the phrase I wanted on my tombstone should read—"She never met a duck she didn't like."

But above and beyond the valued animals in my life, from whom I usually knew what to expect, there were always so many of those unpredictable human beings to deal with throughout all my many decades. For the most part, I knew where I stood with my extended blood relatives, most of whom were always in my corner. However, there were so many people traveling through my lifetime, of whom I had not a clue as to their motives. But nevertheless, I had to deal with them, and so many times my trust in them turned out to be very disappointing—to say the least.

My Mother used to tell me, when I was a young girl, that I was too trusting of people. And as a result, she predicted that I would get hurt many times in my life. Of course, being the "Pollyanna" type of person whom I was, I replied thusly.

"Oh Mother, I believe that if I am good to people, they will treat me well too."

How wrong I was! I should have heeded my Mother's advice. But when we are young, we think we know better, unfortunately.

As it turned out, along the path of my lifetime, I was stabbed in the back—figuratively speaking—so many times, not only by several males of our species, but also by other women, whom I thought were my friends. In retrospect, I now realize that several of those so-called women friends were really jealous of me. Why, I ask myself, should they have been jealous of me, who had to struggle so hard to get through this life? Perhaps to them, I made it look easy—when in fact they had no idea how hard it was for me. Apparently, for many of those women, whose lives were so lacking, they had to put their blame and jealousy toward someone. And I guess I was chosen to be the object of their disdain.

Now, I realize that I had to overcome all of the obstacles put in front of me, by such unkind people. Even now in this Senior era, some of us still experience certain individuals, who come into our lives without our best interests at heart. We should refer to them as "toxic people", ruled by self-centered, greedy, dark forces, who only want to bring others down. To their way of thinking, spreading un-true gossip, over charging & ripping off unsuspecting older people and attempts at character assassination of others is their means toward whatever dastardly accomplishments they espouse. So, it is far better to be on guard for such people, because their very close presence in our lives can literally bring us down—not to mention sometimes separating us from our money.

It has always been a mystery to me, as to why people do not make the most of what God has given them. How much better would it be, for them to spend their energy in wiser pursuits toward their betterment, rather than try to pull others down. After all, we each have some God given talent or ability, that we are good at. If we pursue that, which we have been given, the result could open life's path to our greater destiny.

Many of us might have been thought of throughout our lives as having several talents—kind of like being a "Jack of all trades....but a master of none". Thus, in our older age, we may find ourselves dwelling on a kind of "what if" scenario. What if I had taken a different path, where would I be today? But the truth is, we each live the life that has mostly been pre-ordained for us—with all it's consequences, both good and bad.

Perhaps there is no Senior Citizen, who will not agree that life is hard, and that (to quote a wise song) "Love Hurts". From this lady's point of view this is so true. And I do believe that I am abundantly qualified to speak about this as an expert. Therefore, my heart goes out particularly to women, who are presently living lives of quiet desperation, having to endure so much abuse from men they thought cared about them. But I say to them, consider this. Throughout history, there have been untold multitudes of wives and significant others, who have had to be sexual slaves to the whims and needs of husbands and/or boy friends—men, who regularly pushed themselves on females (against their wills). And these are women, whom they professed to love. Thus, for women, who have had to endure being sexually and emotionally abused by drunk or drugged husbands for years, life can evolve into a mind-numbing existence, where they find themselves just going through the motions of everyday life—in lives robbed of any personal joy. This can be true for women of all ages. In such cases, they run the risk of suppression of their spirits and their very souls becoming bruised from such on-going abusive treatment. Unfortunately, even in older age, some of us have never forgotten the disrespect heaped upon us through such assaults—even many decades later.

As Loretta Lynn said in her big hit song—"Don't Come Home A Drinkin' With Lovin' On Your Mind"— is good advice for any alcoholic man, who wants to keep a marriage together. Because most women will finally say "enough"! True, some of us may tolerate that kind of forced physical and sexual abuse longer than others. But trust me, most women usually have a breaking point! Unfortunately, the residual memory of such forced abuse—for many years within a marriage— can result in psychological and emotional damage that remains embedded in a woman's psyche, often well into old age.

However, if such oppressed women have the courage to get out of an offending relationship, life could get better for them. This is especially so, if one has reasonable good health and an active mental capacity. Personally, I did not begin to feel a down turn in my health until after I turned onto that downward slope into my 70s. So, I look back at my 40s, 50s and even 60s as good productive years.

Of course, along the way I developed a slight cough (when I laugh), which I attribute to having inhaled so much second hand cigarette smoke over many decades. Please understand, I was never a smoker and I was reared in a home where no one smoked. However, every house in those decades had to have ash trays put out for visiting smokers—even in non-smoking homes. Indeed, my lifetime—in an era of the 1930, 40s, 50s,60s, 70s, 80s—was a time when a great majority of adults smoked. So, we non-smokers always had to endure breathing in their second hand smoke in homes and in all public places—in short, everywhere we went! We were in the minority, so we had no clout. Therefore, so many of us have had our good health impacted detrimentally.

Hallelujah! Times have changed and we non-smokers, who are still ticking, have lived long enough to finally see some justice. Now, smokers have to endure being ostracized outside of public places so they won't spread their toxic (and disgusting) cigarette and cigar fumes. As a result, whenever this lady walks by a public building or restaurant and observes those ostracized smokers outside puffing away on their cigarettes, I can't help but giggle a bit at their discomfort. After all, I had to endure such unwanted smoke for some fifty years. Now, it is their turn to suffer the consequences of their own choice to smoke—without inflicting those fumes on everyone else.

So, living long has it's benefits—even if it is just to see some justice done. However, as I said, getting up every morning out of bed does require more fortitude and endurance than it used to. But I have found that grooming one's self each day helps with personal morale. Being a life long career women, who was required to look as good as possible for my office and newspaper jobs, I still continue to apply makeup and make sure I am presentable each morning, before facing the day. Even if I know that I will not be encountering another human being the entire day, I still have the comfort of knowing that I am presentable at all times.

But the root of my grooming behavior goes back—really way back to my young teenage years. A girl friend and I went on a bus trip to New Orleans when we were both about age 13. Arrangements had been made for us to stay with one of my Mother's brother's family in Algiers, Louisiana—just a ferry ride across the Mississippi river from Canal Street in New Orleans.

It was a great few days for the two of us, when we were allowed to take the ferry and go on by street car to visit Audubon Park, and tour the French Quarter, and visit the big department stores on Canal Street—all by ourselves. Of course, those were the days when two young girls could go all over by themselves, without the risk of harm coming to them. Nowadays, that would probably not be a good idea for such young teens.

However, something happened that I have always remembered to this day. My girl friend and I were sitting on my Uncle's front porch in Algiers, talking to my cousin who was older than us (in her late teens). We were watching folks walk by on the sidewalk out front, and we noticed a young boy about our age was staring at us as he walked by. Well, we thirteen year olds were struck by his good looks and we stared back.

After he had passed by, my cousin told us his name and that he lived on this block. She also went on to say that he had told her yesterday, that he wanted to meet us girls. But he especially wanted to meet the little blonde.

Well, this was crushing for my ego, as I was certainly not the "little blonde" he referred to. My friend was the blonde, and she indeed had lovely natural blonde hair. But her face was not particularly outstanding, as one would certainly discover, once the observer got past all that blonde hair. So, I learned early on how the male of the species can be fooled by first appearances, and be impressed by surface attributes. And this lesson never left me.

In fact, that experience went far in affecting my subsequent good grooming behavior. For thereafter, during all those difficult teenage years, I strived harder to be as attractive as possible. And this was not easy, because I had inherited thin straight, "mousy brown" hair, which was difficult to manage. So, this problem started my life-long familiarity with hair tinting and permanent waves, which I endured from time to time throughout most of my adult lifetime.

Later, I became quite adept at the use of makeup, to bring out my best features. And my ability to design and sew some of my own clothes allowed me to be better dressed than most women. As an adult, I did this myself, rather than waiting until I had enough money to purchase store-bought clothes, which were usually too expensive anyway. So, by using my God-given talents in this way, I managed to exude the facade of an attractive gal. This is an example of what can be done, if we realize what our talents are and we make good use of these for the betterment of our lives. Because for me, obstacles throughout my lifetime have usually brought out my inner strength, leaving me with only one question. How can I overcome this?

Looking back, I can see many bits and pieces of good advice, that my Mother gave me. One time when I was a young school girl, I came home feeling very dejected. Mother asked me what was wrong. I replied that there was a particular class project, that I was required to do. And I couldn't see how I was going to accomplish it, because it was too hard. She then asked me if I felt that my classmates would do it. I replied, yes.

To this, she admonished me with these never forgotten words. "Well, if they can do it....you can do it too!" And she was right, for I had worried needlessly about a project, that (as it turned out) after I applied myself, came easily to me. But I had allowed negativity to enter my mind, thereby causing me to question my abilities. Learning to have faith in ourselves, should begin way back in our young years. For believing in ourselves is the key to accomplishment throughout our lives. It stands to reason, that if we do not believe in our own self, how can we expect others to believe in us? It all boils down to this. Whenever we doubt ourselves, we lose faith in our ability to face any situation—no matter how difficult it is.

That is the trouble with so many of us. Throughout our lives, we have worried needlessly about things, which as it turned out didn't need worrying about at all. Thus, we wasted much of our precious energy in such stressful activity—energy that would have been better spent on more productive pursuits. Now in older age many of us realize, far too late, that worrying never accomplished a thing.

In this age of "How To" books, or "Self-Help" books, which profess to tell everyone how they should deal with particular situations, or how they should live their lives, sometimes we have to take much of this advice with a grain of salt. Speaking from the point of view of a Senior, after reading some of this advice, I came to realize that most of these things are written by much younger people. Of course, advice about the power of positive thinking is always a good thing to absorb, as all age brackets could do with more of that advice.

However, when these younger authors try to push their suggestions on us older folks, it often falls on incredulous ears. Such advice often suggests each and everyone of us should wake up every morning with elation, get up out of bed with vigor, and joyfully give thanks for the dawning of another day on this planet. Such joyful exuberance suggests, that those authors are probably not past the age of 60—if that old. This is because if he or she had ever walked in the shoes of the over 75 crowd, then they would realize that, for most Seniors, waking up with such suggested mythical vigor, is a crock of nonsense.

However, no matter how old we get to be, our soul is forever young. Indeed, it is ageless. Yes, inside of that elderly gray haired lady, sitting in her wheel chair at the nursing home is the soul and spirit of that once young girl, who used to radiate such joy when dancing with G.I.'s at USO dances during WW-II. And in the body of this popular (once young) woman, who never missed a dance and could even do a snappy jitterbug a well as anybody, dwells the same soul that is still within her today, albeit in the body of an old woman.

Human bodies deteriorate with time, but not our souls. Our bodies should be thought of merely as "containers" for our souls When the body reaches it's final "exit point", and breathes it's last, then the soul leaves the now deceased, useless container. It is then that the soul goes on to the "other side" and it's spiritual destiny, Our life here on this planet should be looked upon as only a tiny interlude in the history of our soul. It is kind of like "doing time on Planet earth", until we have fulfilled our current life's span. I have to agree with some, who regard our life span each time as a particular version of "hell", where we are supposed to get through all manner of distressing trials and tribulations. Because I believe emphatically in reincarnation, I take comfort as I age, just knowing with every fiber of my being, that I have personally lived many lives on Earth. And this current life is just another one of those lives. Then, at the end of each lifetime, my soul's growth has been enhanced, from the lessons learned during every incarnation.

But before we can leave this "veil of tears" each time, we must endure. Some of us, as we age, are plagued with heart trouble, strokes, cancer, diabetes and such. Thus for some of those folks, the mere act of just living everyday can be an exercise in endurance and painful acceptance. Consider these facts of life. When you look upon a stroke victim, who has become disfigured from partial paralysis, or a heart attack patient who can no longer walk without assistance, or a Diabetes victim with an amputated leg which has curtailed the quality of life, or an Emphysema victim who always needs respiratory assistance close at hand, it is sometimes heart breaking. But these have become common repercussions in old age. However, no matter how disabled those bodies are, the souls are nevertheless intact.

Each soul—even in damaged bodies—represents the "real" person, and is always beautiful to God. No matter what, God sees the beauty of a timeless human soul—not the ravages of an aging container body.

So, it could be asked of those of us, who are now Senior Citizens in that so-called "golden age" group, what are we doing with the rest of our lives? First of all, I can't imaging where that term came from, for there is nothing "golden" about these years. Of course, for some with tolerable good health in tact, there are those endless times spent on the golf course, hitting a little white ball everywhere in the hope of seeing it drop into an unlikely hole, and having to pay exorbitant green fees and Country Club dues for the privilege.

Then, there are those globe trotting folks, who schedule countless trips, in an effort to see as many exotic lands as possible before they die—or become incapacitated. There are others, who have little to no excitement left in their lives, so they spend endless hours playing bingo, or the slot machines at casinos—hoping for the excitement of a big prize. Still, there are the more sedate Seniors, who rarely even leave their houses. And for them, the most exciting outing in any given month is a visit to the doctor's office.

As for this lady, many may find themselves in my predicament. For, like me, they may have chosen to become a recluse. But I do keep busy with artistic embroidery and textile painting, e-mailing, creative writing, gardening outside when the weather is good. So, it is important that we oldsters have something which we are passionate about, in order to pass the time in as productive a manner as possible. If not, we risk the possibility of our brains becoming stagnant.

For many, Bible study is a source of comfort for them—especially in my area of the "Bible Belt". However, personally I am not even a candidate for such study groups. This is because of my belief in reincarnation. Although reincarnation was once a part of those ancient writings, and should have been included in the final compilation of the Bible, it was excluded So, now every Bible reading religious person has been misguidedly taught that there is no such thing. As a result, they tend to look down on those of us, who believe in reincarnation.

There is no doubt about it, many retired Seniors have much time on their hands. As a result, some of us tend to dwell on the past, as we look back at our lives. Besides the big things that impacted our lives, there are many little things that come to mind. For me, things like when I was fired from a job I loved, been stood up for a big event date and he never even called with an excuse. Also, these come to mind—when I was passed over for a promotion I was counting on, lost a high school election for Homecoming

Maid, been betrayed by classmates you trusted, been gossiped about with untrue allegations, and such. Yes, those things were indeed so important and traumatic at the time. But now as seen in the light of present day life, such incidents should no longer matter. Yet, certain bad memories often stick with us for the rest of our lives.

You know it is true, what they say. When people get old, their brains seems to recall so many things from long ago. And it is interesting, that as the saying goes about folks suffering from dementia—"Grandma can't tell us what she did yesterday, but she can relate at length what she wore to a dance when she was age sixteen."

For such folks, those suddenly revived long ago memories had probably been relegated back into the far reaches of their mentality. And these recollections were put out of mind and thought to be forgotten. This was probably to make room for more pertinent everyday living thoughts during the decades of child bearing, rearing and making a living. But as our body ages and changes, apparently some electrical charge must cause those long past memories to once again surface and vividly come to light.

Of course, many of these once revived recollections are not so pleasant. But we must accept the bad, as well as the good memories that surface in later age. Now, after mulling over all my memories that are coming to light, I realize why I had to go through so many things. It was a learning experience for me—a warning of sorts, to keep me on guard and knowledgeable as to how I might prevent such distressing events in my future. It was also a lesson, that makes me more on guard as to the people I let into my life. For there are many dark force people out in this world, who think nothing of taking advantage of others—particularly Senior Citizens, who are usually so trusting. So yes, I did learn from such as this, and as a result have become wiser.

But in spite of it all, some of us older folks will go on to live independently in our own homes until the end—provided some terrible malady does not afflict us. However, in some cases, there are so many middle age daughters and sons, who will be called upon to look after their aging Mothers and Fathers, before their end comes. This can be such a difficult task in many cases, as some old folks can get pretty cantankerous and bitter. So, my heart goes out to those care givers, to whom such a task has fallen.

I know about this first hand, as I took care of my Daddy near the end. And afterwards, my Mother for many months, too. Although I cannot say enough about what a good Mother she always was for me and my brother throughout our lives, near the end she became very difficult. I always considered myself to be more like my Daddy, than my Mother. So, sometimes it was hard for me to relate to her. And this difference became evident, magnifying itself so much when I was her "care giver" near the end.

Even though Mother lived by herself in that big house for several months, after my Daddy passed over, it was a constant worry for me—living hundreds of miles away. But the last straw came, when the phone rang one morning about 7:AM eastern time. On the other end of the line was my Mother's weak voice. I asked in alarm what was wrong. Her reply was, that she had fallen on the bathroom floor and couldn't get up. But she had managed to drag herself into the bedroom and get to the phone. And I was the person she called—me, who was 650 miles away at the time! I told her that I was coming as fast as I could drive that route. But in the meantime, I would call the ambulance, and my Aunt and Cousin, who would come over to let them in.

So, as I said, that was the last straw. And after I arrived to see her in the hospital down there, I told her in no uncertain words, that things had to change. She could no longer live by herself. And she would have to live up here with me part of the time, but alternating back at her home for a few weeks, to keep her as satisfied as possible.

However, during each day of our lives together after that, there was a definite strain between us. I could never do enough to please her. She even found fault with the color of my fingernail polish. Also, my hair do was not to her liking; I put too much roux in my gumbo, and I should quit using so many spices in my cooking. She would suddenly want to chat with me, in the middle of a TV movie I was interested in, and would get mad when I didn't give her my full attention. She admonished me for not resting more and for staying up so late each night to watch TV. In addition, she said I was too strict with her little dog, and should be more gentle with him. She even insulted me further by saying this.

"I'm glad my dog will go to live with my son after I am gone, because he will treat him better than you do."

What a slap in the face that was for me. And this was so bogus on her part. I was strict with him, because I was trying to train him. She had spoiled him so much, he needed a bit of discipline. God knows, my own dog was much better trained. But I loved both of those dogs, and would never hurt them. The trouble was, that she had been so spoiled by my Daddy, and she couldn't even admit that he had done so—even to herself. So, how could she be expected to recognize the fact that she had spoiled her own dog?

But through all of this time of trial with my Mother, I finally realized something. It occurred to me as in a flash what the problem was! It was that I had never measured up to what my Mother thought her daughter should have been—not even when I was a kid and certainly not as an adult. This was difficult to admit to myself, but it explained everything. And it was time for me to face the music, so to speak. My own Mother simply did not even like me as a person, much less as her daughter!

In this regard, I can recall, back in the 1950s, when some of Daddy's siblings & wives would gather after Mass, at Grandma Fangue's house, for coffee and cake. My Aunts, Grandma and Mother would sit at the kitchen table, drink coffee and chat about children & female subjects. But my Daddy, and his brothers—Uncles Ty, Johnny, Elby—would sit in the dining room and talk about politics and national events. Personally, I preferred to sit in the dining room with the guys, because those subjects were of more interest to me. Mother always took a dim view of my behavior, as she thought I should sit with the ladies, and she told me so. Obviously, we were seldom on the same wave length, and I always had the feeling that I was a disappointment for her. Of course, I knew she loved me as her child—even though she never said so—but I finally became convinced, that she never really liked me.

After this realization, I prayed to God that He would give me the strength to continue taking care of her, as each day was becoming harder. There was never a word of praise or a "thank you", or even an occasional compliment. There seemed to be only endless criticism.

I was becoming literally drained of my energy with each day. The only thing I had to look forward to was sleep—falling asleep each night was my escape from this reality. Mother expected me to be all things to her, but I simply could not live up to what she wanted me to be. I did my best, but it was never enough in her eyes.

Yes, it was a thankless job, and no doubt brought down my physical and mental health. Having experienced this, I can only suggest that such "care givers" get occasional relief from these obligations, by having someone relieve them from time to time, so that they can get away from such responsibility—even for an occasional day.

But life goes on—whether young or old—and we must cope with it all. For Seniors this phrase has meaning—"Now the end is near....and I must face the final curtain". So, at our older stage of life, we become forced to deal with our own mortality, and contemplate how the rest of our years should be spent. Personally, it will be a relief for me when my "exit point" comes, for I am not afraid to pass over. I agree with many, who believe that we should celebrate death and mourn when a baby is born. Just think about it! It is understandable why a baby cries when it is born, sliding out from that warm womb where it has been safe and cared for. Then, to abruptly enter a cold place, with bright lights and all those hands reaching for it. And the worse is yet to come for that baby's soul, once again having to deal with life on this difficult planet. Whereas, an elderly person, who finally breathes his or her last, is free at last!

But when it comes to our final time to pass over to our "real home", here is a bit of simple advice for those to be left behind. I wrote this to my son, after he and his sister had to put their stroke-ridden Dad in a home town, south Louisiana, nursing home. After all, there was little else either of my adult children could do for their severely stricken father, because they both lived hundreds of miles away.

"About your Dad, I do not want you to feel so guilty about your not being there all the time. He has several of his family looking in on him everyday. As a result, he is more fortunate than others in nursing homes, where few to no family members ever visit them. Yes indeed, he is blessed to have his siblings and their wives care enough about him.

"You and your sister have done so much for him already. So, don't worry about him passing over alone. We are never alone when we pass over. On the contrary, before that exit point out of this lifetime comes, several spirits/ angels will come to escort his soul, and make sure he has a smooth transition. Besides, terminally ill folks really do not want people fawning over them, as they breathe their last. For coming to the end of a life is a very personal event, and not meant for more human intervention.

"I remember hearing about my Aunt Eula, when she lay terminally ill in a New Orleans hospital. Her only daughter Betty was ever at her bedside for days. Finally, Aunt Eula said to her. 'Betty I want to go....but you are preventing me from leaving. Go home and leave me alone for a while, so I can be at peace.'

"So, Betty, who probably loved her Mother more than words can say, obeyed and went home, but only to eat and sleep for she planned to come back the next morning. But then, Aunt Eula died that evening. Obviously, it was her wish, to be alone when she crossed over.

"I guess we are not doing them any favors by insisting on always being there at the end, in a crowded hospital room, where many eyes are constantly on them.

To put it quite simply, they need their own space, in order to contemplate this personal ultimate act of their earthly life."

☆ ☆ ☆

But long before our final time comes, we can remember that this lifetime did have it's moments. For me, one such event remains ingrained in my memory.

It was in the summer of 1963, when my Mother and I took my two small children on a train trip to visit my brother and wife Nancy in Baltimore, Maryland. It was a lengthy overnight journey, to get there from New Orleans. So, I tried to keep the kids entertained along the way. But we were in open coach seating, so this wasn't easy. However, I would quietly sing songs and urge them to sing along with me, as we gazed at the passing landscape through the train windows. One such song, which seemed apropos was "Chattanooga Choo Choo", because it had lyrics like this. "Read a magazine and then you're in Baltimore......dinner in the diner, nothing could be finer.....than to have your ham and eggs in Carolina". To this, the children joyously chimed in with their youthful voices. And then, we became the hit of that train coach, for this got everybody else smiling and singing along with us. So, we apparently perked everyone up.

But what I remember most about that vacation was the unforgettable excursion we took to Arlington National Cemetery. We walked around Arlington House, on that Virginia hillside, overlooking the Potomac River. And we adults watched as my two children ran up and down the grassy slope, in front of that impressive mansion. This mansion's construction was begun by George Washington's step son in 1802. Later it became the home of Robert E. Lee and family until 1861, at the start of the Civil War. This was when the Lee family had to move away from that Virginia hillside home, which they loved so much, because they risked capture by Union forces if they stayed.

Yes, we did enjoy visiting that lovely unspoiled historical site, up on the hill, which overlooked Washington D.C. But little could we have envisioned on that special summer day what a drastic transition would be in store for that acreage in a matter of a few months. For in November of that same year, President John F. Kennedy was assassinated in Dallas, Texas, And his widow (Jackie) made the decision that he should be buried in Arlington, because as she stated, "He belongs to the people".

So, that special hillside, which we so enjoyed in summer of 1963, was designated as the site of internment for President Kennedy, and later for Jackie too. As a result of this, I always thought about what a privilege my children had, while running across that green, vacant hilly lawn back then—when never for a moment could any of us on that summer day have imagined that it would become such a special burial site. With it's eternal flame now always lit there, this piece of hillside was literally transformed into a place of homage for the countless numbers of people, who have visited there every year since.

No matter how long I live, that special day in 1963 will always reside in my memory bank. But unfortunately, it will also resonate right alongside of my deepest regret at losing JFK—our notable president, who left us much too soon.

Speaking of Jackie Kennedy, there is something else that she was unknowingly responsible for, but is little known by the multitudes in that decade, or since. During the early 1960s, when she was first lady, all eyes were on her impeccable sense of style. Thus, most ladies wanted to emulate her. As a result, many designers strived to copy her apparel in all ways. Of course, this was understandable, but alas, it resulted in an unforeseen consequence.

Coming out of an era when most women wore hats when they dressed up, Jackie limited her head wear considerably. Her favorites were pill box hats and black lace scarves on her head—worn mostly when she went to Catholic Mass. And since women were copying her style of dress, this had a devastating impact on the women's hat industry. I know this, because I had a hat and gift shop at the time. So, I saw for myself how suddenly the women's hat business went down hill. This was because of the cheap pill box hat imitations and $1.98 lace head scarves, that women had begun to buy then. As a result, retailers in that line quite simply could not survive. In fact, even many hat wholesale and design businesses went under, too.

But such is life, and we must move with the inevitable nature of changing times—like it or not! So, we are always at the mercy of what next season, or next year brings into our lives. However, for some of us, as we grow older and have seen more than our share of bad times and bad people in our particular lifetime, we just want to get away from it all in our waning years. I know, that I feel like that.

When I was spiritually directed to move to north Georgia, I so wished to be led to the right plot of land, on which to build my house. A real estate agent took me to a new subdivision with large hilly lots, which were just beginning to be carved out of a previously undisturbed forest. No houses were built there yet, in fact, the roads were not yet paved. As I walked on one particular piece of land in this thick forest, I noted that it was filled with tall old oaks, maples, sycamores, poplar and a few pines. And while treading on the crackling, thick fallen leaf carpet below my feet, I was reminded of those times when the native Creek and Cherokee Indians walked that land in their moccasins, so long ago.

But it was difficult to decide which 3/4 acre lot to choose, and I wanted a sign to direct me to the right one. Then, through this thick forest, I saw a misshapen tree, that had apparently been bent over long ago, and subsequently had righted itself, to grow in this fashion. Somehow, I knew that this was a significant tree, and had to be saved. So, after I selected that particular piece of land, I pointed at the special tree, and told my contractor to save it. In fact, I told him to save as many of those magnificent trees as possible on this lot, and only cut down the very minimum of trees—only on the space where the house, driveway, septic tank would be built. I told him I wanted to enjoy the feeling of living in a virgin forest, and I did not have enough years left to wait for trees to grow.

I well knew how so many builders literally stripped the land of just about every tree before they built a house. This is because it made it easier for their heavy equipment to move around thereon. But, what a disservice they do to Nature, by needlessly cutting down so many trees.

As it turned out, it was a good thing I did specify this, because they had already drawn up the plans as to where to construct this house, and it had included the cutting down of that "special" tree I had found. When I told him that would never do, he altered the plans, specifying the driveway be moved a few feet over, to save the tree.

As it turned out, after doing some research, my feeling for that special tree was justified. It is one of thousands of what they refer to as "Indian Trail Trees", that literally dot the southeastern forests of our country. Because the American Indians had no road maps, they relied on old trails when traveling through the thick forests. But they did have their own style of road direction signs. They would take a sapling of about ten feet tall, bend it over in a certain direction where they wanted it to point as it grew. Then they would fasten it to the ground with rawhide strips. Afterwards, the young tree would try to right itself as it grew, but a part of it would always point in the direction intended by the Indians. In this way, those trees directed subsequent generations of Native Americans to find their way to creeks, lakes or Indian villages. In this case, my tree pointed toward a fresh water beaver pond, located a short distance further in the forest.

So, in my own small way, I helped to spare a piece of history, that few people are aware of. This is not to mention the many numerous tall hardwood trees on my property, that would have been destined for the chain saw, had I not intervened. I do feel good about that.

I also feel good about living on a property, that after twelve years, is thick with lush tree foliage throughout. In fact, with each passing year, it is getting more difficult to even see my house from the street, so thick has this beautiful foliage become.

Perhaps, a psychologist might suggest that with such behavior, I am trying to hide from the world in my own way. And they might be right. Because at this point in my life, I prefer to be surrounded by nature and it's creatures, rather than to be around crowds and commercialism in the real world. I take great delight in suddenly coming upon a beautiful doe deer, standing on the other side of my backyard fence, where she and I can stare at each other for a few glorious seconds before she bounds off into the trees. It is revolting to me, how anyone can shoot such a lovely creature.

I also find it fun to see so many squirrels scurrying about in my yard, searching for acorns, in their ever constant pursuit of places to hide these. However, I do look with some disdain when these little rascals eat the still green peaches off of my trees, and partake of my tomatoes before I can pick these. But this is all part of Mother Nature's natural scene—like the occasional nighttime sightings I am privileged to see, of a scared possum on my back deck railing, with it's eyes reflecting red in the glare of my flashlight. However, all of these creatures seem to know, that I am no threat to them, so we can co-exist together. The trick for me is, to hold back my ever present doggie companion, when she wants to chase the possum.

But I consider my constant companion German Shepherd/Chow mix dog, as my true "friend". After all, we two old ladies compliment each other. And in "doggie years" she is even older than this 75 year old lady, at her age of 84. So, we are a good team.

Yes indeed, there is a lot to be said for getting back to Nature, after a lifetime of struggle and stress in the real world. For no doubt about it, peace and quiet has it's place, when one is trying to come to terms with personal mortality.

In regard to all those difficult people, who have passed through my life, I have also come to terms with their presence. Indeed, I constantly have to remind myself, that all those who caused me trouble and sorrow this time around, came into my life for a reason. They were written into my life chart, to pass through this incarnation of mine, so as to provide my soul with the challenges needed to aspire to a higher level. For without such difficulties to deal with in life, we are not provided with the necessary hard lessons, from which to learn. And without these struggling life challenges, our souls would not be able to aspire to greater levels in God's realm. I suppose we could say, that toxic people and dark entities provide the obstacles, from which we learn to overcome.

But as long as we aging humans are still in this lifetime, we must make the best of it. Personally, I have bestowed on myself one big reward, for four years in a row. I have treated myself to one expensive vacation each year since 2004, and thus gave myself something to look forward to all year long. And it is so important that we all have something to aspire to, or else our life becomes too drab.

So, cruising the Atlantic, Pacific and Caribbean has become my yearly reward—on luxurious cruise ships where they treat me like a queen. But then, I figure that I deserve such treatment—just for having survived this long from my tumultuous lifetime. For now that I have the time and financial resources to cruise in style, I even book a cabin with it's own private balcony, which is such an added treat. However, when I booked my last cruise and told the young lady, who was taking my reservation over the phone, that I was traveling as a single lady and wanted a private balcony cabin, she replied thusly.

"You are traveling alone.....and you still want a balcony?"

I assured her that I did, and wondered if she thought that in order to enjoy a balcony at sea, a lady should be traveling with a man? Of course, she sounded young and had still to learn the ways of the world. Because nowhere is it written, that a lady has to have a man along, in order to enjoy a vacation.

After all, I do believe that first rate night club entertainment, four star meals beautifully served, high teas and art auctions, swimming pools & hot tubs, not to mention taking a few turns on the dance floor to live music, comes under the heading of enjoyment. And what's more, a lady does not need to have a man to dance with on those ships. She can get up and dance to rock and roll, as other ladies do, if she so chooses.

But a word of caution is given here, about booking certain shore excursions, that are sometimes much too strenuous for Seniors. I learned the hard way, while struggling up a hill to see the Mayan pyramids in the country of Belize. Indeed, while huffing and puffing with others in my group—all of whom were much younger—I soon found myself trailing behind them all. And I thought my heart was going to give out, as my lungs struggled to pump enough air in and out to keep me going, amid that jungle humidity. So, as much as I love the pursuit of history and historical sites, my brain cannot always be allowed to ambitiously dictate to my aging body, pushing it much too hard in order to get me where I want to go. After all, as soon as we gals get it through our thick skulls, that we "old gray mares ain't what we used to be many long years ago", the better off we will be.

However, of all the many trips I have taken over the decades, the one that stands out the most was my 1979 genealogical journey to the birth place of many of my ancestors—Acadia—now known as Nova Scotia, Canada. Yes, standing on the shoreline of the dykes, which those industrious French people built way back when, was such a revelation. To be there, where they were forcibly taken onto English ships, after being robbed of their farms and possessions in 1755, evoked such a feeling of awe, that has never left me.

But then, I have always been driven to search for my ancestors all my life. And just recently, I enjoyed another such humbling experience. I saw for myself where another of my Theriot ancestors was during the Civil War in 1863. And it was so amazing to literally stand at the top of a hill, where he and his comrades (of the 26th Louisiana Infantry—Confederate States of America) held the high ground against attacking Union troops. This was at the battle and siege of Vicksburg, Mississippi—back then called the "Gibraltar of the South".

So, we Seniors, who still have some get up and go, can continue to enjoy certain highlights in our lives. But finding those things we enjoy, and that our bodies can endure, is the key. I know it is not yet my time to exit, so life must go on for me in as positive a manner as possible. But it is sometimes frustrating, that I do not fit in anymore. This is in spite of the fact, that within my very being I still have the same inner spirit as I did at age 40 or 50. Those are the decades when many of us felt that we had gained enough maturity, to be considered somewhat wise. Of course, there are some exceptions.

For occasionally I have been privileged to meet a very few people—much younger than me—who seem to be on the same wave length. And I do so feel comfortable with them. I attribute those rare folks to souls, who were with me in previous lives, or we were previously together on the "other side". For such souls, whenever I have met them, we always hit it off so well. I realize they care not how old my container body is, because they are wise enough to know deep within, that our souls are ageless.

My daughter is one of those souls, whom I have shared other lifetimes with. So are her two children, my grandkids. I feel this strongly, for those teenagers do not view this grandma as a boring old lady,. On the contrary, together we can talk about anything, I am happy to report. But I have never talked down to them. Rather, I have always regarded them as intelligent young people, with souls as old as mine, whom I feel an obligation toward to inform and teach, about life and spirituality. After all, they are my "seed". Along with my son, my daughter and her children, these are—for the most part— the reasons for my continued existence in this lifetime.

Yes indeed, along side of this current mission of mine, other things seem to have lost much of it's previous meaning for me. Now that I am in this era of life, I can relate to the motives of some other Seniors. How often have I heard people say, that a certain elderly lady or gentleman were no longer taking as much care with the up keep of their house and yard, as they used to do. Well, I can guess why. In fact, I know why.

In senior Citizen realm, our bodies no longer have as much stamina, as before. So, Seniors want to save what they have left, to do the things they still enjoy doing. So what, if their house is not as straight as it used to be.

So what, if their yard is no longer manicured. At this stage of their lives, they do not have to prove anything to anyone. Of course, such folks should always keep their lodgings clean and their yards not an eye sore. And most do. But many of them no longer want to risk depleting all their stamina in such pursuits.

My Mother, who was an immaculate housekeeper in her day, became much less so in later years. During those years left for her—health permitting—she preferred to work in her flower beds and yard, as opposed to doing house work. I understand that too, for I particularly like to use my available stamina, to do the things that are enjoyable for me.

When I lived in SW Florida, I knew a delightful, aged, retired couple, who were in their middle 80s. He delighted in growing potted palms and tropical plants, which he sold at ridiculously small prices to fellow gardening friends, who would come by to see him, and get his advice about growing tropical species. His wife spent much of her time inside at her ham radio setup, where she talked with people all over the world.

True, if you were to walk into their home then—although it was presentable—the rooms were cluttered and not straight and tidy. Their yard needed much weeding too. But these two beloved folks chose to use what stamina and energy they had left to them, to pursue the things they truly loved to do. For their time was fleeting, and they knew it.

However, I can only hope and pray, that throughout my 80s I will still have the energy needed to pursue certain favorites of mine. Indeed, if I am able to have the physical energy needed, that a certain elderly gentleman I remembered had, it will be enough. How well I remember him, that nice man, who lived down the street from my parent's house. He so loved to plant a garden each spring, that even in his elderly years, he found a way to continue. Toward the end of his life, I used to see him in the spring, when he had managed to plant three rows of his vegetable garden. Although he was in failing health and walked hunched over, he would go out there to hoe those rows of veggies. He did this, by having one plastic lawn chair set at one end of the rows, with another at the other end. And by the time he would hoe one row, he would sit down to rest in the chair at the other end, and repeat this over and over again, until he was satisfied with his work. Such is the unrelenting persistence of a true gardener—no matter what the age.

My wish, also, as a life long writer, is that someone will bring a lap top computer to my death bed, as I near my last days on this earth. This is so that I may type some final words. Wow, talk about having the last word! However, what better, or more satisfying, way for a professional writer to exit this life?

But no matter what our age, there is one ingredient, that we should all nurture in our individual personality. That is a sense of humor! Because without the ability to laugh at ourselves, we risk becoming bitter and unlovable. After all, no one wants to be around anyone, who constantly feels sorry for themselves. That's no fun.

"Woe is me......I'm old!" Many remark over and over. Well, join the club, because the Senior Citizen category grows every day, and there is no end in sight. After all, time is our enemy and takes it's toll on our bodies, relentlessly. So, even you youngsters out there will someday be old. There's just no stopping it!

Ah yes, there are always new—and not always good—things to get used to when thrust into this Senior realm. Not the least of these for me is the fact that I am shrinking more with each passing year. Amazingly, I am no longer the 5 foot 3 inch petite statue I used to be. Yep, when I look into my full length mirror, I am distressed at that much shorter old lady, who stares back at me. Now, I even have to sit on a combination of two foam wedges on the driver's seat of my car. This is in addition to adjusting the seat forward as far as it can go. All of this is necessary for me to sit up high enough to see over the dashboard and hood.

But we old gals go on in spite of such obstacles. Yes indeed, for years now, I have become adept at taking myself out to dine alone in restaurants. Because so many previous pursuits have been taken away from me with age, now, tasty food has become even more of a comfort than it used to be. So, I seek it out regularly. Even though I am a good Cajun cook, who prepares a special meal each day for myself, sometimes I like to go out and be served in a good restaurant. Heaven forbid, that I ever have to be on a diet! For then, I will have little left to make life worth living anymore. My favorite restaurants (besides Cajun) are Mexican, where the atmosphere of south of the border—down Mexico way—music and decor greet me as I enter. Some how, whenever crossing the threshold of such a cafe, my spirits are instantly lifted. It is as if an overwhelming reminiscence of another era takes over me. As a result, I have chalked these experiences up to having lived other lives in Mexico, in some of my previous incarnations. Even if such experiences are just cell memories, it always leaves me with a good feeling.

But no matter where I go now that I am in this "old" category, I do notice the difference as to how I am treated by the males of our species. Previously, when I was younger—even in middle age and still somewhat attractive—whenever I was out and about, men stared at me, waiters hovered over me, mechanics couldn't do enough for me. But now, men who glance at me hurriedly look away, as if they had seen something they do not want to dwell on. Some waiters are respectful (I guess hoping for a good tip from this old lady), but others are cold and distant. And mechanics and home repair guys look at me as if I was some old gal, whom they could rip off. Yes indeed, during the past eight years, about the only male of the species who looked at me with some interest was a decrepit little old man I passed on an aisle in Walmart. But then, I decided that his interest was strictly because he was looking for some passable woman, to take care of him in his old age. Fat chance, I say to that!

As to how long I will be living on this planet, I know not. But I do know this. If it would be possible (and affordable) for my kind of funeral (when the time comes), I would wish for a New Orleans Dixieland Marching Jazz Band, to lead my procession to the grave. And they would play at the wake after my burial, where I would have left instructions for everyone to dance, laugh and celebrate the fact that I had made it through yet another journey on this planet. But there is one thing I want to make perfectly clear. It has to do with the name inscription on my tombstone. My original maiden name—Beryl Ann Fangue—is to be used there on my final marker. This is because that is who I truly am. Any other names added on, because of marriages, do not reflect the real me. When I came into this life I was given that name, so I want to go out with the same name.

And as my soul hovers over such festivities, looking down I would be so glad and satisfied that such a send off celebration was taking place, as per my previous expectations. However, if any of those present would be moved to shed a few tears at the loss of my presence in their lives, that would be fine. But do not cry for me, just for the fact that I have exited at last! For at that moment in time, I will be happier than I have ever been in this life. My loved ones present could celebrate my life, if it makes them feel better. But I want them to also rejoice, that I am finally out of here, and going to that more treasured destiny, where I will be anxiously waiting for them to join me.

But because I believe strongly in reincarnation, there is something I already dread. It is the possibility that my soul might be foolish enough to volunteer to be reborn again into yet another lifetime on Earth. To that possibility, all I can say is this.

Say it won't be so, as I honestly do not want to come back here again—to this troubled planet, where mankind never seems to learn from their own mistakes. They just continue to repeat those mistakes over and over again, causing more war, death and destruction within every century. It is just too hard, living here..... so I have no wish to incarnate on this planet again.

✬ ✬ ✬

CHAPTER - 13
I Know What It Means To Miss New Orleans

There she sat, this petite, elderly, gray haired lady, at a restaurant table near the booth where I was about to order my lunch. It was a Friday in 2006, and we were part of the crowd at this north Georgia seafood restaurant. After I gave the waitress my order, I looked over at that lady and felt her loneliness from across the room.

"Go over there and introduce yourself," said the telepathic voice in my head. I knew it was my Spirit Guide talking to me, as she did at different intervals throughout every day of my life, since March 1994.

"No," I mentally replied. "I do not wish to intrude..... maybe she is expecting someone, and would resent my interference."

"She is definitely not expecting anyone....she is alone....and we will not stop with our entreaties until you go over there. I assure you, that she will welcome you." Thus, went the reply from my very persuasive Guide.

So, while waiting for my meal to be served, I got up and walked over to that lady's table, and said to her. "Hi.....we don't know each other, but somehow I was urged to introduce myself." I then told her my name, and she said that her name was Emily.

She looked up at me and smiled, and continued. "I'm not from here, you know.....read this, it will explain my presence here better than I can."

Then she handed me a couple of typed sheets of paper, and invited me to sit down with her, as she went on to say. "I'm from Louisiana.....and only recently came to live up here."

"Wow, that is great," I exclaimed. I am from Louisiana too. What town are you from?"

"New Orleans," she replied. "I am up here because of Hurricane Katrina. It has become so much trouble to tell my story over and over again to everyone I meet, that I wrote it all out so that they could read about what happened to me. It is easier that way."

Needless to say, my curiosity was really peaked by this time, as I glanced at the printed sheets she had just handed me. What I read there really amazed me, as it probably would anyone, who has occasion to learn of her story. It goes somewhat like this.

On Saturday, August 27, 2005, news of Hurricane Katrina's track looked pretty ominous, so Emily tried to make arrangements to leave New Orleans. But by that time, it was too late, as residents could no longer get out of the city. So, after speaking by phone with her daughter, who lived out of state, Emily was urged to go to a neighbor's house before the storm struck.

Her elderly neighbor Jack, to the back of her property, had a two story house and he invited her to take cover there, in order to ride out the storm. On Sunday afternoon, she made several trips back and forth from her house, bringing things she thought would be needed for what was expected to be a stay of only a couple of days.

Then after a stormy night, Monday, August 29 dawned. It was her 81st birthday, but there were no presents to be had on that terrible day. For when Emily and her neighbor went out on the upper porch, a horrific sight met their eyes. There was water everywhere! As they looked over at her yard, they saw for themselves how high it was, because the water was almost over the top brick of the six-foot fence around her home. Then, began their time of waiting.

Because at that moment in time, there were no sounds or signs of any rescuers anywhere around that flooded realm, where they now found themselves. As it turned out, it would be days before they would see any signs of help coming their way. But at that time, they had no way of knowing this. So, by way of trying to signal to any planes or helicopters, that might be coming, Emily made an effort to call attention that they needed help. She had previously brought from her house, a CD player that contained a small flash light at one end. So, for three nights she sat on that second story porch, with that beam of light aimed at the sky.

Then, on the morning of September 1—Thursday— a helicopter did appear and try to come down. But Emily said the noise was so deafening and the air was like a cyclone, so they went in and closed the door to ward off the wind. But Jack did not open the door again, and they could not hear the voices calling down to them from the copter. So, it flew off and left us, Emily said.

After this failed attempt, at midnight Emily went back on the porch to keep her flash light beam going— shining up in that black sky. She could remember thinking to herself.

"If this was said at the worse time in the whole world, I must say it too,—Father forgive them, for they know not what to do." Then she prayed. "Forgive them for leaving us; forgive me for closing the door; forgive Jack for not opening it. But God works in strange ways,

His wonders to perform. And as the lines of a song say—"Leave it with Him for all the lilies and they do grow".

At that point, Emily fell asleep in a chair.

Early on Friday morning (7:AM September 2), she reported that along came their "savior" Tommy in a motor boat. He lived blocks away, but often when he used to walk his dog, he had stopped to converse with Jack.

Even though the water had receded somewhat, both Emily and Jack couldn't walk in the water. Luckily, Tommy had brought wheelchairs for use when the water was too shallow for his boat. In this way, he rescued several stranded folks. Emily said, that even after he rescued her and Jack, Tommy went back to get more people.

After they were put into the few police vans, which were picking up anyone in need, they were taken to the Convention Center, which was not the greatest place. It was just okay, Emily remarked. If the helicopter had picked them up, she learned later, they would have been taken to the Superdome, which as it turned out had become an over crowded, horrific place.

On Saturday—September 3—Emily, Jack and many others were taken by helicopter, across the Mississippi River to a naval base. Then, on Sunday, September 4, she and Jack were among others, who were flown to Knoxville, Tennessee. From Knoxville, the Red Cross had them taken by bus to Oakridge and then to Methodist Medical Center. Everyone had to be checked over, as the hospital personnel did not know what each of them needed. But Emily reported that most of them did need help. They found her to be dehydrated, due to very little food or water over several days.

At that center, they tried to take care of each person. According to Emily, "A nurse washed everything I was wearing, and set it aside for me. I still have the plastic case marked 'for a patient'. The next day, a nurse went and purchased a housedress from K-Mart for me. I still have that one too."

During her stay there, Emily was able to phone her daughter, to tell her where she was. Then, her relatives drove up to get her, to take her to the town in north Georgia, where her daughter lived.

Since then, Emily has become re-settled in a condo in that town. But it was not easy, starting over with next to nothing—literally starting from scratch. But by September 21, 2006, she finally had her own place. Her daughter and grandchildren helped Emily to get some furniture to put in her new condo home.

Emily's own words show her strength of spirit reflected. "I remember that old TV program 'One Day At A Time', and that is what I am now trying to do. And the many, many, many acts of kindness people have shown me along the way, will never be forgotten. Most of all, something my Daddy used to tell me resounds— God provides."

Emily had included, in her written account, a tribute to a particular unsung hero, former Vice President Al Gore, who financed airlifts for some 270 evacuees on two private charter flights from New Orleans to Knoxville and Chattanooga, on September 3 & 4. This case was another effort by those, who saw on news reports what was happening in New Orleans, and realized the federal government was not acting fast enough to save all those stranded people. So, they took it upon themselves to help.

Even former Secretary of State Colin Powell had this to say. "I think there have been a lot of failures at a lot of levels—local, state and federal. There was more than enough warning over time about the dangers to New Orleans. Not enough was done."

Since those terrible days from August 29 to September 4, 2005, after which she was relocated, Emily said several months later she was taken back to New Orleans, to see what was left of her old home in the city. She reported what a sad occasion that was, seeing her house, as well as block after endless block of formerly viable homes in deplorable, unlivable condition. Indeed, most of the city's structures became unlivable, because of the flooding caused by Hurricane Katrina. However, Emily was able to retrieve a few of her personal possessions, that had been kept up on high shelves, above the water line. The rest was irretrievable. Sometime later, the ruined moldy furniture, walls and such in the interior of her home were removed. Now, her house just sits there, in that destroyed neighborhood of New Orleans. And it is for sale—AS IS .

Remembering What It Was ....Not What It Is Now !

Yes, when we say "we know what it means to miss New Orleans", we are speaking of that former city (circa pre-Katrina), when it's cultural history, glory and energy was still intact. Because what that city is nowadays is barely a shadow of it's former self.

Pity, that most visitors to New Orleans only think of the French Quarter, when that is just a small section of this metropolis. Yes, tourists see New Orleans in an entirely different light, than those of us who are from south Louisiana, and for whom that city was an integral part of our lives. Even though so many of us did not live in the city, it was our destination as the largest city in our state. I was reared some 95 miles west, via Highway 90 from New Orleans, but we went there regularly.

Sometimes, it was to visit our city relatives. Sometimes it was for a great meal and a stroll in the French Quarter, but also because of Audubon Park, Ponchartrain Beach, Mississippi River cruises, the yacht basin, as well as all the great shopping to be had there. But what made New Orleans a great city, was the people. There was such a diversity of people in that city, all of whom added to the flavor and texture of the atmosphere. Yes, there was no place quite like it anywhere in the world.

Way back when, there used to be so many excuses for driving over to the Crescent City, that we kids became indoctrinated with the route there, long before we were old enough to drive. So, when we came of age, driving to New Orleans became almost a matter of pointing the car in the right direction and guiding it along that familiar route.

Since Katrina, I have driven through New Orleans along Interstate 10 a few times, going back to and from my home town. However, each time I am filled with an ultimate degree of sadness, when viewing the destruction along both sides of that highway. It looks in many sectors as a ghost town, with empty ruined houses, apartment buildings and businesses. In so many neighborhoods could be seen a place where grass and weeds were growing between concrete cracks in sidewalks and streets. There were few to no cars driving in those countless ruined neighborhoods in New Orleans East and other hard hit sectors.

My last visit through there was February 2007, and it appeared to me that most of the city was still deserted. Even a year and almost a half later at that time, most of New Orleans still looked like a disaster area. And in fact, it still was. Because half of the population has relocated to other places in Louisiana, and into other states in this nation. As a result, most are now picking up the threads of their lives elsewhere, and have no plans to return. Even if they could return, there are few to no livable and—for many folks—affordable homes available there anymore.

But there is no doubt in my mind, that all those relocated folks (even as they go on with their lives elsewhere), will carry with them the heritage and love of that city. How can they not, when we consider the preponderance of varied ethnicity that made up the population there—particularly the French, Spanish and African heritage, that is so rooted there. Indeed, this varied ancestry contributed to the unique ingredients, that made up the delightful "gumbo", that was New Orleans.

As a result of this lady's life long love of that city, and the fact that so many people like me have ancestral French ties with that place, I looked with dismay at those, who tried to put France—and anything French—down, when that country had the good sense not to go along with Bush and his cohort's Iraq War. To express their dislike of France for not going into that war, certain people had the audacity to pour expensive French wines down the gutter, and tried to change the name of French fries to "Freedom Fries". This was just to make their statement, albeit an expensive one with the wine. These war-backing folks wanted to remind France of who saved them in WW-I and WW-II. But they failed to remember their Revolutionary War history, when if not for France coming to the rescue of the struggling American colonies, that war would have been lost, and we would never have had a United State of America.

So, being one of those people, who was against the Iraq war, I felt empathy for France at that time. After all, like many of us, the French government could also see the folly of backing that illegal war. So, look who is now able to say—"We told you so"!

As for the value of the City of New Orleans to these United States, it's importance cannot be measured. And yet, it still appears that not enough attention seems to be afforded to the rebuilding of that important city. It is almost like it is now off the radar of consideration, except for occasional blips in the news. Our country extends obscene trillions of dollars to bomb, destroy and then rebuild places on the other side of the world. Yet, it obviously fails, when it comes to taking care of so many of it's own people.

However, no matter what, there are countless numbers of us, who will always know what it means to miss New Orleans. But we miss that city the way it was....not the way it is now!

✵ ✵ ✵

CHAPTER - 14
Doing It My Way?

Through all the ups and downs of my life, my soul has really had a learning experience. But then, that is what our souls are supposed to do. And now, even after so many decades of strife, I realize that there are still more years yet to come. Therefore, I can relate somewhat to those lyrics (in the words of a classic Frank Sinatra song). "Now the end is near and I face the final curtain.... and I did it my way."

Those words are certainly apropos for me much later in life, when I finally refused to allow others to call the shots for me—although some were still trying to chart the path they wanted me to take in my own life.

But for several decades in earlier life, I did not do it the way I wished I would have. Few of us ever had that option, because as teenagers and young adults, we were expected to adhere to religious and social expectations—often times ruled by guilt.

As a former "good little Catholic girl", I was made to feel guilty about so many things. Thus, in order to get some relief, I would go to Confession, to confess my so-called sins. Imagine, if you will what dastardly sins a twelve year old sheltered girl would have to confess. But that was the way of life back then. I guess man-made Confession was put in place as a way of easing the unreasonable feelings of guilt we had to carry within—all for having done what men of the church told us were terrible sins. But what were in reality little to no offenses.

Then after my failed marriages, I was plagued with guilt for having failed again and again. The thought even entered my mind, that if only I would have tried harder, maybe the outcome would have been better. With each marriage, it was my hope that this particular man would be the answer to my prayers—a good man, who would offer me and my children a better life. I kept trying to make each of those unions into what (I finally came to realize) was my impossible dream. Yes, no one can say that I didn't keep trying to find the right man for me. Now, I have come to believe that there is no "right" husband for me in this lifetime. And that is all right with me. But it is a pity, that I could not have accepted this earlier.

However, over these many years since, I have looked back at the unwarranted guilt I had heaped on myself, and saw it for what it was. In hind sight, I realize how manipulative certain of my spouses were. And how, because I wanted to be a good wife in hope of keeping the marriage together, I went along with certain dictates when I really did not want to. However, consider that I was dealing with an alcoholic, another with extreme jealousy problems, another who didn't like children and detested my son, and another who had over-the-top controlling issues. Therefore, I now see that such problems were not my fault. So, I shouldn't have ever continued to beat myself up about those things, which were not my problems, but theirs. Admittedly, I certainly have my faults too, but nothing like those guys. However, I look back and see myself, almost as if I had a sign around my neck that said—"Choose me..... I'm here to be your whipping girl."

But there are other origins of guilt, that have stayed with me. Believe it or not, I still carry a feeling of guilt whenever I consider purchasing a new dress for myself, or something that I might not really need at that moment. This is a throw back from all those years of supporting two children and myself on 1960s/1970s woman's wages. Back then, even if I spent $10 for a new store-bought blouse for me, the guilt would overwhelm me, because I felt the money should have been spent for my children's clothes. So, there was no end to the guilt that was a part of my emotional baggage. And to think, even today—all these decades later—still some of those feelings occasionally pop up from my "file 13" mentality.

I fully realize, that the readers of this literary epic of mine, can't help but notice how much I have zeroed in on the lack of rights I have experienced in regard to the females of our species. But for me, this inequality had it's origins way back in childhood. To be reared as a proper "Southern girl", meant that there were unequal expectations for girls, as opposed to boys.

When I was about ten years old, wooden stilts were popular among the kids. My Daddy had made a set for my brother, but when I asked for mine too, Daddy said that I was a girl and shouldn't be doing such things. When I was seventeen years old, I wanted to learn to drive. My brother, who was three years younger than me, was being allowed to drive in and out of the driveway by himself, so he could get "used to the car." However, that privilege was not given to me. When finally, after my begging got on her nerves, Mother decided to take me out to the old gravel road outside of town, so she could teach me to drive. The trouble was, that my Aunt Co and Aunt Lil came along too.

Now, I tell you this. Never be in the company of three emotional women in the same car at the same time, when you are learning to drive. Back then, most cars were of the shift variety, so it was harder to learn how to drive those. But when I took over the wheel and went through the motions of learning to drive for the first time, you would have thought I was taking them all to their doom.

"Oh my God! Watch out....you are curving too near that ditch....you are swerving too much and you'll hit another car!" This was the screaming voice from my Aunt Co only minutes after I took the wheel. Considering there was not a car to be seen anywhere as far as the horizon of this lonely old road, she was overacting considerably. As for my Aunt Lil, well she was even more demonstrative, when she shouted out.

"Oh God....help us......please don't let us die!"

So, that was the end of my first lesson, which ended in failure, because I couldn't concentrate with all those emotional tirades to contend with. It wasn't until after I married, when my husband taught me, that I finally learned to drive.

There were so many other examples of how differently girls were treated back then, as opposed to boys, who were more privileged. My younger brother and his friends used to dive off of the wharf into Bayou Teche. This waterway ran along the banks of my parent's new property, in Bayou Vista outside of town, where Spanish moss hung ancient live oak trees lined the shoreline. I asked Daddy if someone would teach me to swim, so that I could dive in the bayou too. But I was told, because I was a girl, that it was not necessary for me to know how.

It appeared that all of this was a throwback from the "old South", when women were supposed to be "protected", and not meant to be portrayed as participating in what was regarded as masculine pursuits then. It was the macho southern males, who were continuing the misguided tradition of "protecting the flower of southern womanhood". What they were really doing was causing us girls a disservice, which in fact did not prepare us for the new and changing world, that we were all too soon to be plunged into—totally unprepared.

Yes, later on in life it became excruciatingly clear to me, that I had never been prepared for the role of my destiny. There were no warnings of a future, soon to be filled with so much inequality and injustice, that would become facts of life for me—as for many other women of that era, as well. But my Mother taught me to always present myself in a positive manner— no matter what. She said that people are always impressed with those, who appear to be prosperous in their lives—rather than those, who put on a poor front for all to see. Again, she was right! So I strived to follow her advice.

With three people to support on my limited salary, back in the 1960s & 1970s, sometimes the asset and liability columns of my household accounts teetered barely on the edge of making ends meet—sometimes not even coming close to paying all the bills.

In fact, just recollecting back to those times, an old spiritual song, that we used to sing in high school chorus, comes to mind. It was "Nobody Knows The Trouble I've Seen....", and that title sums it all up for me during those times. Even though my children and I always looked prosperous, little did people know how hard life was for me. As for the kids, I tried to shelter them, so they would never know how difficult it was for this head-of-household Mother.

On occasion, during certain of those divorced years, I would be invited out to a fine dinner with a gentleman caller of mine. And I remember on a couple such occasions, when I had ordered a fine expensive steak and would only eat half of it. Then, I would ask for a "doggie bag", to take the rest home. Of course, that is standard for some folks. But for me, it was different. Because the next day I would chop that steak into little pieces, make a roux, put in chopped onions, bell pepper, carrots, potatoes and spices. And this would miraculously turn into the very best beef stew on rice, that one could partake of anywhere. Thus, my children and I had a great meal, as a result—and that fine steak did double duty. "Waste not....want not", was always another motto of mine.

Every summer, we would take a one week vacation trip. Once we went to Panama City, Florida. Another time, we drove to Denver, Colorado, and still on another occasion we drove into Mexico, across the border from Texas. Usually, it was just the three of us, but a couple of times, I invited their teenage baby sitter to accompany us. Sometimes, I would book a room with a kitchenette, to cut down on the expense of eating out so much.

One might ask, where did I get the money to do this? Well, along with my income tax refund money, and my Shell gasoline credit card, those trips were made possible. Of course, the only reason I had a Shell card was because I worked for the company for some years. Had I applied for such a credit card, as a divorced woman without this employee connection, chances were I would not have gotten one.

In those days, I often mixed canned evaporated milk (what I call cream) with water, to make whole milk for my children's cereal. On our vacation trips, I did this particularly for breakfast in the motel room, where I also boiled water to make instant grits or oatmeal. It didn't seem to be a problem for the kids—not so I noticed. In fact, recently my daughter told me of her remembrances of those times. And I apologized to her for not having provided regular milk on those journeys for her and her brother. She then said this to me.

"Mom....that didn't matter to us.....we were happy to be on those trips.....and you always made things so much fun!"

So, those instances are examples of how I did it "my way", so that the three of us could get the very best I could provide out of life—with very limited resources. It is just another instance of how this "Southern Belle" chose to use her common sense "get up and go", ingrained attributes to good advantage.

That was then, and this is now. But this lady still has to do the best she can, with what she has left. Unfortunately, along the way, I still have not completely come to terms with all of my lifetime emotional baggage. However, wouldn't it be really great if we all could let go of our personal emotional baggage? However, for most of us this is easier said than done.

Thankfully, during my career, I got caught up in more things than just my personal dilemmas and observed that there was no end to injustice in this world, as most of us have discovered. But seeing how bad it was for so many of the world's people, I felt blessed. Indeed, I was blessed with a good childhood and good parents. It was only when I became an adult, that life became so hard. But then, I was never one to blindly follow, without often questioning. "Why?" Even though I was taught to be a proper southern young lady and act with dignity, underneath I felt as though there was a streak of the "rebel" within me. It was a streak of individuality, that would so often cause me to go my own way in life, be my own boss and speak my own mind. Indeed, those qualities became an integral part of what went into making me the person I became later in my life.

Yes, those qualities were necessary when I became a newspaper columnist in five southern states, over four decades. Indeed such attributes allowed me to flourish in my career, which provided me with a "soap box" of sorts. This stage was necessary for published opinions, where I fought for many worthwhile causes.

This was especially so, during those years in southwest Florida, when I published my own monthly newspaper. This afforded me a big "soap box" from which to fight for worthwhile causes in that sector. I allowed regular space in my paper, to promote that county's foster children program—hopefully to reach would-be foster parents, who were so in need at that time. Also, free space was regularly afforded to the area animal shelters, in an effort to find homes for dogs and cats.

Then, when an oil company proposed to build a fuel tank farm along one of the palm tree lined scenic rivers within that Florida community, I went all out through my paper, to fight against this. After all, dealing with oil companies was something I knew about. Those oil company people insisted, that their fuel tanks would not be an eye sore, because they planned to landscape with tropical plants and palm trees. My reply to that was, no matter how many palm trees you plant around a fuel tank farm, you can't disguise such a huge eye sore facility, that will always be a blight on the environment! Thankfully, as a result of the area folks becoming informed, through my periodical, there was an uproar of disapproval from people in that sector. Meetings about this proposal were held, votes were taken, and those oil company executives were sent packing.

There were also numerous other environmental issues—especially about saving the manatees, that were becoming endangered—which got much free coverage in my publication. Ah yes, it was good to be the editor & publisher-in-chief in those days!

Samuel Adams once wrote. "It does not require a majority to prevail, but rather an irate, tireless minority keen to set brush fires in people's minds."

That is what I often tried to do. "Set fires in people's minds", and plant seeds in the mentality of so many people, who were often times erroneously sold a bill of goods about things that matter. There were many things, throughout those decades, that needed more attention from the American people. Pity, that most regular folks usually continue to go on in their own "business as usual" limited environs, giving little credence to so many things that matter in this world. Indeed, it still appears that even now, in this era of global instant news, too many folks are apathetic to such things as illegal wars, earth & climate change, environmental polluters, government corruption, and such.

It has always been my feeling, that we should all pay more attention to what is happening in the entire world—not just in our own personal backyards and hometowns. And more people should stand up and be heard about such things. After all, Planet Earth is the only home we have in this lifetime, and all of us residents should have a say in the preservation of it's good health.

Martin Luther King, Jr. once said. "A time comes when silence is betrayal."

And I certainly agree with his wise words. Pity though, that so many folks choose to follow the herd, never deviating from a certain leader's dictates—no matter how failed that direction has been shown to be. Thus, all too few people ever have the courage to stick their necks out, and voice their own opinions. And quite simply, just stand up for what they believe.

Many people believe in destiny. Certain others believe only in the here and now. Some ultra religious types believe we always make our own choices in what they believe to be this one and only lifetime. Others attribute the impact of reincarnation as our set courses in several lifetimes. Personally, after participating in my own current lifetime, I choose to believe as a certain 1930-40s famous lady singer did. She endured a very painful life, wherein she successfully overcame many obstacles. It was that great lady, Lillian Roth, who had this to say about that.

"My life was never my own......it was charted before I was born."

☆ ☆ ☆

CHAPTER - 15
Never Be The Same Again

"You know....since you started hearing those telepathic messages in your head, you have changed."

My previous husband said this to me, while we were driving on an RV weekend jaunt down to the Florida Keys in 1995. Remember the RV, that I was spiritually told we must purchase? Well, this was the vehicle we were in on that day—this RV which was taking us on a three hundred mile trip south from where we lived in SW Florida. Funny, how he was always so dubious about the information I had shared with him from my spiritual source. It was just the RV idea he truly accepted. But this was only because he always wanted one.

After his strange remark to me, I looked at him incredulously and replied.

"Of course I have changed! How could anyone in my situation not change?"

Over and over again, I tried previously to explain this to him, but he never quite got it. I guess he was never meant to understand my plight, because he did not have to live with those spiritual voices in his head everyday of his life.

On some days, I would be driving on the main highway, leading to the closest big town from my home on the SW Gulf Coast of Florida, and while driving I would peer out toward the river and horizon beyond to the Gulf. At that moment, the voice would announce these words to me.

"As far as you can see, and beyond, will be under water in times to come. It is coming and cannot be stopped. That is one of the reasons why God wants you to move to higher ground. He wants you to go on, and be in good shape in order to continue on your path for Him. Much more is expected of you before you pass over. And we will always be with you, to help you accomplish what must be done."

But my Guide would never tell me how far in the future, when such an inundation would happen. However, this is the kind of communication I have had to live with on a daily basis, and it has continued now (as of this writing) for some thirteen years. So, of course I am not the same. How could anyone be the same, after living with such as this?

Since 1994, and into the following years since, much has been revealed to me. No longer do I look at my life the same as before. No longer do I see the entire concept of life, and what happens after we pass over in the same light. For now, I realize that what I had suspected for a long time is true. Those religious teachings, that were so much a part of my life, I now see as so lacking in many aspects, when it comes to both life and death. And certain of the so-called terrible sins, that guilt-riddled my life since a child, were nothing more than man-made rules, and certainly not God's dictates.

Also, what I learned through my research, coupled with what I have been spiritually told, I now realize that so many ancient books, that should have been included, were left out of the Bible, because of the patriarchal attitudes in ancient times. Therefore, it is understandable that modern day religions do not want any of those once suppressed ancient writings—especially those that speak of reincarnation as fact—to alter the way of thinking for the multitudes in their congregations. Such a revelation would alter Christian religious teachings for all time.

Of course, all that guilt many of us carried from religious teachings certainly kept us in line. But in the end, it did much damage to people, who wanted nothing more than to have a place to pray—a place where their spirit could be elevated, rather than diminished.

All those things wandered through my mind on that long RV trip to the Keys. But on that jaunt, I also remember appreciating God's beautiful natural creations, and felt His presence along the way. For He was everywhere along that journey. From what I observed, for me, there was no church necessary to be at peace with the Lord. That beautiful land and water would suffice as a place for any amount of praying. I paid special attention to the passing views of land and water along the way. Driving along Alligator Alley in the Everglades, I relished in the sight of the stately Cypress trees, lush green swamp Maples and Sabal Palms lining this route. Then, all I could think about was that this low land will be lost beneath the salt water in times to come. It was so hard for me to accept, that there would someday be no everglades.

On the return trip from the Keys, after driving the full length to the end, I realized how little water rise it would take to cover the Keys. Those small areas of mangrove covered coral mounds are less than a five foot sea level rise away from being inundated.

Since my "spiritually reached" date, I have spent much time, researching "Earth Changes", that were beginning to come into the main stream then. And amid this new learning experience, I discovered facts about the already on-going sea level rise, due much to the melting glaciers. And then there were the droughts, that would probably continue to become facts of life. This is not even to mention the ever stronger hurricanes and tornadoes, that would result in this era of climate change. Since that trip in 1995, we have all seen many of those things come to pass—with still many more disasters yet to come.

Being at sea level in many places along the Keys, made me realize even more about certain facts of life. Of course, at that time I was still struggling with those dictates, that urged me to move further north. But the more I saw of that low land, the more I could accept the reason for moving further inland. This is because the sector where I was being directed to move is situated some 1200 feet above sea level, high on a ridge in the north Georgia foothills of the Smokey Mountains. So, this finally made sense to me. But it was still hard to accept, because I always loved the seashore and wanted nothing more than to spend my last years near a coastline.

However, observing changes to our planet was not entirely new to me, at that time. For I have always been somewhat of an environmentalist, even back in the 1970s, when I sported a bumper sticker to "Save The Whales". I have contributed (and still do), to causes to save the seals, the wolves, the polar bears, the bison, and all manner of God's wonderful creatures. So, it has always been my contention, that if we sit by and allow the unchallenged extermination of so many of God's beautiful creatures, it will be a loss from which we will never recover.

Thankfully, it does not always take spiritually reached people, to urge others to take action to save what we can. Many of this world's governments are seeing this "Earth Changes" handwriting on the wall, as being inevitable. And they want to do what they can to stop it, or even just slow it down. But shamefully, after the 2000 elections the United States GOP Administration seemed not to acknowledge the seriousness of this situation as much as they should. They opted more to maintain economical progress, rather than address predicted ecological disaster. Why do they not realize that without our environment being stabilized, there can be no economical progress?

Our climate is changing, and the accompanying detriments are happening. As a result, we must address the changes and adapt to such repercussions. In some sectors, this is happening in our country. Seven states already realize the seriousness of drought. Southwestern states, that are dependent on water from the Colorado Rive for the very existence of much of their population, have already been experiencing a long drought period in that region. The water from that river has already been lessened, and in the not so distant future it will not provide what will be necessary for that growing population. So, the leaders there have drawn up plans to offset this anticipated problem. They are acting, and not leaving their heads in the sand, as so many in the realms of higher government power seem to be doing.

It is notable that retirees, particularly in Florida, have seen how much milder the winters in certain of their former home states have become, so they are choosing to live year around there. Certain species of mammals, birds and butterflies are extending their usual range, to many miles further northward. This reminds me of what a gifted psychic told me several years ago.

"So much warmer will the climate become, that there will be palm trees growing outside in and around Atlanta, Georgia."

Now anyone, who lives up here in the foothills north of Atlanta, knows that no such thing is presently possible. This is because when winter comes, we plant lovers have to bring in our exotic plants, for their protection against cold temperatures, in which these cannot survive. So, certainly no palm tree planted outside up here can survive, at these current winter temps.

Of course, as we are all seeing in current times, it is not just Mother Nature, whom we have to deal with. It is the distressing economical state, that is causing so much distress for so many people. Although the President and some stock market gurus often proclaim, that such unfortunate financial times are just a bump in the road, regular folks are nevertheless still struggling to keep their family's head above water.

However, in the not too distant future, there will be a new slant to the world's priorities. Because as droughts widen, crops fail and nations begin to suffer more from loss of coastlines, there will be less resources for the ever expanding poor populations throughout the world. In such times to come, the fight for water rights will overtake the previous struggle for oil.

No doubt, there will be several terrible wars still to be waged—resulting in nations being ruined, as well as cities being destroyed, causing the deaths and maiming of multitudes of people in many parts of the world. Why? Because so much of mankind refuses to address climate change.

Now, some might ask, what gives this lady the right to prophesize such gloom and doom? Has her way of thinking been influenced by the large number of modern day mediums and psychics, who are regularly on TV and in the news in recent times? Not so, I say. Remember, it was way back in spring of 1994, that I was first reached spiritually. At that time, I had no knowledge of most of the modern day psychics, who are now in the mainstream. True, I follow some of the reputable ones, in order to get a handle on their predictions. But for content in this book, I have mostly set forth instances, that I have personally researched and been privy to.

So, for purposes of discussion here, about all we can do is pray and hope that most of the prophesized events, that are possibly yet to come, will be altered for the better. And that nations will be blessed with intelligent and compassionate leadership, who will be qualified to deal with planet Earth changes—before it is too late. Most of all, we need leaders, who are wise enough to truly accept that these changes are real, and that this state of affairs is only going to get worse with each passing year.

I am reminded of that most remarkable heroic leader of India, Mahatma Gandhi, who said some memorable words several decades ago. These are words, that we should all remember, when our world seems to be getting worse and so many inept leaders fail us.

"When I despair, I remember that all through history the way of truth and love has always won. There have been tyrants and murderers and for a time they seem invincible. But in the end, they always fall!"

And so it has been throughout history. We see inept leaders come, and we (by the grace of God) ultimately see them go. But take heart, for there are also some good prophesies coming, that will go far toward the betterment of mankind.

However, for those of us, who have been reached spiritually, we have heavy burdens to carry. So, I say to those of you, who would wish for such communication, be careful what you wish for. Even though in my case, some of the things I am being told do not always sit well with me, and I have struggled against such, I have accepted that this is my path for the rest of my life here on earth.

So, it is obvious, that I will never be the same as before this personal spiritual intervention. But then, I am not supposed to be the same ever again.

That is the point!

✫ ✫ ✫

CHAPTER - 16
Unexplained Happenings Abound

When it comes to "unexplained" happenings, that many more people are reporting these days, is it because there are more of these events? Or is it because more people are speaking out and reporting their experiences?

It used to be, that folks would never speak of such things as seeing ghosts, spirits and generally unexplainable things. This is because they feared being made fun of, or thought to be "seeing things"—and therefore, deemed to be going off the "deep end" of sanity. But it is far different in these modern times, especially since we entered this new century.

Personally, I do not remember any such experiences as a child or teen. But later on into my life, things did happen to me—things that I could not explain. When I gave birth to my son, I now believe that the feeling I had while almost bleeding to death was accurate. Because it was akin to a feeling so wonderful, in those moments of being encompassed in such a comforting light, that it was much like what some people report as a "near death experience".

When my two teenage children and I lived in our memorable apartment in the early 1970s, there were many unexplained happenings in those rooms. My teenage son saw a vision of a filmy gray lady with flowing white hair. She was peaking at him from behind the dining room doorway one Saturday morning, while he watched TV in the living room. As a result, he was so emotionally affected by this experience, that it took my daughter and I quite a while to comfort him, until he stopped shaking from fear.

Once, on the occasion of a small party I hosted in that apartment, while I was busy in the kitchen getting more canapes and drinks for my guests, my cousin walked over to me, holding a framed picture in his hand. I asked him what was wrong, and why he was holding one of my framed pictures? He said that it came flying off the wall, and hit the head of the young woman whom he had brought to the party. I went over to the wall, where it had been hanging, to see if the nail had come loose off the wall. But it had not, and the string on the back of the picture had not broken either. So, there was no reason why it had come off the wall all by itself. But then it didn't fall; it flew off the wall—this framed picture of Jesus Christ. To this day, I wonder if that was a message meant for that young women.

But then, there were so many unexplained instances, happening during those almost five years we lived there. Once, my daughter reported having locked the back door, with the dead bolt intact, and when she checked again, the door was standing wide open with the dead bolt sticking out. Another time, there was a plastic soda pop bottle, standing on the kitchen cabinet, which literally exploded one night. And shadows were seen on the walls of the middle hallway there, when no one was present. Indeed, it was a place of many strange occurrences.

However, somehow (with the exception of my somewhat traumatized son and his "gray lady"), we never felt threatened while living there. On the contrary, we learned to co-exist with what were probably ghosts of deceased people, who had not as yet found their way to the "other side". But they never hurt us, so we did not fear them.

At one time, we attempted to conduct a seance in the dining room, in an effort to bring them through. There were six people around the table, and we started out in a very serious mode. Unfortunately, one of those people was my Mother, who really never believed us when we spoke about our "ghosts". So, in the middle of this (what was supposed to be a serious affair), she began to giggle and couldn't stop herself. Well, that ended our seance experience right away. For if there is one thing I know about the spirit world, they do want us to take them seriously.

Another, particularly notable experience, comes to mind from members of my extended family. Aunt Margaret and her family had a new house built on the shore of Bayou Teche outside of Patterson, Louisiana, several decades ago. But they lived there for only two years. Why? Well, so many strange things happened during that time, that my Aunt could not stand to live there anymore. According to her, there were unexplained noises within that house—chains rattling, glass breaking and such. Her children experienced those things too. Her daughter even saw an apparition out of the corner of her eye, and her son was terrified by the sounds of rattling chains. They all reported often feeling ice cold air within, along with overall feelings of dread. Her husband, Uncle John worked offshore, so was often away from home. One time, Aunt Margaret recalled, he came home at night, to find her sitting on a chair, outside in the yard, just so she could get out of that house and away from those spooky happenings, for a little while. Of course, he didn't believe her stories of those happenings, because he had never experienced such. But one night, finally, he heard some unexplained noises for himself. And he didn't doubt her anymore.

I heard tell, that there had been a farm house or barn on that particular site, back in the 20s or 30s, which was torn down. But even though their brand new house was built on that same site, in such cases the land can still harbor unsettled spirits of those, who have not completely passed over. And of course, many stories abounded, about the source of such unsettled spirits, in this case. Some folks even believed those ghosts to be left over from the old swashbuckling days, when pirates sailed up the bayou, to bury their treasure along those shores. Thus, leaving some of their own deceased members, also buried thereabouts. Over the years, along those shores, many have dug countless holes in the ground, searching for pirate buried treasure. And still in modern times, some people have even been known to retrace that sector along Bayou Teche with metal detectors. But it isn't likely, that we will ever know what happened there, way back when.

☆ ☆ ☆

Now, let's talk about another unexplained phenomena, that many people are familiar with. It is UFOs (Unidentified Flying Objects), that have been talked about since that 1950s Roswell, New Mexico event. As I have said before, never did I believe that we, here on Planet Earth, are the only beings in God's vast planetary realm. I always thought how arrogant of mankind to even think, that this planetary life is all there is! However, even though I wanted to, I never personally saw a UFO—that is until the early 1990s.

I was standing on my small wharf on the lake in back of my SW Florida property when it happened. It was a beautiful day, with vivid blue sky and no clouds—except for one puffy little one to the left of my range of vision. The sun was shining, and all seemed right in my world. As I looked up to admire the blue of the sky, I saw it. There it was—a shiny silver glimmering saucer shaped object. It was not moving, rather it appeared to be just hanging in one spot, as if suspended there. The shape of this craft looked amazingly like the pictures I had seen in numerous magazines on "flying saucers". At that moment, I was so elated, as I continued to gaze at it.

Then, I felt the sting of one of those pesky mosquitoes on my leg, and hurriedly reached down with my hand to slap it away. It was a matter of a couple of seconds, and when I looked back up, the UFO had disappeared. I searched the sky for some sign of where it had gone, but saw nothing. No doubt about it, I thought, no man made flying machine could accomplish such a disappearing act in those few seconds.

Even though, to date, I have not been privileged to see another one as yet, back then I was so excited that I wanted to share this event with everyone. However, other than my daughter, who knows me well enough to know that I would not make up such a thing, no one else in my family took my sighting seriously. I was almost in tears, trying to emotionally tell of my observation, but to no avail. So, I soon discovered, that most people really do not want to hear such a story. It is as if they have long ago shut their minds to the possibility that we are not alone. But the beliefs by so many, that there "is no such thing" are bogus. Take it from one, who has seen a UFO!

✵ ✵ ✵

Another unexplained subject, that I guess should be included in this chapter, has to do with reincarnation. A couple of years ago, I was hypnotically regressed by a licensed spiritual hypnotist. She regressed me back to previous lives that my soul has lived, back in history. Two of those former lives came in loud and clear for me. I saw myself in a work house type orphanage, which looked to be a century or two ago in England. Rough stones rimmed the walls of the large cold room, that I could see. There were several long rough tables, where countless disheveled raggedly clothed young children sat on crude benches, eating some kind of gruel from wooden bowls. A feeling came across me, that I was one of those children. But that feeling also brought forth the realization, that I did not live very long in that lifetime.

Then, my mind was propelled abruptly into what I perceived as another lifetime, which I took to be in late 1700s France. It appeared that the time period was before the French Revolution, because of what I saw. What was revealed to me was the sight of a beautiful ballroom, lit by countless candelabra. The occasion appeared to be a delightful ball, where the strains of beautiful music could be heard from the musicians there.

And there I sat, at one of the many elaborately decorated dinner tables, in all my finery. I saw myself as a young lady of perhaps eighteen years of age, all attired in a lovely brocade satin gown and a white wig (which was the style in that era), and I looked very pretty—from what I could see. Also, I was surrounded by three handsome gentlemen, who were in lavish attire also, They, too, wore white wigs. And they were attired in brocade coats, lacy shirt cuffs and satin knee pants with silver buckles atop their silk knee stockings. Much to my delight, they were all obviously fawning over me, trying to get my favor. To put it simply—they were flirting outrageously with me. And of course, I appeared to be so happy with all that attention. Indeed, it looked like I was indeed one of the "belles" of that ball. But then what young woman would not have been happy with such attention? However, that pleasant scene ended after the ball was over, and I had to go home with my parents in their horse drawn carriage.

The reason why I perceived, that this last scene was in pre-French Revolution times, was because the people at that ball were obviously upper middle class or richer, judging from their fine attire and the elegance of that event. Had it been after the revolution, the lives of such well off French people would probably have already met their end, by means of the infamous guillotine.

So, there you have it! At least I know of two of my previous lives, and had not the session's allotted time ended, I would have found out even more. But I did learn, that I am now on my 48th lifetime.

Hypnotic regression particularly worked also for my daughter. She had struggled with an unexplained phobia from the time she was old enough to walk. She was always afraid to go into the water at the beach. I first noticed this, when I took her by the hand and attempted to walk with her into the shallow surf at Grand Isle, Louisiana. Whenever I tried to get her to walk with me there, she would scream and cry. Then, she would try to run away from me, away from the water. It was obvious that she was terrified of the Gulf salt water there. Later, as she grew older, on the beach trips she would usually only stay on the sandy beach, and venture only into shallow waves.

So, during a hypnotic regression, that took her back to a particular previous life, the reason for her fear became evident. When hypnotically propelled back in time, she saw herself standing on the heaving deck of a sailing ship in a previous lifetime. Her attire was the fashion of an earlier past century, and in her arms she held a baby. The ship had ventured into an intense storm, and the relentless wind, waves and pelting rain of this turbulence seemed to envelope the ship and all aboard. So, she saw herself and the baby being thrust overboard into the darkness, where they both drowned. Obviously, this satisfied my daughter's life long question as to her fear of water.

During her hypnotic regression, my daughter also discovered something about her own daughter, in this lifetime. My granddaughter, starting in her middle teen years, developed severe discomfort in her neck area. It was so uncomfortable for her, that we even had to be careful when we hugged her. This malady appeared to crop up out of the blue, when she was about age 16. But even a doctor could find no reason for this painful neck affliction, that she professed to have. However, the answer to the problem was discovered during a regression. It was shown that in a previous lifetime, she had been strangled by an older man, when she was in her middle teens. So, in this lifetime, the affliction had literally come back to haunt her, at the same age as in one of her soul's previous lives. After becoming aware of the reason for this neck pain, my granddaughter has since felt a lessening of this affliction.

Apparently, for some people's souls, memory of a traumatic event from a previous incarnation can sometimes become evident in their present day lifetime.

Thus causing them problems, that no doctor can diagnose.

For many people, hypnotic regression has become a great tool, in their search for possible reasons for their physical and emotional ailments in their current incarnation. This does not always successfully afford everyone the answer they are looking for, but for many, who have exhausted everything else, it is worth a try. Yes, we believers in reincarnation have become cognizant of the fact, that our individual souls are ageless, and that we can learn so much from some of the lives we have lived before. In addition, during regression certain subjects sometimes become tuned in to some of the time they spent on the "other side"—in between incarnations here.

But even now in our present lifetime, our deceased loved one's souls can reach out to us on occasion. Case in point, was the time my grandson (when 3 years old) accompanied his parents back to the home towns for the funeral of his paternal Grandpa E.J. A couple of days after the services, he was playing in the backyard of my parent's home, when his mother called him, because they were leaving. When he came running to her, she asked what he had been doing.

He replied, "I was talking to Papa E.J. over there in the yard. Didn't you see him?"

There are so many recorded instances of souls, lingering after death or coming back at different intervals before they continued on to their destiny. And usually children are more able to see them, than us older folks. But I did have a message from my Daddy after his demise.

After Daddy's funeral had been over for a couple of days, I was left alone with my Mother, who would have to go on living in their house alone. So, I decided to plant a row of tomato plants in her backyard (so she could have some fresh tomatoes in early summer), before I began my long drive back to my home. That night, my Astrologer/psychic friend Doris telephoned me from SW Florida, from my former town of residence. She had a message for me from my Daddy.

"He wants you to be careful with that shovel you were using today, to plant those tomato plants, as it has a crack in the handle. And he doesn't want anyone to get hurt using it."

I asked her why he chose to give the message to her, rather than straight to me? She said that his spirit could make better contact through her, rather than directly with me.

Now, it was in early evening when she called me, and only Mother and I were there watching TV. But after I got her call, I abruptly got up and went out to the shed where the gardening tools were kept. I picked up the shovel I had used, and examined it, finding that yes, it did indeed have a crack in the handle. With no little amount of excitement, I carried that shovel into the living room, to show my Mother. Needless to say, she thought I had gone off the deep end, carrying a shovel into the living room at eight o'clock at night! I explained to her what had happened, and showed her the crack in the handle. Now, this has to be believed, because only Mother and I knew, that I had planted those tomato plants in her backyard that day. And it was so like my Daddy, to be so caring of my welfare that he reached out to me, through my friend. He took this detour, because sometimes passed over souls are not able to make direct contact with certain loved ones, so they will try in other ways.

But it was not like that for me, after my Mother died. She came straight to me, as it turned out. Although, during her last couple of months in her earthly life, she and I had our differences. As I said before, she had become so difficult, and there was no pleasing her. There was never a word of comfort or praise coming from her to me. That is except for one night, about a month before she passed. I had gone into the room, to her bedside at my home, to make sure she didn't need anything, and to say goodnight. She seemed to sense how down I was that night, after our particularly difficult day together. It was then, that she said those memorable words to me—words that I had wanted to hear more of from her, during my entire life.

As I tucked her in, she looked up at me with her sad eyes and said. "I love you....you know."

At that moment, I felt so elated. Finally, my Mother said she really loves me! Now, I know that seems like a little thing to most people. But for me, it was such a gift to hear those words from her. This is because throughout my entire life with her, I can't remember hearing that from her—nor did I ever hear those other words, "I'm proud of you".

It is my contention, that most of my life has been spent, striving to do something that would make my parents proud of me. But never did I hear those words from them. Of course, my brother and I always knew we were loved, because they took such good care of us. But never did they say those words directly to me, and these should be said to children, who hunger for such.

However, that was not to be Mother's last emotional reaching out to me. Because she made a special visit, in person after her death. It was about eight months after that terrible summer of 2000, and I was still trying to get my strength back from that second surgery. I was laying on my sofa in the living room, up here in north Georgia where I was continuing to live alone after my husband had left some moths before. It was a depressing time for me, and I was still suffering emotionally and physically. I knew I had to go on. But my future looked so dim, from my point of view at that time, and I seemed to be slipping ever more into depression.

At that moment, my dog, who had been laying on the carpet next to the couch where I was, got up and began to bark continuously. I looked over at "Ronnie Bonnie", and reprimanded her, because I could see nothing in the living room that she should be barking at. But she continued to look toward the middle of the room and bark.

As I got up into a sitting position on the couch, shouting at my dog to stop barking, I saw her. It was my Mother, standing in the middle of the room. She had on her favorite black and white sweater. Her hair was dark and wavy like it was when she was young. In fact, her face was young too. No longer was she that same 89 year old lady, who had passed over a few months ago. No longer was she bent over and decrepit, as in old age. She looked as if she was about 30 years of age, and in her prime. But there was something more in this vision. Her face was beautiful and it radiated with a glow that cannot be described with earthly words. But the best part of all, was that her eyes were so full of love for me.

Her arms were outstretched toward me, inviting me to come to her for a hug. Suddenly, becoming jolted from my state of shock, it struck me that this was real! My Mother was really there; it was not a figment of my imagination! She smiled, and beckoned for me to hurry to her. Her eyes were soft and glowing with such a loving light. Her continence and bearing were both relaxed—not at all like she had been in real life, when she often appeared to be up tight and on edge. All of that was gone from her, and my Mother's face glowed with the beauty and ease of what we might imagine how a soul would appear, when all cares and woes of this world had been erased from a continence. I hurriedly got to my feet and took two steps toward her, exclaiming with delight in that moment, as if I had reverted back into her little girl, who once again was reaching out for my mommy.

"Mama......Mama......it's really you!"

But as I hurried into her outstretched arms, she disappeared! I was so devastated to see her just vanish from my vision in that instant. I flailed my arms around the spot where she had been, in a useless effort to find her again. But even while I was doing these fruitless motions, I knew deep within my being, that she was gone.

After I reflected on what had just happened, it's meaning struck me loud and clear. When she appeared to me, I was so alone and so down, still struggling to get my strength back and questioning whether or not I could go on by myself. So, she had taken the time and effort to appear to me (from the "other side"), during that time of distress for me, in order to give me hope. As a result of her effort in my behalf, it was not in vain. Because her "visit" was like an emotional shot in the arm for me. For after that experience, as I recalled the joyful celestial beauty of her vision, my spirits were lifted and my very being became infused with a special brand of optimism. It was an optimism, that reflected the fact, that I most certainly had what it takes to go on, because my Mother believes in me.

Since that momentous vision from my Mother, I have learned that I must fight against depression and negativity every day of my life, if I am to go on in any worthwhile manner. I have also learned, that my body could be likened to a volcano. For when we keep worry and stress within and carry it with us everyday, we are harboring negativity inside of ourselves. And unfortunately, "negativity begets negativity" as they say. So, in this internalization of stress and depression, we are also attracting more negativity to us, which keeps on building up. So, as in the case of a volcano, which becomes so full of lava and blows it's top on occasion, so do our human bodies do much the same. For all that bad stuff that we keep inside will eventually explode, as well. But in the case of we humans, it will erupt as an illness in the body.

✫ ✫ ✫

Other unexplained occurrences in our lives should come under the heading of our dreams. It is said, that all of us dream every night, but some of us dream more than others. However, most of these dreams are not remembered upon awakening. But there are also some intense dreams, that stay with us long after we awake, and even remain in our psyche for weeks, months, and even years later.

Astral traveling while asleep is part of this scenario. It is believed by many, that we go out of our body on trips to other places, while we sleep. Pity, that we are usually not allowed to remember where we travel when our spirit vacates our sleeping body. Haven't you wondered why so often you feel very tired when you awaken? You know you have slept, and there should be no reason to be tired, so could Astral travel perhaps be one of the reasons for this?

In recent years, I have had the feeling that I have astral traveled many times while sleeping. Because recollections are so strong, that I have perhaps visited the "other side", and been among many of my beloved deceased loved ones. And it has always been such a pleasant experience.

Personally, there are what I call dreams, that I have had over the years, which were inhabited with several of those "passed over" beloved souls of mine. Even though some of them had passed over years ago, there they were in my dreams, looking remarkably alive and much better than I remembered them. Most of the time, when such dreams happen to me, I am there with them usually at a party or reception—places where everyone is so joyful. Such dreams are so vivid, and could perhaps be interpreted as Astral trips to the "other side", that I took during my sleep state. But apparently, I have been allowed to remember some of those.

During such episodes, I seem to have been catapulted (through dreams or Astral state—which ever) to such joyous receptions, where those deceased loved ones of mine are always so happy to see me. And the joy on their faces is unforgettable. It is as if they are showing me what awaits, when it is my exit time—such a wonderful place to look forward to. It appears, that in these dreams the wonderful souls, who are therein, are endeavoring to assure me that my time on earth is but a short interlude. And that my real home is there with them. Usually recollections of most of these happy dreams (or Astral travel instances) have stuck with me, occupying a very special place in my memory.

But there are also prophetic dreams, that happen to those of us, who may be worried about something or someone. By way of putting our minds to rest, sometimes a special dream comes to us for just such a purpose. I remember in the early 1990s, when I was planning a long anticipated island hopping cruise to the eastern Caribbean. At the time, my parents were both getting up in age, and I knew that I had to always be available to travel to their side, should they have an emergency health issue. So, it was difficult for me to plan long trips, where I would be out of the country for a time. For I always had that worry in the back of my mind, that I would not be reachable if I was needed.

But I went ahead and planned that trip, hoping nothing would happen. However, each day thoughts of "what if" never left my conscious mind. It was as if a bitter sweet pall was distracting me from the sheer anticipatory enjoyment of my special trip. Finally, one night in just such a special dream, my worries were alleviated.

In the dream, I was going up the staircase at my parent's home, and my Daddy was coming down the stairs toward me. In between the space where we were about to meet on the stairs, through the banisters I could see a glowing Angel looking directly at me. Then the message from this celestial being entered my head.

"Do not worry.....it is not his time yet!"

Upon hearing that message, it was as if a huge weight had been lifted off of me. Now, I would be free to enjoy my trip without fear, and I did.

Personally, I do believe in such prophetic dreams, as well as Astral travel. Because a few years ago, I awoke in the morning to find myself suspended about a foot off of my mattress. I was just laying there in the air. I remember a feeling of shock, to find myself in such an unexplainable situation. But there was also a very pleasant feeling permeating my entire body at that moment. And while I hovered there, I saw a beautiful light blue and silver pulsating glow, surrounding my body. Just as I was beginning to consciously enjoy my predicament, my body was abruptly dropped onto the mattress.

Needless to say, it was difficult for my wide awake conscious mind, to accept what had just happened to me. But it did happen, and I shall always remember the wonderful feeling I had while hovering there. As for an explanation of what really transpired, it is my opinion that my soul was returning into my sleeping body after Astral traveling, and my conscious mind woke up too soon— prematurely before the transition was completed.

Some people might scoff at such an event, as a figment of my imagination. But I know what happened on that morning. I lived it! Indeed, critical people should never attempt to judge another person, until they have walked in their shoes—or in this case, hovered with me above my bed.

Not long ago, I awoke from a dream about a person, whom I had never thought about in over 50 years. But the dream triggered my memories of him, back then as a young man, who had been drafted to serve in the Korean War. His initials were J.H. and I recalled, that since birth, he had been somewhat intellectually challenged, and was unable to keep up in school. A comparison could be made to Forrest Gump and his friend "Bubba"— beloved characters, who were depicted as drafted into the Vietnam War.

Here was a case of a young man, who had difficulty fitting into the real world. Yet, our government had no qualms about drafting him to serve as cannon fodder on the front lines of that terrible war. And as it turned out, J.H. was captured by the North Koreans, and was a prisoner of war for some time.

Later, when other POWs were freed, he was among one group that finally came home. And what a reception the town of Berwick held for J.H. In my dream, I was catapulted back in time to the front yard of his parent's home, where people of the town were overflowing from the house. The Mayor and town officials came out to welcome J.H. home, as did just about every resident in his home town. It was a joyous event, because one of our own had returned.

But then in my dream, the questionable reality of the aftermath of this celebration became real for me. True, J.H. was the man of the hour on that special day, after all he had been through. But what became of him, after the last "hoorahs" were shouted? We all knew of his limitations since birth, but now he had to also overcome the horrors of what happened to him as a prisoner of war in North Korea. In my dream, I was given no answer as to what happened to J.H. All I can surmise from this dream is that it was a reminder that he should never be forgotten. And now, I certainly will never forget him.

✳ ✳ ✳

At this point, I have to interject another of my mysterious experiences, but it was not a dream. This happened while I was fully awake. The father of my children passed away on a May day in 2007—just four days before his granddaughter was to graduate from high school. I did not travel the 650 miles to attend his funeral, but I did write a eulogy for him, which my daughter bravely read at his service.

On the Saturday after his funeral, we gathered at a restaurant luncheon up here in north Georgia, to celebrate my granddaughter's graduation, which was set for later that afternoon. As everyone prepared to go to the car, to drive to this ceremony, I decided to go to the ladies room of the restaurant before I left. I was the only one in that room when this happened. Just as I entered the ladies room, some piped in music came over the intercom system. The song was "Cry" by Johnny Ray, who was also famous back in 1950 & 1951, for "Little White Clouds That Cry". This was a song, that I had not heard in decades, and it was certainly never played anymore.

It had been my first husband's favorite song, and only I would have known that. Not even his children knew this. So, I stood there and listened to the entire song, and just knew that this was a message of some kind from him. Later, my Spirit Guide Olivia told me, that it was meant to let everyone know—through me—that he had made it to the "other side", and was not earth bound.

So, some times messages from beyond not only come to us in dreams and through Astral travel, but also while we are fully awake. Another case in point was a favorite music box of mine, that started playing a couple of times on it's own (without being wound up), not long after my Daddy's passing. The song it played had also been a song, that I had requested to be sung at his service—"Wind Beneath My Wings".

As we all know, many times our dreams are not pleasant, causing us to wake up with a distressful feeling.

Of course, some of our dreams are merely conglomerated bits and pieces of our unconscious minds. These dreams we usually do not remember any length of time after we awaken. But the ones we do remember, are the ones we should pay more attention to. For those are the dreams that might possibly be important to us.

Once not too long ago, after taking my trusty companion dog out for her 7:AM potty visit to the backyard, we came in and went back to our respected beds for a couple more hours of sleep. Before closing my eyes on that morning, I asked my Spirit Guide or whoever else was listening to any entreaties of mine, to allow me to have a happy dream. And they did.

In this dream, I was in a waiting room with several other ladies, whom I did not know. A man came up to me and asked if I would like to have a special evening gown designed and made especially for me? It appeared that this man, along with others there were clothes designers of the highest caliber. So, I said yes, and sat down to wait.

After a short time, he came out with the gown they had made for me. It was magnificent! And the cloth was one of my favorite colors—maroon. The bodice was made of the finest velveteen, designed with off the shoulder straps. The full long skirt had alternating panels of that same maroon velveteen, intermingled with the finest of maroon colored tulle. They handed it to me, and I immediately held the dress against myself to get a feeling of it's grandeur. I discovered that the skirt was hemmed an inch from the floor, just as I like it. Because for this lady to wear such attire, meant I would also be dancing in that dress. And you can't dance properly in a dress that drags on the floor. So, it was truly a dress made especially for me. It was as if this heavenly designer knew everything about me—my likes and dislikes, my love of dancing, a favorite color of mine, the most flattering design for me. Indeed, they seemed to know me better than I even knew myself, thus they incorporated it all into this fantastic dress.

Then, the man told me to go behind the screen and try it on. I looked at him with amazement, that he should tell me such a thing. After all, the dress was not this elderly lady's size, and although quite beautiful, the design was not appropriate for someone my age. It was more like the size dress I would have worn when I was about age 30. I say 30, because that was when my figure was at it's best. Unfortunately, time had marched on for me, and now my figure of long ago was just to be seen in photos taken back then.

But he insisted that it would fit, and I should put the dress on. He continued to assure me that it would be fine. So, I did what he said, and lo and behold as I put the dress on, it was as if my figure was being transformed to the one I had in my prime. The designer had been right. This magical dress had transformed my body to fit perfectly, and as I looked into the mirror I was even more pleasantly shocked. There I stood in this beautiful dress, and saw that not only my figure, but my face as well, had been transformed back in time. I was age 30 once again!

Needless to say, I had been granted a very pleasant dream, as per my request, and it lifted my spirits so much. Although I am not a morning person, I am here to tell all of you, after that dream, there was a smile on this lady's face when I woke up—and that never happens in the morning.

✢ ✢ ✢

However, for the most part, I find some of the dreams I am having at this more advanced stage of my life are so strange, and these oftentimes leave me with more questions than answers. I used to look forward to sleep, during all my hectic bread-winner years, when I was pushed almost to the limit, trying to get everything done. Indeed, back then, I regarded sleep as my only escape from reality. But no more!

In recent years, I have come to somewhat dread the prospect of sleeping, because of the extensive dreams I have. Of course, as most Seniors soon realize at this stage of life, the mere process of falling asleep has become a challenge. This is because, for some of us, oftentimes our bodies do not relax enough to allow us to fall asleep when we are supposed to. However, when I do finally fall asleep, it is almost wall to wall dreams for me, especially in recent years. Most of these dreams are of no consequence, but many appear to often have illusive meanings—some of which escape my comprehension.

Yes, more and more people from my past have been appearing in my nightly dreams, since gaining Senior status. Some have crossed over many years ago, others not so long ago. The other night, William from my high school graduating class played a part in my dream. This is another fellow classmate, whom I had not seen in over fifty years, but whom I had heard passed on some years ago. Then, there was my good friend Herman (now deceased for a few years), who came to me in a dream, where the two of us sat and talked for what seemed like hours. He appeared young and handsome—not like he was in his 70s, when he passed over. Even my first ex-husband, who expired in 2007, showed up in one of my very vivid dreams recently. When I saw him in my dream, I walked up to him and asked pointedly—"What are you doing here?" To this, he answered that "he was just checking up on his family". That seemed apropos, as the setting for this dream was my granddaughter's college dormitory, where we had apparently gathered to get her settled for the freshman year.

So, what am I supposed to learn from all of this, I ask myself regularly Never before, in my youth and mid life, did so many deceased people ever appear in my dreams. Is it because I have outlived so many of my friends and family, that they want to check in with me on a regular basis, just to say "hello, I am still with you"? Or do these dreams contain messages, that I am supposed to decipher? Or perhaps these are familiar deceased folks, whose souls are merely passing through my dreams while on their nightly Astral traveling junkets. Or could it be that I am the one, who is Astral traveling—visiting them in my sleep state?

Whatever the reason, I am now hesitantly retiring each night with some misgivings, as to what lies in wait within my dream state, during the hours when I am supposed to be sleeping. But I will continue to pay attention to my most emphatic dreams, as I endeavor to seek answers within these unconscious visions, that venture into my psyche during those slumbering hours. For you never know what message or warning we may be able to gleam from certain of our dreams.

Remembering back to one of the most memorable dreams I have ever had, it was a recurring one. It recurred three times during a hectic time in my life, and it was always the same. This happened back between 1971 to 1974, when there did not seem to be enough hours in my day, to accomplish all I had to do, as sole bread winner for my children. It seemed that I was always on the go. But fortunately my good health held up well through those years, considering the rigors of this demanding schedule. Of course, my positive state of mind had a lot to do with my body's good health, believing as I did (without question), that I could do all of those things. The term "Super Mom" comes to mind. However, sometimes the mind boggling responsibility would get to me. And it was then, that an overwhelming fatigue would encompass my body. It was just at such times, when this recurring dream would come to me during sleep.

In the dream, I was shown a room, the walls of which were filled with book shelves from ceiling to floor—crammed with so many books. There were books of reference, history, philosophy, prophesy, historical novels—you name it. Also, in that room was office furniture, a couch and desk. On the desk was a state of the art electric typewriter (no one had home computers then). There were stacks of typing paper also, ready to be used, along with all the office supplies needed. Although I could not see beyond this room, I sensed that there were other attached rooms—bedroom, kitchen, bathroom. Then, a voice from an unseen source would speak to me.

"How would you like to live here, where you could use your writing skills however you wished? You would never have to venture out, unless you wanted to. All your bills would be paid, and you would not have to worry about making ends meet anymore, when you live here?"

Of course, in this dream I didn't even have to hesitate with my answer. Because so tired was I, on the occasion of these recurring dreams, that I would readily say "yes" every time.

That was almost forty years ago, when this recurring dream occurred, and I remember it like it was yesterday. And now, I realize that for the last seven years I have been indeed living just such a scenario in my current reclusive lifestyle. The difference is that the dream scene room has been updated to include an office computer (instead of a typewriter). As for not having to worry about bill paying, this has come to pass by means of Social Security and investment status.

Even now, I am still able to play that dream over and over in my mind—just as experienced decades ago. And every detail of that well-equipped "writer's dream" room is still vivid to me. Although, this prophetic dream took decades to become reality, I am happy to report, that it finally did.

It is understandable, that widows/widowers may see their deceased spouses in dreams. But even in cases of divorce, former spouses may cross paths during dream sequences. Of course, it goes without saying, that former spouses will always remain in our memory banks. But don't be surprised when they pop up in your dreams, as well. Because, let's face it—divorce not withstanding— we are never emotionally free of our former spouses. Take it from one, who knows.

Over the years, since I was married to them, each one has shown up on occasion in this lady's dreams— even decades later. Yes, just a few years after my last "ex" removed himself from my premises in late 2000 for good, he was in a most vivid dream of mine. In this dream, I was sleeping in my darkened bedroom and he came through the door. And without giving me even a glance, he went to the other side of the bed where he used to sleep. Then he pulled the covers over him, assumed a fetal position, and went to sleep.

The next day, I thought little about this dream at that time, but then I received a call from his son, telling me that his Dad had been stricken with a massive stroke, and the prognosis was grave for his survival. Now, being a believer in Astral travel, it was my analysis that in my dream his soul had traveled out of his damaged, hospitalized, container body (some 500 miles way), back to a place where he had previously felt safe—in the bed we had shared for almost 17 years.

This was proof for me, that his soul still regarded being in my presence as a comforting place. And why not, since I had taken such good care of him for so long? I took great satisfaction from this dream visitation event, even though at the time he was already living with another unsuspecting gal. Incidentally, he did survive the stroke, and I learned that his long rehabilitation, care-giving became the duties of his new woman, to take care of this invalid guy—something she probably had not bargained for.

So, as I said, we never seem to be free of our "ex's", sometimes even long after the final papers have been legalized, as they often come back in our dreams. And even if at the time, the meaning of such dreams is not clear, give it time, and perhaps you may get the message.

Besides the means discussed here, there are other ways, spirit visitation has been reported by many. While lying in bed, have you ever experienced the edge of your bed become indented, as if someone was sitting on that spot, but you can see no one there? I have! But I may never know who was visiting me on those occasions.

And let us not forget about all those deceased pet animals, that so many of us have loved in our lifetimes. They have souls too, you know. And there have been reports of many of those, coming back to visit their former owners. One night, my daughter and hubby heard guttural meow sounds in the hall, during the dead of night. It could easily be explained as being from their elderly cat "Missy". The only trouble was, that this cat had been deceased for some time then.

So, I do believe that spirit entities (whether human or animal) often times visit many of us—mostly through dreams, Astral travel and visions. But sometimes evidenced by sounds. Indeed, the spirit world uses varied methods to make their presence known, and we should pay attention. For we never know, who is trying to reach us.

✫ ✫ ✫

CHAPTER - 17
Never Forget About Angels

Each of us has Angels around us, in addition to our Spirit Guide. These Angels stay with us as our guardians, who are there to protect us in life-threatening situations and to help us through difficult emotional times. The number of these wonderful entities, assigned to each of us, varies from person to person. Some people have as many as five and even many more, who come to protect in especially difficult situations. These awesome Angels have been assigned to us by God, but are not meant to be worshipped. Rather, Angels should be honored and thanked for their service to us.

In Luke-4:10, Angels are referenced to thusly. "For it is written, He shall give His Angels charge over thee, to keep thee."

Throughout history, there have been Angels sightings, and many people have been (as the saying goes) "touched by an Angel". Joan of Arc was just a simple teenage girl in her era of history, yet she was reached by angelic direction from God. She claimed to be directed in battle by Michael the Archangel himself. So strong was her beliefs, that when she was persecuted after literally saving France in battle, she refused under severe duress to renounce her angelic communication, and was subsequently burned at the stake.

Because Angels have become such important elements in my life, I have done much research about them. Of course, there are more Guardian Angels than other more elevated levels of Angels, because there are so many humans to protect. But others of higher angelic strata can be called upon to come and help the Guardian Angels, in severe cases where more assistance is needed. As far as the hierarchy goes, the top of the roaster lists St. Michael the Archangel, who for me represents the "big gun" of all. Others in the higher group have names like—Uriel, Raphael, Raguel, Sarakiel, Gabriel, Ramiel and such. And of course, most of us have heard of the Cherubims and Seraphims, who play a special role in God's celestial choir.

Then, there are countless reports of Angels taking human form, coming to the aid of many. Indeed, we should all pay heed to the advice given in Hebrews. "Be not forgetful to entertain strangers; for thereby some have entertained Angels unawares."

But for the most part, our Guardian Angels are meant to protect us from harm and adversity, amid the pitfalls of our lives.

All of this reminds me of a time, just a few years ago, when I was traveling to south Louisiana, to do research for one of my books—"Escape From The Guillotine". I had taken an unfamiliar route through Baton Rouge, so as to travel toward Lafayette. This meant I had to drive over the newest bridge on the Mississippi River there, and afterwards onto the highway which went across the great Atchafalaya Swamp.

A few miles before getting to the approach of that bridge, the sky grew black and it began to rain. It was dusk and visibility was already getting bad. Then, when this terrible storm came up, seemingly out of nowhere, the wind was so strong that the rain was pelting all the vehicles on that bumper-to-bumper route unmercifully. I could only grasp the steering wheel with all my might, to keep my car on the road and to follow the one in front. To make matters even worse, I could see nothing past the blurry thick rain on my car's hood, except for the red rear lights of the car ahead of me. Even though this congested traffic had slowed down considerably, because of these adverse conditions, I was literally at the mercy of that car in front for guidance.

I don't mind saying, that I was terrified, and literally praying out loud. Yep, I called upon every heavenly entity I had ever heard of, from God, to Jesus, my Spirit Guide, the Saints, all the Angels—especially St. Michael the Archangel—to send help to keep my car on the road and me safe. I kept saying to myself, between praying, if I can only make it to the other side of that terribly high bridge—to the other side of the Mississippi River—I would be safer. But after finally coming off the bridge, I found that there was no place wide enough to pull over, as that highway rolled on, taking all the traffic along it's byway. The vehicles had to keep on going, until an exit presented itself. However, first we had to travel over that great swamp, before there was any land high enough to support an exit. Because for miles and miles, there was no place to pull over, and nothing to be seen on the side of the highway past that driving rain. That is except for when the lightning repeatedly struck and lighted the sky, illuminating the dreary, Spanish moss hung, ghostly cypress tree vistas, standing guard in the awful blackness reflected from that deep swamp. There were no lights to be seen anywhere, and no signs of civilization for miles. What was worse, there continued to be no wide enough places on the side of the highway, where a car could pull over in safety.

Finally, several miles later, as this line of vehicles creeped along precariously, still enduring this terrible zero visibility storm every inch of the way, the first exit appeared. It goes without saying, that I took it, for nothing more than to get off of that deadly highway and pull myself together. I have to say, that it had been years, since being in such a dire situation, where I had literally felt so close to another of my life's exit points. To put it bluntly, I had bad feelings throughout this entire route. And I feared that this dire traffic situation would result in a massive pileup—because every vehicle was just following the one in front for direction, in this zero visibility. All the front vehicle had to do was to slam on the brakes, and every other car for hundreds of feet behind would likely crash into the one in front, causing a terrible chain reaction traffic disaster.

After checking into a motel at that exit, I turned on the TV, to learn that my foreboding had not been wrong. It seems that just minutes after I had exited off of that terrible highway, there had been a multiple car pileup, which resulted in several casualties. At that moment, I humbly thanked all of those magnificent entities, who had literally heard my prayers and kept me safe before urging me to take that exit—to save me, from quite possibly being a part of that disastrous event.

Another memorable happening reinforced my angelic beliefs on yet another occasion. A few years ago, I was in a store parking lot, standing at the back of my car, loading some purchases into the trunk. Upon finishing, I slammed the trunk cover down, and at that moment I felt a strong push on my back, which caused my body to be jerked away. After the initial shock of this, I pulled myself back to my feet and turned around, to see who had pushed me. What I saw was frightening. Another car had apparently backed out and didn't stop until it hit the back bumper of my car, where just moments before I had been standing. But as I brushed myself off, I realized that there was not even a scratch on me anywhere, even though my legs should have been crushed between those two bumpers. The driver of the other car hurriedly got out when he realized what he had done, and came over to me, to see if I was all right. Even though still shaken from what certainly should have been a disastrous experience for me, I fussed at him to be more careful in the future. But there was no doubt in my mind that my Angels had put themselves between me and those two car bumpers—to save me from terrible injuries. There is absolutely no other explanation.

Then, there was another time when I was riding in the passenger seat of my friend's car. We were driving along a particularly curvy two lane highway, when we spied a car trying to pass another on coming auto. It was obvious to us that there was not enough space for this approaching car to pass and get back over in the proper lane, before our car reached that spot. To make matters worse, it happened as we approached a small bridge with railings on both sides, so there was no room to take the shoulder.

As our eyes were glued to that on coming car, it looked like there was no way for us to avoid a head on collision with that offending vehicle. Because it was coming so fast, we would not be able to clear the bridge or stop in time. Anyone, who has ever been in such a situation where it appeared that death was imminent, because there was no logical way out, can certainly relate. I remember my throat being dryer than it had ever been, my eyes were staring in horror at what was being hurled our way head on, and my brain seemed to be shutting down in disbelief. All I could think to say was, "Dear God......help us!"

Then, as if by magic, the on coming car speeded up over that little bridge, and made a sharp turn immediately where the railings ended—just between there and our approaching car. His abrupt turn caused him to crash down into the highway embankment ditch, to the right of our car, as we went speeding by. It was such an unimaginable close space, where he was propelled through, that it must have taken a bit of paint off our car in the process. Needless to say, we both breathed a sign of relief afterwards, and counted our blessings. But I knew that we had been spared by some unseen force, that today I call Angels.

However, there are many times when we see danger approaching and do have time to call on the "big guns" for help. For if our entreaties are sincere and we really need them, Angels will come to help us. They have done so for me, many times in my lifetime.

They do indeed come when we call, particularly for events of great magnitude in human endeavor. Reportedly, at the time of the 9/11 disaster, there were reports of people observing Angel sightings that day. Several people professed to seeing large Angels in the sky above the twin towers. Although that tragic 9/11 event was destined to happen, many Angels were apparently waiting there. It is as if they were summoned to come and escort thousands of souls, who were destined to leave their human bodies and pass over to the "other side", on that memorable day in September 2001.

On another amazing day in September of 1914, astounding sightings were reported. A London newspaper ran the story of this event, with details of the Battle of Mons, Belgium in the First World War. At that site, the German army was fighting the British and French armies, which were about to retreat from Mons, because the battle was going against their forces. As it was subsequently reported in that newspaper article, there were sightings (from soldiers of both sides) of angelic figures coming to the aid of the distressed British troops. Some claimed that what they saw was in the form of Saint George and medieval archer spirits, who helped repel the German forces.

Several others from that battle said that these sightings were of warrior type Angels, clad in white and carrying bows and arrows. They all seemed to be directed by what they thought was Michael the Archangel on a white horse. Those witnesses reported that the Germans fired continuously at this leader, who was obviously an easy target. But no shell ever brought him down.

Even more witnesses in this battle said that the horses of the Germans, upon seeing the white horses of these angelic adversaries, bolted and stampeded away from the front lines. A particular Corporal reported that he and other troops around him watched with awe for almost a half hour, viewing these angelic figures with their out-stretched wings as they advanced on the German lines.

Of course, when this story ran in the newspaper in Britain, many tried to debunk these sightings as hallucinations on the part of the battle weary soldiers. But in following months, it was reported that wounded German soldiers from this battle were still ailing as a result of arrow wounds, sustained during that confrontation. This raised the question as to how these German casualties sustained wounds from arrows, which were not standard weapon issue on either side during the First World War.

And so it goes, sightings of Angels have been with us throughout history. Yet, so many people still attribute little importance to these fantastic beings. Even some religious denominations, that profess to follow the Bible, fail to extend expressed honor toward Angels. It has been my observation, that many Christian denominations seldom even mention Angels, except once a year at Christmastime, when an Angel is included in the nativity scene.

Yet, Angels have been sighted by multitudes of people throughout the ages. And these sightings have come from all over the world, even from those of different religious backgrounds. Indeed, there is no doubt that Angels have always been a fact of life in the chronicles of human kind.

My Mother once told me about a game she and her brothers and sisters used to play, back when they were kids—something quite hazardous to their health, to say the least. There was a wide pasture near their farm, which was the domain of a big, bad, fierce bull with long horns. And these children would see, who could run fast enough across that pasture, to the fence on the far side, before the bull could catch up to them. Luckily for each child, none of them tripped and fell during their flight for life run against the speed of that bull— otherwise not one of them would have lived to maturity, without being gored. No doubt about it, here is another case where Guardian Angels were on the job.

As a five year old child, I can recall memories of a terrifying event, that I experienced. There was a house on the corner next to the home where my family lived at the time. And in that house resided an older woman and her grown son, whom she had taken care of since his birth. By that time, he was probably in his 30s. As children, we used to walk past that house and see him on the screen porch, attired only in a shirt and a diaper. The screen porch was crisscrossed with reinforced slats up and down, so he couldn't get out. But he used to hollow and scream at us when we passed by—not in words, but in hair raising, indescribable shrieks—because he was incapable of speaking. You see, he was completely insane from birth, and only his mother could take care of him. Because he would assault anyone else, who attempted to get close to him. She used to tell everyone, that this son was sent as her "cross to bear" in this life. And rather than put him in an insane asylum, she chose to devote her life to caring for him.

One day, as I was walking to my house from down the block, I decided to take a short cut across the fenced in backyard of the house where that man lived with his mother. Their yard and ours were side by side, and on that day their gate was not locked. Thinking that he was probably sitting on the porch, as he usually did at that time of day, I started across their yard. About half way across, I saw him, coming out of their back door. When he saw me, he started screaming at me in his horrid guttural voice, as he began running toward me. Of course, I was terrified and ran as fast as my little legs could take me, toward the safety of our fence. By that time, his mother had heard him and she came out of her house and was running toward him, in an effort to keep him from getting to me. And as I ran with all my might, I could see my Mother, who had come out of our house upon hearing his screams. She was trying with all her might, to get across our fence in an effort to save me.

Thankfully, he tripped , which allowed his mother to reach him just in time—when he was only a few feet from catching me. Had he gotten to me, this tiny little five year old would not have stood a chance at the hands of such an insane grown man.

Again, here was a case of those wonderful Guardian Angels, who were there with their protection before it was too late for me. Indeed, they have had their work cut out for them during my lifetime,. And this is true for most of us, who would never have even survived childhood without such protection, in order for us to go on and fulfill our earthly destinies. There are quite simply no other answers for many of those close calls in our lives.

To tell it like it is, I do believe that this remarkable, world-renowned, spiritual gentleman, Edgar Cayce, said it best. "Each person, who is now on earth, is here to potentially assist the earth in it's spiritual transformation and evolution to higher consciousness. Not that the way will be easy, but all who seek to bring about this spiritual renaissance will indeed be shown the way, through dreams, intuition, meditation. Some may even have the experience of direct communication with Angels."

✮ ✮ ✮

CHAPTER - 18
Living With My Spirit Guide

Since I was "contacted", my life has literally been altered to adhere to the guidance of my Spirit Guide "Olivia". At first I fought against her directives, because at the time it did not fit what I thought I wanted for the rest of my life. But with the passage of more time, I began to see the wisdom of her guidance.

I know that she is from God, as she has assured me over and over again. Because she always encourages me to pray, impressing on me how important prayers are. In fact, on a few occasions after going to bed, when I had forgotten to kneel at my in-house altar to say my prayers, she would not let me rest. Her words would fill my head and she would literally nag me into getting up to pray. Also, never has she ever told me anything bad to do. Always, her telepathic words were those of encouragement, urging me over and over again about the things I am expected to do, to safe guard what is left of my family, before I pass on. Of course, by the same token, she never tells me what she thinks I want to hear. On the contrary, many times I did not want to hear what she told me about the direction of the years remaining in my life. But my arguments did not change anything, as she has always stayed on course—continuing to stress the several difficult tasks left for me to do.

"Times on this planet will continue to get harder," she says to me. "And you are destined to provide protection for your seed, before you pass over."

Never would I have ever used the word "seed", as a description for my children and grandchildren, before I met her! But even though it is somewhat of an archaic term, I must admit it is apropos. She always assures me every night and day, that my Angels are keeping me and mine safe—and no harm will come to us, that is if we don't do something stupid. It would appear that our Spirit Guide can be likened to the foreman on the job, with our own personal Angels on hand to do the heavy lifting of protection for us, when we need their help. As set forth before, there have always been close calls for each of us—close calls, that we wondered how we were spared? There is probably not one of us, who has not had a near-miss auto accident, or a terrible swimming or boating accident, not to mention a fall that might have killed us. But it was not our time to exit, so our wonderful protectors saved us from disaster.

I asked Olivia why it took until March 1994, before direct contact could be made with me.? And she told me this. "I have always been with you, as have your Angels, who have protected you through several life threatening events in your life. Whenever you felt what you called 'feminine intuition', or that 'gut feeling', that was me trying to advise you. Usually, most human charges are too busy and their mentality is filled with so much worldly activity, that it gets in the way of their Guides coming through. But most Guides still struggle to get in anyway—usually to no avail. For you, it was time that you be reached in a more definite way, because you were not where you were supposed to be living on this planet. And since time was getting shorter for you at your age, it was necessary for us to literally push our way into your consciousness. Because there are more things for you to accomplish, before you are through."

Olivia impresses on me, that certain of my "seed" are meant to go on to important destinies in their future lives, after I exit. But my efforts in their behalf are imperative toward their survival. So, she has revealed to me a few priorities that I must accomplish before it is my time to exit. On the many occasions, when I have asked her how I am expected to do these things, as well as where will the money come from to accomplish such, she always says that it will be provided, when needed—reiterating again, that all things are possible with God.

As a result of this close spiritual communication with my Guide every day and night of my life for some thirteen years now, I have come to have great affection for her and my Angels. Although I am not permitted to see them, I feel their presence. We go everywhere together, and they never sleep. Olivia warns me to be careful when driving, when going up and down stairs, or when I work too hard in the yard. And now, I hardly ever play my car radio, in case she wants to have a conversation with me. Usually such quiet time, while I am driving my car, allows for uninterrupted communication between us.

Every night, in addition to thanking her and my Angels in my regular prayers, for helping me get through yet another day, I also say an additional "thank you" to them just before I close my eyes in sleep. At such times, Olivia always replies thusly. "It is good to be thanked."

She says that it is a pity that more humans do not thank their ever vigilant Guides and Angels like I do. But I can understand why that is. Because most people do not even realize they have such personal heaven-sent protectors around them at all times.

For years now, she told me I would write a special book. Even though I have written other published books, she insisted that this one would be the most important. She insisted it would be written to help other people, who might have had similar things happen to them in their lives. She emphasized that by sharing my life's story in this book, it would also show how so many obstacles can be overcome, if we are strong. And by my efforts at telling it as it was (and is) for me, many would be given hope and the strength to strive toward perseverance, so they can also fight against negativity in their own lives. Olivia would tell me time and time again, that the inspiration for this book would come to me, at the right time.

Of course, I remembered that several years ago on two different occasions, two reputable psychic ladies had also revealed to me, that I would write an important book. But still, this concept seemed like an impossible project for me.

So, Olivia had her work cut out for her over several years, trying to convince me over and over, that I would write just such a book about my life and it would be published. But my belief that this would ever come to pass was often strained. Because for me, it was still unbelievable that anyone would want to read my life story. But she continued to encourage me, in an effort to make me believe that this would indeed happen. In fact, it got so monotonous for her, that one day she became so irate with me at my refusal to accept this premise, she just suddenly shouted out to me.

"Humor me! Just write the darn book......and let the finished manuscript sit there. Things will fall into place."

As it turned out, one day I did suddenly sit down at my computer and began typing away. The inspiration just came through me and into my fingers, to be transferred to the printed page. Many of my long ago memories, as well as present day realities, were made known to me to be included. The inspiration seemed to come to me out of the blue on a particular winter day, when I began this literary epic.

Several of my family and friends have asked me how they might go about getting in touch with their Guides. All I can say is it is different for every person. Some people are never meant to make contact, as it is not in their destiny. But there are many others, who might possibly get in touch with their Guides if it is meant to be. They could perhaps meditate in quiet times, and open their conscious minds to the premise that these protectors do in fact exist. But the most important thing is that you must believe.

However, believing in my Guide is one thing, but there is something that has caused much dismay over these past years. Whenever I speak to Olivia, to ask her for the date of any of the prophesies that she gives me, the result is often misleading. This is because timing in the world of spirit and timing on our earthly plane is not the same. When Olivia would tell me, that something would happen "soon", I found that this could mean tomorrow, next week, next month, or next year. So, I finally asked her not to use that word "soon", as it was misleading for me. She agreed. Now instead, she uses the word "eminent", if it is close at hand. This has proven to be better.

I can recall one particular day, sometime in 1998, when she told me about what she called a "very big event", that was going to happen in this country. She said it will have to do with tremendous explosions, that would greatly affect those in the places where it would happen. But it would also affect everyone in all of our nation, as well as people in other countries. Then, she hastened to add that it would not be happening anywhere near where I would be living at the time of the occurrence. So, not to worry about that. But Olivia went on to reiterate that as bad as it would be, it must come to pass—"is is written in stone and cannot be stopped!"

Of course, I anxiously inquired of her as to when this would be. But she would not tell me, except to say it would be within the next few years. Nevertheless, I kept asking her to tell me more, but she would only say that it was forbidden for her to impart such to me at that time.

I searched my mind, to try and come up with a likely scenario that might fit this predicted horrendous event, that was supposed to happen. Mostly, I thought of big oil refineries blowing up, or nuclear plant accidents, and such. Then, I remembered a big event that happened when I was a teenager, that today few people know about. Something like that terrible event might be similar to what Olivia was telling me.

I remember it well. It was Wednesday, April 16, 1947, and the day dawned with bright sunshine and pleasant temperatures. I was in my room upstairs at my family home in Berwick, Louisiana, when all of a sudden every window in the house began to shake. Indeed, each pane of glass, along with the window frames shook and rattled, to the point of almost breaking. The resulting loud noises clanged and clattered. I ran downstairs, to see what was happening. Mother ran to me, obviously just as bewildered as I was, for neither of us had ever experienced such a thing in our lives. Neighbors ran out of their houses, only to encounter others, who were also in search of an answer to this strange event.

Unfortunately, we did not get an answer until we turned on the radio and listened to the news. It seems that there had been horrendous explosions of freighter ships and docks at a particular port. What was so amazing was that this port was about 300 miles to the west of us in Texas City, Texas. Yes, so intense had those explosions been in Texas City, that it caused people to be knocked off their feet ten miles from there, in Galveston. The shock wave shattered windows in Houston, 40 miles from that site, and rattled our windows hundreds of miles away and beyond.

We later found out that the SS Grand Camp ship had blown up, while docked at the port of Texas City—a busy port that also included a very large complex of industries and oil storage depots in the same general vicinity of those docks. The resulting explosion caused other ships nearby to catch on fire, particularly the SS High Flyer freighter. The flames enveloping that ship could not be extinguished, so hours later another horrendous explosion resulted when the High Flyer blew up.

Those ships had been loaded with thousands of tons of very volatile ammonium nitrate, and there were tons of this same potentially dangerous substance stored in warehouses, along where those vessels were docked. Thus when the ships blew, a chain reaction was set in motion, causing dock side buildings and storage facilities, filled with even more volatile material, to explode. So, all together this was a recipe for disaster just waiting to happen. And it do so, on that fateful day in 1947.

Later, we found out that over 500 people had died in the explosions, and many thousands of others had been seriously injured. Countless bodies were never found, because those folks had been incinerated. So strong were these explosions, that a tidal wave was caused to flow, inundating that town of about 16,000 population back then. After the relatively short flooding, the water receded, leaving mud and debris everywhere.

Several still photos exist today, showing the extent of the devastation there. In some of these, the scene is indescribable and can only be likened to photos of the immediate aftermath of Hiroshima, Japan, after the atomic bomb was dropped.

Of course, this happened before television sets were a part of every household, so our only reports of this horrible event were to be gotten from radio news, or from the new reels at the movie theaters. As a result, the full impact of this horror was glossed over.

But then it happened just two years after the end of World War-II, and the public had pretty much become apathetic when it came to more horrible news, having seen so much of it during that war. People in 1947 just wanted to get on with their lives, after those difficult war years. Therefore, the Texas City disaster was not afforded the attention from the masses, that it was due.

So, this was the kind of severe disaster, that I pondered on after being told by my Guide to expect a really "big event", yet to come in our nation. Of course, as she had warned me, it would come in just a few years, and it did. When it finally happened a few years later, I then realized, that it was the terrorist attack of September 11, 2001, that she was warning me about. When I asked her if it could have been stopped, once again she emphatically reiterated the same thing, that she had previously told me.

"It was a disastrous event, that had to happen. There was no stopping it....it was meant to happen. So, whenever I tell you something that is yet to happen, and I say it is written in stone and cannot be changed, then you will know that this is an absolute coming event."

So, you can see how difficult it is sometimes to deal with what is being told to me by my Guide. Because the timing of such prophesy is never exact, and the details are sketchy. But the content almost always has come true—especially the big things. However, because of the difficulty of pinning down times and places of many prophesies, I often refrain from sharing some of what I have been told, with my daughter and her two teenagers. By the way, all three of them believe that this granny has, in fact, been spiritually reached. They have never questioned the validity of this. But I do not wish to confuse them, with inexact information.

However, it is so comforting to know that they are in my corner, and believe in me. This is because usually I have to pick and choose with whom to share any spiritual revelations of mine. As Olivia has told me time and time again, be careful with whom you confide. For unfortunately, most humans on this planet have been so brain washed in certain religious dogma, that any way of thinking, which is different from their beliefs, is bogus to them. So, to save myself from the insults and put-downs from many, who refuse to open their minds to the spirit world, it was best to still pick and choose in this regard. But now, I am letting it all hang out in this book.

Above and beyond the responsibility, that comes with having attained Spirit Guide direction, there is a fun side to it all, as well. And there is much comfort, that comes with this personal realization from the spirit world for me. For just knowing, that I am never alone— even though it appears so to worldly eyes—is such a blessing.

And how wonderful it is, that in a quiet moment, I am able to invite my Guide into my consciousness— to converse with me, whenever I want. Of course, sometimes she pushes her presence into my mind, when she has something to tell me—no matter where I am. But it is like having an extra special, kindred, close friend with me at all times. It is even better, because she knows all about me and as a result can counsel me in my times of distress, like no other entity can. She also makes me laugh sometimes—even when she does not intend to do so. But she calls herself a "no nonsense guide", who was appointed to watch over me and to get the job done.

Indeed, there have been nights, when before I closed my eyes to sleep, I have asked her to be sure and not let me over sleep in the morning. And sure enough, she would wake me at the appointed time, although often her methods are unorthodox. Sometimes, she will ring the phone with one ring. There are times, when she has nudged my body while I slept, to wake me up. And one morning, she used a different method. As I slept, I heard a strange voice in my mind. It went something like this—"Aaaaaah.....Aaaaaah", and I immediately woke up to this unusual sound. So, I never know how she will awaken me, for those times when I ask her to do so.

Pity, that I have no memory of my Guide talking to me as a child. Because children are better candidates for spiritual communication, than adults. But I know she was there with me then, long before I realized who she was. I am reminded of my daughter, when she was a child. She regularly chatted with what I now believe to have been her Guide, back then. She would refer to her invisible playmate as "Miss Doffie". This was decades before my belief system is as it is today. But somehow instinctively, I believed back then, that my daughter's "friend" was indeed real, even though only she could see her. Therefore, I treated this entity with all due respect, and never told my young daughter what most parents usually say at such times—"You are just imagining this!" Pity, that more parents can't respect the reality of their children's communication with the spirit world. It is such a special time for children. Because as we age, usually those earlier communication abilities fade.

I remember asking my little daughter on several occasions—"How is Miss Doffie today?" And she would reply, that her friend was fine. When I would open the car doors for my two little kids to get in, I would ask my daughter if Miss Doffie was coming with us today. She would say yes, and I would keep the door open long enough for her invisible friend to get into the back seat. And I would not back the car out of the driveway, until I was told Miss Doffie was settled in her seat.

Looking back, I believe my young daughter needed her communication with what I referred to as her "imaginary friend". For even though she and my son were just ten months apart, they were as different as night and day. And I have always marveled at the reality of how two children, from the same parents, reared in the same home & atmosphere, went to the same schools, had the same extended family, could each turn out to have such different personalities and abilities. So, I guess playing with her little brother was not enough

363

for her. She was a very shy little girl, then. Therefore, her guide probably came into the picture, to keep her company.

In my case, Olivia often defines certain warnings I experience. One hot July day, when I was almost age 75, I attempted to cut the backyard grass with my electric lawn mower. As I huffed and puffed, pushing the mower, which only makes a deep humming sound—not the loud obnoxious noise of gasoline type mowers—I was literally assailed by the loud chirping of a single bird, that I could not see. Now, when I had started this chore, there were no birds to be seen or heard anywhere around my property. Yet, all of a sudden here was the shrill unrelenting call of this bird, trying to get my attention.

I endeavored to ignore the bird's loud noise, as I continued on with my chore, although quite out of breathe as I pushed my body to it's limits. But the unseen bird only chirped louder, as if to say "pay attention to me"! And when I say this bird's chirping was loud, I mean it, as it's volume was far and above that of normal bird calls. So, it finally hit me, that I should stop and take a break, sit down and drink some water, before continuing on. I then turned off the mower and went over to a shaded lawn chair. And amazingly, just as soon as I sat down and started to drink some water, the bird stopped it's shrilling. It was then that I realized, that the bird was trying to warn me to stop pushing my body so hard.

As I sat there, in my moment of revelation, I telepathically asked my guide what that was all about. Olivia piped up and told me this. "That bird was sent by someone, who loves you very much—someone who has passed over and is now on the 'other side'. It was that spirit's way of trying to protect you—trying to warn you about pushing your human container body too hard and putting your health in jeopardy."

How wonderful, I thought, to get such validation from my Guide, whenever something unexplained happens to me! Indeed, she is just a mental thought away from me all the time, and is readily available whenever I need immediate answers to my questions.

This is so comforting for me, to know that I am always being watched over by unseen entities—in addition to my Guides and Angels—who really care about me. But then, I have heard that sometimes certain of our deceased loved ones send birds and butterflies to flutter around us. It is their way of reminding us, that they are still around. However this time, I guess they didn't want to be as subtle as that. This time, they had to be more emphatic, by sending that loud bird to literally fuss at me for being so careless with my health.

So, this was another instance when my Guide was there, to explain things that perplexed me. But then, I marvel everyday as to how well she knows me. Indeed, this Guide of mine never ceases to amaze, with her wise incites and knowledge.

Another example of this happened while I was shopping at a garden center. At that time, I noticed a potted "Bridal Wreathe" bush. And my memory was propelled back to long ago, little Catholic girl days, when all the children used to pick spring flowers out of their yards, to bring to the church, in honor of "May Devotion". Usually sprigs of white Bridal Wreathe were always a part of my contributed bouquet. So, I really wanted to grow such a nostalgic bush again. When I saw the price, it was very cheap at $6.98. So, I picked it up and took it to the check out counter. But when the clerk rang it us, it was really $16.98, and I really did not want to pay that much. However, I was too embarrassed to back out.

So, I paid for it and carried it toward the car—all the while fussing at Olivia for not alerting me to the fact of that higher price. "Why didn't you tell me it was ten dollars more, Olivia?" To this, she replied.

"If I had told you, you never would have bought it."

Sometimes, even when it appears as though I am entirely alone while shopping in a department store, looks can be deceiving. But at such times, I must always be on guard, not to appear to be talking to myself. One day in such a store, I purchased a few items of clothing for myself. I paid for these, picked up my bag of new clothes and began to walk toward the door. It was then, that the dreaded guilt feeling (ingrained in me from long ago, when it was so hard for me to make ends meet) started to surface in my mind. Yes, it was that recurring guilt, that I used to feel whenever I bought something for myself. So, Olivia instantly warded off those approaching guilt feelings, that were trying to enter my mind, by saying this to me.

"Enjoy yourself....it's later than you think!"

As I chuckled to myself over those words of hers, it was difficult to suppress my laughter, as I remembered the rest of the words of an old song, that she was quoting. "Enjoy yourself, it's later than you think. Enjoy yourself, while you're still in the pink. The world goes by as quickly as a wink. Enjoy yourself...enjoy yourself....it's later than you think!"

It was her reminder of this old song, that I thought I had long ago forgotten. And it caused me to laugh to myself, all the way to my car in the parking lot.

Oh, how much incite, fun and laughter she has brought into my life, with her wise and sometimes funny remarks—remarks that usually hit the right tone for me, causing me to laugh on so many occasions, when I definitely needed to.

So, from my soul's very beginning in this lifetime, when I slid down my Mother's birth canal, into the waiting hands of that dear old country doctor in 1932, my Guide and Angels have always been with me. They have protected me, every time I needed protection. They have comforted me, when I needed comforting,. They have been sad when I was sad—and happy for me when joy was in my heart. And most of all, they have never been away from me throughout all my trials and tribulations. What an ultimate gift God has bestowed on each of us, in assigning these wonderful beings to always be at our sides!

Indeed, life with Olivia is something I have come to treasure. Because I now realize how lacking my life was—before she made contact with me.

✫ ✫ ✫

CHAPTER - 19
Spiritually Speaking........Am I Worthy?

Have I suffered enough? Have I tried hard enough? Did I—too many times—bite off more than I could successfully chew? Has my track record for endurance been enough? These are the questions I ask myself over and over again. This is because since 1994, I have wondered why I was deemed worthy, to be reached spiritually in this lifetime.

My big question is just exactly what makes me special enough, to be among those so reached? This was what I asked in the first chapter, for the readers of this book to discern for themselves. My Spirit Guide tells me over and over again, that it is because I am a communicator and must prepare a safe place for my "seed" to go on after my exit. But most of all, my Guide insists that this spiritual connection came about, because God knows my heart, and knows that I can be trusted to fulfill this destiny.

But I do know this. Since my entry into the world of spirituality, I had this overwhelming feeling that I should share my experiences with others, who might have become "reached" too. Therefore, my hope is that those of you so reached, will take comfort in knowing there are others out here in the world like you.

Reports have it, that similar spiritual out reach sometimes runs in families. But I could see no correlation in my case. That is until I remembered, that my Grandma Landry was a healer. She had the ability to lay her hands on ailing people, and help with their healing. I know, because she did that for me when I was a child. Back then, I had fallen hard and bitten down half way through my tongue, which resulted in profuse bleeding, that would not stop. But Grandma knew what to do. She placed her hands over my mouth and prayed. Then, amazingly the bleeding stopped.

However, my Mother did not have that ability, nor had she been spiritually reached anytime during her life. But in recent times, my 18 year old Granddaughter has revealed to me, that she has also begun to be the recipient of telepathic messages. And at her young age, this has been a not so great experience, but it continues. Indeed, recipients of such communication may find this "gift" a heavy weight to carry. So, obviously these things may run in families, but often times could skip a generation—affecting certain ones in every other generation.

As a person, who believes that we write our own charts before we come into life on this planet, I realize that those dictates must be fulfilled before I can take my final exit—and I am striving to do this. I have also come to believe, that there is a "Mother God", who is the feminine side of the Almighty. And also, that as we progress into this new century, Her influence will began to become much more evident.

Now, that I am on the down slide of this life, I look back and see all the obstacles I have overcome, and wonder how I came through it all. But I know it was all necessary, in order for my soul's growth and enlightenment. However, it was a great price to pay in anguish, betrayal, sorrow and disappointment—and there is probably more still to come. Yet, I am not afraid of the future, because I have gained knowledge from the past. So, my demise (whenever that comes) holds no dread for me. On the contrary, I look forward to that time, when I will be free of this traumatic lifetime.

Yes indeed, there are many things I have learned along the way. I have learned that love does NOT conquer all. I also now know, that just because I am nice to them, all people will NOT be nice to me. And it is true, as the old saying goes, that bad things DO happen to good people. But in spite of all these lessons, I know with all my heart, that the years of life we spend on earth, is temporary and fleeting. And that someday, we will all be free of the confines of this difficult planet. Because our real home is on the "other side".

However, until our exit times come, we must make the most of this earthly life of ours. And we must follow our paths here. As for me, one of the major things I have been spiritually directed to accomplish, before I leave, is to provide a state of the art, concrete enforced, safe home—away from big cities, deep valleys and coastlines—so as to insure the survival of my descendants. For there are some difficult times coming from Mother Nature and man-made events, that will test the resolve of mankind to go on. But this is nothing new, for Ancient Indian seers and prophets, as well as Biblical texts, have been warning the world about these coming times, if we do not change our ways. And from the looks of current events, most of mankind has no intention of changing their ways.

But this lady has long ago seen the environmental light, and I want to do what I can to help the only home we have right now—Planet Earth. Indeed, we should all accept that we need to do our part, by getting an ecological attitude adjustment for our future.

Long term survival, of course, will necessitate an ecological revamping for people. More of us have to learn to protect Mother Earth and it's species. More of us should learn to work the earth, to provide some of our food. Pity, that too many folks laugh about "old school" ladies, like me, who wash used tin foil, plastic picnic plates, utensils, plastic bags (except for those that have held meat, fish or onions), and reuse these. And let's not forget about using those new fangled electric light bulbs, that last for years This is reported to be another small way to help the planet.

Personally, as previously said, I have purchased an electric lawn mower, that is powered by batteries that are plugged into my house receptacles, to be re-charged, when the mower is not in use. Thus, I need not buy gasoline or oil, as I used to do, for my previous mowers.

Another important way to save on energy, is to install solar panels on all new houses. In fact, if our government powers-that-be would stand behind their many promises to reduce energy reliance on oil, they should have long ago made it mandatory, that solar panels be on the roofs of every new building in this country. Because the sun comes up everyday, it should be harnessed as our primary energy source in our homes. But then that would reduce our reliance on the "big oil & coal companies", and their profitable bottom line. So, as long as the traditional energy lobbyists continue to influence the leadership in Washington D.C., we will see little progress in this regard.

But even if our leaders refuse to see the light of a coming oil depletion future, each of us in our own small way can contribute to the continued well-being of our precious planet. So, we should make a concerted effort to do so—even in some of the smaller ways mentioned here.

In the case of nuclear energy, those plants still make most folks uneasy. Because we have seen what horror transpired when one of those plants self-destructed. As far as our present leadership even considering the use of what is referred to as "limited" nuclear weapons in warfare, how distressing is that? In some speeches, just such has been suggested as "being on the table", possibly to be used against certain other nations. What are they thinking? And just what could possibly be considered as "limited nuclear", anyway? That would just be opening a "Pandora's Box" of retaliation from other upstart countries, who already have some nuclear capability.

Just such a scenario of horrific warfare could only be imagined. Indeed, if this man-made idiocy comes to pass, combined with what Mother Nature will be throwing at us in years to come, in the form of hurricanes, tornadoes, droughts, earthquakes, volcanic eruptions—you name it—the people of this planet will pay dearly.

We should take a lesson from the continent of Atlantis, several thousand years ago, when this advanced civilization got too big for it's technological britches. Reportedly, the scientists there had harnessed a special power, but pushed it too far. So, their man-made "pushing the envelope" technological miscalculations, coupled with natural upheavals from Mother Nature, proved to be the end for that advanced civilization.

For we mere mortals on Planet Earth in this new century, we will be seeing combinations of mass migrations and evacuations in years to come. Perhaps, some will transpire within what is left of this Senior lady's lifetime—with most to occur in decades yet to come.

However, a word of caution is offered here. When traumatic events strike, we must all learn to accept these happenings as facts of our life, and know how to go on from there. We will not have time for all that "woe is me" stuff, if we expect to survive. We will each have to accept responsibility for our own self and family, and not look to the government to solve all of our problems. You saw what happened with Hurricane Katrina and Rita, when outside help did not come for several days. So, in some cases it is better to evacuate from danger if possible. In other cases, having stock piles of canned & dried foods, as well as sufficient quantities of water, could make the difference between life or death. Let's face it, doesn't it make good sense to—in the words of that old Girl Scout motto—"always be prepared"?

I offer these suggestions as part of my communication duties, which is still a part of my path in this life. This is meant only as constructive suggestions for your consideration.

At this advanced time in my life I have accepted, what before was considered unacceptable, to me. It is the fact, that Planet Earth will always be a sphere where pain, struggle, injustice and negativity exists, as long as God permits it to spin in this universe. Yes, after infused spiritual information, much research and experience, I have come to accept emphatically that our planet is a place of learning for our souls—a training ground of endurance, so to speak. And with each incarnation here, our soul is destined to struggle as best it can through the adversity set forth for a particular span, which is the length of life for it's human container.

What is even more distressing, is that no matter how much we try to help others, how much money we donate to the starving people in Africa, or other places where people are so in need, it seems to be an endless pursuit toward the betterment of mankind. This is because of the negativity of this planet, where whenever people in one sector are helped, there always seems to be another region where even more help is needed. Of course, we should never stop helping our fellow human beings. But we should also be prepared to realize, that there will always be more and more people in need. Such is the nature of the planet, on which we live.

There is no denying, that so much horror that fills our TV screens each day of our lives, is distressing. Many of us abhor the killing brought on by that unnecessary Iraq War—a war that so many of us never believed in. Every Sunday morning on TV, they list the names, home towns/states and ages of those of our military, who were killed the previous week. Whenever I read this, it makes my heart hurt, just to see the words on the screen—words that reflect what used to be fine young people (mostly in their late teens and early 20s). Sometimes, it is 15, 20 or even as many as 37 or more killed in one week. And I can't stop feeling that the lives of these young people, who hardly had a chance to start living, have been ended for such a dubious cause.

However, we have only to look back at the history of this violent planet, to see that war, violence, suffering and persecution have always been here. Personally, I have come to regard Planet Earth as a particular version of hell, that our souls have to get through.

You know, often it appears to this lady, that we are all but pawns on God's chessboard of life. For it is a fact, that in many cases—especially now—certain people are being directed to move to other regions. Usually, the reasons given are for new jobs, family changes, retirement, necessary relocation from disaster areas, and such. As in this lady's case it was a move to higher ground, in order to fulfill my destiny. But you better believe, that wherever people are being directed to move, it is because a particular sector is where they are meant to be at that point in time. For each person's destiny is different.

As I said before, I have accepted this premise, as it now makes sense to me. This is especially so, since I realized that everywhere I go, I am accompanied by my protective Guides and Angels—not to mention the many spirits of deceased loved ones, who drop in and out to see me from time to time. Indeed, my Guide tells me, that I would be astonished if I were allowed to see all the "now deceased" family, friends and acquaintances, who regularly visit me. This is a great comfort for me, and it should be for all of you, knowing that your protectors are ever with you.

But the unanswered question still remains, as to whether or not I have experienced what it takes, throughout this lifetime of mine, to qualify? Have I been dismayed and betrayed enough? Have I been deceived, disappointed & discouraged enough? Has my mistreatment, humiliation & vilification been sufficient? Does the fact, that I have been slandered, slighted, trivialized, overlooked, intimidated, surgically butchered, misled and cheated on in this lifetime count? This is not even to mention, that I survived the plague, a near death experience as well as six major surgeries— with all the accompanying pain and suffering. Also, does the degree of having been used, abused and confused enough to qualify my soul, as worthy of such special spiritual contact?

Well, the preponderance of experiences, set forth in this literary epic, should say it all, in regard to "why me"? Because the answer should be a resounding "YES"! Yes indeed, I am as worthy as anyone else, to have been "spiritually reached". After all, have I not paid my earthly school of hard knocks dues in this life? Am I not a spark of the divine God, just as all His children are? But most of all, throughout my life of adversity, I have never lost sight of Almighty God as our supreme being. Even in my lowest moments, God was always in my heart. So, YES, I am worthy to have been the recipient of this gift.

But now, as my exit time from this life draws ever nearer, I can't help but ponder thoughts of my own mortality, and how I want to be remembered. In a previous chapter about animals, I mentioned a quote, that I would like on my tombstone. But I now take that one back. For after seeing the celestial expression on my Mother's face when she appeared to me in spirit, months after her passing, I know without a shadow of a doubt that the "better place" people are always talking about does in fact exist. For my Mother is there, along with all my deceased family, friends, and all those doggie souls, whom I loved so much in this lifetime. So, that is where I will be going when it is my time. And what a joyous reunion we will have, while we await the return of the rest of our loved ones, whom we will have left behind to finish their allotted time on this planet.

Therefore, I request the words of a beloved old song, to be sung at my service. And these apropos words to be inscribed on my grave stone, when my time comes. The words from that beautiful old song are—"I'll Be Seeing You".

Because it is true........I really will be seeing you!

✵ ✵ ✵

A Final Note From The Author

It is wisely said, that "there are more things in heaven and earth than that which meets the eye". This is so true, as evidenced by the experiences of the author as portrayed in this book.

Although, there will be some who shall doubt these personal happenings, that is your privilege. However, all the experiences of this lady, as set forth in this text, actually happened, and more are still happening. Indeed, communication with my Spirit Guide will no doubt be on-going until the day I pass over to that anticipated "other side". So, for those, who doubt the existence of the spirit world, and only believe in what they can see, hear and touch, they are fooling themselves. Such naysayers should take their heads out of the sand of denial, and acknowledge the existence of their Guides and Angels. And it wouldn't hurt to say a proper "thank you" to them for all they do.

In recent times, more has been revealed, particularly about the need for me to forgive those, who have trespassed against me in this lifetime. But not only am I supposed to let go of the hurts from this life, I must also forgive all those numerous ones, who have hurt me during my past lives, as well. This must be done, I am told, before my soul can successfully go on into a higher realm of growth.

Now, this task seems overwhelming for me, because I have not been allowed recollections of previous lives, except briefly for two lives under hypnosis. And considering that I am supposed to now be on my 48th lifetime for this soul, this seems like an impossible task.

I have been told, that some of my past lives were lived as far back as on the continent of Atlantis, as well as in Mongolia, Greece, Egypt, Palestine, France, England, Spain, China and many other places. I even lived a life as a pre-Columbian American Indian. In several of these incarnations, I apparently suffered much abuse, torture and violent death. And it seems that certain of those hurts, from way back, have been carried over into this lifetime as cell memories. So, some of that has contributed to my path this time around—influencing my faults, talents, sufferings, benefits, attitudes, etc.

But such a "blanket forgiveness" is no little accomplishment for anyone. However, I recently had a personal epitome, resulting in an overwhelming desire to accomplish just that. Because of that revelation, I have sent out my declaration of forgiveness into the Universe—to every person (past and present) who has ever transgressed against me. Afterwards, it was as if a weight was lifted off of my heart.

However, no one can make a person forgive, if they do not want to. Such a person has to decide for herself/himself, that they sincerely want to forgive. It is kind of like trying to change an Alcoholic, who doesn't want to stop drinking. It will only happen when that Alcoholic decides for his self or herself, that they sincerely want to change.

But forgiving does not mean that we are ever expected to forget. Because those hurtful memories will probably remain ingrained in our brains for the rest of our lives. And it doesn't mean that we have to like an abusive person, or seek to be in the company of those, who have hurt us. Even our Lord Jesus did not like everyone, but He could forgive the ones, who inflicted horrendous trespasses against Him. I believe that He forgave their souls, rather than the actions of their human containers.

Of course, sometimes we may find ourselves having to be in the brief company of someone, who has previously hurt us (and whom we have already forgiven). So, it is at such times, that we have to be on guard, so as not to be their victim of abuse once again. After all, it is wisely said that past experience can often be a foreteller of future behavior. So, we certainly should not seek to be around such people, who have brought harm to us in the past. But we can forgive them, and go on our way.

To continue blaming someone, for slights of the past, can eat away at us like an open wound. Only forgiveness can heal that wound.

In the final analysis, I have forgiven them all. However, I will avoid (whenever it is possible) being in the company of people, whom I discern as those, who are capable of bringing down my very spirit. For the possibility of having such happen to me again and again is too high a price to pay.

I just call that self preservation.

✵ ✵ ✵

EPILOGUE

Babies are born into life with a blank slate,
Knowing nothing about their charted fate.

Children play with so much exuberant fun
With no care in the world under the sun.

Then those difficult teen years come on their
scene,
Often showing the world to be so mean.

But it is the adult years that test their all,
With struggle and strife, and some of them fall.

In yet older age they say—we are still here,
For to be forgotten is their big fear.

Near the end, they can see the last of all mirth,
Time to let go, their path followed since birth.

But babies still come in with their new rebirth,
Back in to serve their time on Planet Earth !

—Beryl Ann Fangue

www.ingramcontent.com/pod-product-compliance
Lightning Source LLC
Chambersburg PA
CBHW030909090426
42737CB00007B/140